PLAGUES OF THE MIND

To Kirk and Sunny—
with memories of Kelee
and Elderhostel!

Regards,
Bruce Thornton

PLAGUES OF THE MIND

The New Epidemic of False Knowledge

BRUCE S. THORNTON

ISI BOOKS
Wilmington, Delaware
1999

Cataloging-in-Publication Data

Thornton, Bruce S.
Plagues of the mind : the new epidemic of
    false knowledge / by Bruce S. Thornton. —
    1st ed. —Wilmington, DE : ISI Books, 1999

p.   cm.

    ISBN 1-882926-34-X
1. Rationalism—History. I. Title

    B837 .T46 1999   99-64337
    149/ .7—dc21   CIP

Printed in Canada

BOOK DESIGN BY MARJA WALKER

Published in the United States by:

ISI Books
P.O. Box 4431
Wilmington, DE 19807-0431
www.isi.org

CONTENTS

PREFACE

Thus, I say, must these authors be read, and thus must we be read
our selves, for discoursing on matters dubious, and many contro-
vertible truths, we cannot without arrogancy entreate a credulity, or
implore any farther assent, than the probability of our reason, and
verity of experiments induce.

— SIR THOMAS BROWNE[1]

Any book that claims to identify and expose false knowledge
must be willing to submit itself to the same scrutiny to which
it subjects others. Let me acknowledge from the start that the following pages deserve to be analyzed and examined, their errors identified and exposed. My aim—however much I may unwittingly
betray it—is not so much to assert a positive, true doctrine that
should replace the false one, but rather to incite the reader's own
critical eye to examine more carefully the many received truths and
elements of public wisdom circulating in our collective mind. If this
means that my own ideas are subjected to the same scrutiny, then
this book has achieved its aim.

A second question may arise in the reader's mind—my own "ideology" or "situation." A particularly dangerous half-truth widely popular these days is that objectivity is a self-serving chimera, since "everything is political," the expression of one's social and economic privilege. There is no truth, only fictions woven by power to justify itself. Since we all grind our political axes, we should at least be honest about it and identify "where we're coming from," as we used to say in the sixties. I will deal with this bit of false knowledge later. For now let me say that on occasion my own "prejudices and prescriptions," as Thomas Browne puts it, undoubtedly intrude into the discussion. Exposing them is left to the reader's critical scrutiny I mentioned above. Yet I believe that my conclusions are based on a rational assessment of the evidence and on a critical examination of the assumptions lying beneath much of the false knowledge in which we trade. If those conclusions appear to some to be "conservative," then so be it—though I would want to know exactly what is meant by that term. "Liberal" and "conservative" these days have become question-begging epithets rather than descriptions of coherent principle. That is why we have illiberal "liberals" and radical "conservatives." Given that imprecision, I hesitate to reduce my beliefs to such vague and shifting categories. There is, however, one conservative assumption to which I will admit: the tragic limitations of all humans, especially their propensity to choose evil simply because they can. The strange belief in innate (rather than learned) human goodness that animates much so-called "liberal" thought seems to me a delusion that even a cursory familiarity with human history and human nature should expose.

One of the pleasures I enjoyed while doing my research was discovering the many first-rate books and articles out there that survey, analyze, and critique some aspect of our social and cultural scene in fresh and insightful ways. I have acknowledged these works with generous quotations in the text and with references in the notes. One of my intentions has been to bring together into a coherent narrative these disparate investigations of our various problems. My hope is that the reader will then be incited into investigating further the various issues raised and will repair to these resources.

Again, I am not so much interested in getting readers to agree with me as in getting them to look beyond the received wisdom and to exercise their own reason. Then readers can determine for themselves how much credence they should give the many "truths" to which too many of us grant "credulity" and "assent." Only that free and independent reason can keep us from "swallow[ing]," as Thomas Browne puts it, "falsities for truths, dubiosities for certainties, fesibilities for possibilities, and things impossible as possibilities" (1.5).

ACKNOWLEDGMENTS

I owe much thanks to Jeffrey O. Nelson of the Intercollegiate Studies Institute for his support of this project; to Victor Davis Hanson, not just for reading the manuscript, but also for his friendship and beneficia too numerous to name; and, most important, to my wife Jacalyn and my sons Isaac and Cole, without whom not much would really matter. I dedicate this book to my parents, in gratitude for all they've given.

INTRODUCTION

Let thy studies be as free as thy Thoughts and contemplations; but fly not only upon the wings of imagination; Joyn Sense unto Reason, and Experiment unto Speculation, and so give life unto Embryon Truths, and Verities yet in their Chaos. There is nothing more acceptable unto the Ingenious world, than this noble Eluctation of Truth; wherein, against the tenacity of Prejudice and prescription, this century now prevaileth.

— SIR THOMAS BROWNE[1]

The inspiration for this book, Sir Thomas Browne's *Pseudodoxia Epidemica*, or "Vulgar Errors" as it was more commonly known, appeared in 1646, midway through the century that, literary historian Douglas Bush suggests, started more than half medieval and ended up more than half modern.[2] In the still-fresh light of the dawn of science, it seemed to optimists like Francis Bacon and Thomas Browne that the human mind was on the brink of realizing the rationalist dream that had begun with Greek philosophy: Through its own experience and power, human reason could develop techniques of discovering the truth about humanity and its world, and this truth would at last liberate the human race from the miseries of both its institutionalized "Prejudice and prescription" and its enslavement to the vagaries of a natural world, whose innermost secrets would soon be illumined by the light of individual reason alone. So it was appropriate that the physician Browne—by profession and temperament committed to the individual's "experience and reason" as the "surest path, to trace the Labyrinth of Truth,"[3]— should follow the suggestion of Francis Bacon for a "*Calendar* of Falsehoods and of Popular Errors," an almanac designed to explode the many instances of inherited "false knowledge" saturating the mental universe of both his learned and unlearned contemporaries.[4]

We moderns, of course, live on the other side of the fulfillment of that dream, in the kingdom created by science's astonishing conquests. The average high-school student today knows more that is true, and less that is false, about the natural world than the most educated intellectual of seventeenth-century England. Even Browne had to suspend his judgment of whether the earth moved around the sun, since that fact conflicted with the divine authority of Scripture (1.5). And he confesses, "I have ever beleeved, and doe now know, that there are witches."[5] More important, that immense knowledge won by science since Browne's time has had practical effects in our world of which earlier philosophers would not have dared to dream. We in the industrialized nations are so sated with technology and its benefits that only the most spectacularly glamorous invention—cold fusion, say, or cloning humans—can excite us. We take for granted advances like electricity or antibiotics that would have awed our ancestors, and that have given us a level of material existence—nutrition, sanitation, health-care, security and freedom of our persons—that earlier people would have imagined existed only for the blessed immortals. Indeed, we of the so-called advanced nations are so spoiled that we must be the only people in the history of the planet who would consider televisions and indoor plumbing and automobiles bare necessities. In short, we see around us every day the proof of Bacon's assertion that knowledge is power, for scientific knowledge has improved our lives and altered our environment to such an extent that it is tempting to think Satan right when he promised Eve that if she and Adam ate from the Tree of Knowledge they would become as gods.

But even at the birth of the New Science certain voices were troubled by the dislocations the new knowledge brought in its wake. The early seventeenth-century poet and divine John Donne wrote that "new philosophy calls all in doubt," leaving behind a world "All in pieces, all coherence gone;/All just supply and all relation." The later Romantics, living amidst the "dark Satanic mills" conjured into being by the New Science's knowledge, felt this dislocation even more urgently. By 1849, when scientific progress was beginning its quantum leap towards the modern world, the English essayist Thomas De Quincey was warning of the need for some force that could resist the "vast physical agencies" unleashed upon the world, the need for "counter-forces of corresponding magnitude,— forces in the direction of religion or profound philosophy that shall radiate centrifugally against the storm of life so perilously centripetal towards the vortex of the merely human."[6]

But we of the late twentieth century now know that the realized dream brought with it a nightmare beyond anything Donne could have imagined, beyond any counter-force De Quincey could have dreamed up. We know that the price of our knowledge is not Satan's "divinity," but the fall into an ever more debased mortality; that the proto-Romantic visionary poet William Blake may have been right: Science is the Tree of Death. Our interventions in the natural world have wrought devastating consequences for our environment from which our species may never recover. An imperious science, driving from our consciousness every other meaning and truth-bestowing worldview, has left in its wake an anxiety and dread we desperately—and fruitlessly—beg that same science and its pseudo-scientific bastard offspring to alleviate. And perhaps worst of all, our knowledge has created weapons of a destructiveness whose monstrosity justifies, even more than in Jonathan Swift's day, the horrified evaluation of humans given by Swift's King of Brobdingnag after he hears Gulliver's delighted description of how the power of artillery can grossly insult the human body: "The most pernicious Race of little odious Vermin that Nature ever suffered to crawl upon the Surface of the Earth." No wonder that two of our most powerful and sinister mythic figures are both "doctors," learned men: Dr. Faustus and Dr. Frankenstein, one the seller of his soul for nature's secret knowledge, the other a meddler in nature's powers who creates a monster.[7] Both appear over and over in our popular cinematic myths, these days in the guise of the mad or naive scientist whose meddling with nature unleashes horrific destruction, as in the recent movie *Jurassic Park*.

More to the purpose of this essay, the "horizontal" spread of knowledge, its dissemination through widespread literacy, universal education, and high-tech media of transmission, has *not* banished ignorance, false knowledge, interested error, or institutionalized lies. The increase in facts and data has simply created a glut of decontextualized information that is *inimical* to knowledge, let alone wisdom. As culture critic Neil Postman puts it, "Information has become a form of garbage, not only incapable of answering the most fundamental human questions but barely useful in providing coherent direction to the solution of even mundane problems."[8] So Browne's main purpose in writing his book and his hope for rationalism, the banishment of "vulgar errors," remain unrealized. After three centuries, despite being awash in information, we are just as prey to misinformation, half-truths, gratifying superstitions, pleasing myths, and outright lies as any seventeenth-century Salemite reaching for a torch as he eyes suspiciously the neighborhood crone.

I am not just speaking, as one might think, of the outré fantasies that divert the average supermarket-tabloid reader and New Age spiritualist—the space-alien autopsies, Elvis sightings, two-headed babies, comet-watching suicide cults, photographed guardian angels, government-suppressed cancer cures, global corporate conspiracies, and various other gaudy hallucinations at which the "educated" elite sneer.[9] The hopelessly ignorant we have with us always. Rather, I am concerned in this book with the more respectably received ideas that many of those same "educated" folks believe and repeat from their privileged perches in universities, in the media, and especially in popular culture. These are the "thinking people" whom Thomas Sowell the columnist recently has called the "anointed," the caretakers of the "prevailing vision" that is rarely "confronted with demands for empirical evidence."[10] Those ideas are the plagues of the mind, the intellectual diseases creating the new epidemic of false knowledge that these pages examine.

First, like Browne, I will look at the various forces that singly or in concert facilitate the spread of false knowledge. Some are the same age-old human failings that were current in the seventeenth century, such as Browne's first cause of error, our "deceptible condition," resulting from the Fall and the further machinations of "an invisible Agent, and secret promoter without us...the first contriver of Error, and professed opposer of Truth, the Divell" (1.1, 1.10). We do not have to endorse Browne's Christian theology to recognize that a general human intellectual weakness, what Browne calls an "erroneous inclination" (1.3), accounts for much of the false knowledge we believe. Whether or not, as Browne thought, this infirmity is the fault of Adam and Eve and their disobedience, most of us today are still prone to believe things to be true, not because we have any logically defensible reasons for believing so, but because it is easier and more psychically gratifying than performing the hard work of reason that makes a belief well founded.[11]

Not long ago the media treated us to a classic example of people's "deceptible condition." In September of 1995 the Associated Press reported that obscene subliminal messages had been discovered in three Disney films. This rumor spread quickly and led to a deluge of letters to the Disney corporation and untold numbers of trashed videocassettes, despite the fact that none of the messages could be clearly seen, even with the help of a VCR pause-button. When the *Wall Street Journal* tracked the rumor down, it was discovered to have spread among conservative Christians whose predisposition to believe that Hollywood is Satan's personal propagandist facilitated the suspension of critical judgment.[12]

Believers, however, by definition put more stock in faith than in reason, like the churchman who refused to look through Galileo's telescope, and so at least they have a rationale for muddled thinking. Who are you going to believe, God or your own eyes? And I'm not so sure they're wrong about the Devil's devious machinations. But many people who sneer at ideas like Original Sin and the Devil are still just as prey to the intellectual weaknesses that Browne catalogs.

Like Browne's contemporaries, we all rely overmuch on sense perception, "led rather by example, then precept, receiving perswasions from visible inducements, before intellectual instructions" (1.3). Our minds are "further impaired by the dominion of [our] appetite, that is, the irrationall and brutall part of the soule" (1.3); thus frequently we are prey to our desires and passions. Rather than believing what we *know* to be true based on sure evidence, we believe what we *desire* to be true, or what makes us feel secure by making the world a meaningful place, or what advances some appetitive aim, or especially what gratifies our secret psycho-dramas, those private operettas in which we are the heroes unjustly hounded by a vast and shadowy conspiracy of spiteful disbelievers in our excellence. And so we are vulnerable to con-men of various stripes, "subtler devisors" (1.3) who can manipulate our ignorance and insecurities to peddle their own brands of intellectual snake oil.[13]

Then there is the false knowledge resulting from "ideology," our modern equivalent of what Browne's inspirer, Francis Bacon, called the *idolon theatri*, the "idol of the theater," those errors of thinking caused by accepting without examination a preformed intellectual system or structure of ideas. French social critic Jean-François Revel has defined modern ideology as an "intellectual dispensation" that fosters untruth by "retaining only facts favorable to the thesis one is defending, even, if necessary, inventing them, and [by] denying, omitting, or forgetting others to keep them from becoming known."[14] No better example of the truth-distorting effects of ideology presents itself than the century-long, baffling, passionate faith in Marxism of various stripes to which numerous Western intellectuals stubbornly clung—and in some cases *still* cling—in the face of the numerous facts demonstrating Marxism's complete and bloody economic, social, and political failure every time it moved from abstract theory to practical reality.[15] This adherence to ideology is a modern version of Browne's "mortallest enemy unto knowledge," what he called "a peremptory adhesion unto Authority" (1.6).

The predisposition to believe what is false underlies and facilitates the other causes of error that we will examine later. But here another cause of confusion Browne mentions should be noted: the numerous logical fallacies and errors of reasoning that humans have no doubt indulged since they first began to speak and dispute (1.4). These too will be shown to be implicated in some of the causes of error detailed below, but since numerous books already identify and define these fallacies, I will mention only a few here. One frequent mistake is the so-called "availability error," which means judging by the first thing that comes to mind, especially if it is a spectacular dramatic and emotional event publicized by the media. People who worry about being murdered by a stranger rather than dying of heart disease or in an auto accident are guilty of the availability error— the publicized emotional drama of the relatively few cases of murder obscures the much more frequent but less publicized and striking deaths due to crashes and heart attacks.[16]

Then there are the logical fallacies first identified by Aristotle, replete with forbidding Latin names.[17] One of the most frequent is called *petitio principii*, "begging the question," that is, asking to be granted the "question-at-issue" that one has set out to prove: those who argue for the existence of God by quoting the Bible—or the soundness of psychotherapy by quoting Freud—are "begging the question." Another frequent fallacy is *secundum quid*, or hasty generalization, the neglect of necessary qualifications. Any discipline, such as psychology or sociology, that claims to offer *scientifically* valid knowledge of human nature and society is necessarily prey to this fallacy. Human nature is simply too complex, partly because it is expressed through *practices* that result from "human decisions and actions" and that "are a function of human intelligence interacting with environment." Human decisions are not determined by unchanging laws, as are the processes of nature, and so most generalizations about human nature are bound to be too broad to satisfy the probative requirements of science.[18]

Then there are the numerous fallacies identified with the Latin preposition *ad*. One of the most frequent—and effective—fallacies in our public discourse, the *ad hominem* attack, can take two forms: alleging that some circumstance of your opponent's life and character is inconsistent with his argument, or avoiding the issue by attacking the character of your opponent.[19] The latter variety has shamefully become acceptable in American political and social discourse, especially as it involves the "question-begging epithet." This is the trick of sticking on your opponent an emotionally charged label that automatically saddles him as well with the assumptions or beliefs associated with that label. Back in the fifties, calling someone who advocated, say, detente with the Soviet Union a "communist" or "fellow traveler" was a way of simultaneously ignoring the issues and tarring an opponent with a decidedly sinister brush. In the sixties "fascist" was the epithet *du jour*, usually shouted by people who didn't have a clue what fascism stood for, and who apparently didn't know that World War II had effectively ended the fascist threat. These days, of course, the number of such epithets is legion—"racist," "sexist," "lookist," "ableist," "homophobe," "speciesist," "ageist," and, recently, such usually descriptive terms like "liberal" or "conservative," which have been transformed from descriptions of political principles into epithets. Even a seemingly neutral descriptor like "white male" has become an insult, denoting a genetic predisposition to be "selfish, uncaring, egotistical, paternalistic/patronizing, and inconsiderate".[20]

The use of these labels has now become so promiscuous and indiscriminate that they are virtually meaningless. "Sexist" no longer describes someone who thinks women are naturally inferior. It means instead someone who doesn't talk about women's issues in the ritualistic phrases and pieties established by the Gender Industry, the professional "feminists" in the media and universities who function as the caretakers of the revealed last word about female nature and the relations between the sexes. Likewise "racist" no longer describes someone who believes that race determines human capacities and traits and that one race is superior to another. "Racist" these days almost always means a white person who takes a position on issues contrary to that determined to be correct by the Civil Rights Industry, that congeries of academics, pundits, bureaucrats and activists whose job is to establish the correct ideology about race in America.[21] Likewise with "ageist" and the rest. They have degenerated into an intellectual white noise that provides cover for self-interested or logically indefensible arguments, making easier the belief in false knowledge.

As I said, these errors of reasoning and logical fallacies are important contributors to the existence and spread of false knowledge. Thomas Gilovich, in *How We Know What Isn't So*, has recently identified some other mechanisms of "flawed rationality" that, like those noted by Browne, facilitate our acceptance of untruth.[22] Our useful cognitive ability to discern order and patterns in phenomena often leads us to see a spurious regularity in random events: "Our difficulty in accurately recognizing random arrangements of events can lead us to believe things that are not true—to believe something is systematic, ordered, and 'real' when it is really random, chaotic, and illusory."[23] We also get into trouble by basing conclusions on insufficient or unrepresentative data, ignoring evidence that denies our hypothesis in favor of evidence that confirms it, or failing to dig up relevant information that may be hidden. And we all more readily see what we are already predisposed to see because of various emotional or psychological needs.[24]

In subsequent chapters we will find the "causes of error" identified by Browne and modern writers like Gilovich implicated in the other forces that foster erroneous beliefs. These important, typical "causes of error" will not be the focus of this book. Rather, I will concentrate on other causes of false knowledge unique to our own historical moment, the larger historically determined received ideas that have shaped the modern world and whose assumptions when unexamined make us receptive to false knowledge. These ideas and their history will be the main focus of Part One.

Part Two will examine three representative "errors" that can be found in the popular imagination as well as in the media and, *terribile dictu*, the universities. Here we will see specifically how the "causes of error" documented in Part One combine to make possible beliefs whose bases are self-interested fashion, or emotion, or a misplaced reliance on dubious authority, especially one tricked out in the meretricious glad-rags of various pseudo-sciences, not reason.

Two such misleading ideas have already appeared in this Introduction—the descriptions of science as *either* blessing *or* curse.[25] As we will see, both of these views of science are widespread in our society, and one of the great paradoxes of the modern age is that most of us manage to endorse both simultaneously. Each, of course, has something to recommend it, though the humanist discomfort with science and technology is very often overblown and fails to distinguish between science and scientism.[26] In the next chapter we see how the Enlightenment faith in the power of rational knowledge to improve human life prepares many people to believe much that is doubtful and mischievous. But despite the limitations of rationalism and its abuse by scientism, I cautiously share at least one assumption of the optimistic view of science: that knowledge of truth is liberating, even if ultimately, as Socrates asserted, all we can know of what we are—and of what is good for us—is that we know nothing, what the French essayist Montaigne called "the most certain fact in the school of the world." But even if reason cannot discover for us the absolute truths about humanity with the same assurance with which it has discovered the truths of the natural world, it can at least eliminate error. As Lactantius said, "The first step to wisdom is to understand what is false."

Moreover, it is the enslavement of science and reason to destructive passions, not science and reason themselves, that has accounted for the horrors of this century, upon whose walls, the German novelist Robert Musil said, the dead cling like flies. Too *little*, not too much, thought has been our bane, breeding monsters while reason sleeps. One of our most perceptive historians of the Enlightenment and its limitations, Isaiah Berlin, has recognized this truth:

> But the central dream, the demonstration that everything in the world moved by mechanical means, that all evils could be cured by appropriate technological steps, that there could exist engineers both of human souls and of human bodies, proved delusive. Nevertheless, it proved less misleading in the end than the attacks upon it in the nineteenth century by means of arguments equally fallacious, but with implications that were, both intellectually and politically, more sinister and oppressive.[27]

Today many of these same "arguments" and a whole host of others cloud our thinking and muddle our political discourse. Hence we are in even more perilous straits than the condition in which Browne saw his fellow Englishmen: "We are almost lost in [Error's] disseminations, whose wayes are boundlesse, and conferre no circumscription" (1.2).

Our situation is more dangerous, not just because high-tech media multiply exponentially the mischief that falsehood can work, but also because we are a democracy, and as Jean-François Revel has written, "democracy cannot thrive without a certain diet of truth. It cannot survive if the degree of truth in current circulation falls below a minimal level. A democratic regime, founded on the free determination of important choices made by a majority, condemns itself to death if most of the citizens who have to choose between various options make their decisions in ignorance of reality, blinded by passions or misled by fleeting impressions."[28] In short, without truth, democracy's immune system, we are vulnerable to the plagues of the mind, a whole panoply of intellectual diseases creating the new epidemic of false knowledge.

PART ONE
Of the Causes of Error

CHAPTER 1 ▪ KNOWLEDGE IS VIRTUE

Tell me, who was it who first declared, proclaiming it to the whole world, that a man does evil only because he does not know his real interests, and if he is enlightened and has his eyes opened to his own best and normal interests, man will cease to do evil and at once become virtuous and noble, because when he is enlightened and understands what will really benefit him he will see his own best interest in virtue, and since it is well known that no man can knowingly act against his best interests, consequently he will inevitably, so to speak, begin to do good. Oh, what a baby!

— DOSTOYEVSKY[1]

We in the West have an unshakable faith in the power of knowledge to solve any and every problem that besets us. When confronted with destructive human behavior—whether violent or sexual, whether aimed at ourselves or others—we immediately turn not to the philosopher or poet or priest, but to some social or psychological "scientist," and we demand that he give us a solution based on his expertise. We then instruct our "educators" to devise curricula and information campaigns that disseminate this "knowledge" as widely as possible, for we maintain our faith that those who know what is good for them will avoid those acts that are *not* good for them. Only the recalcitrant forces of ignorance and atavistic religious superstition prevent us from creating a social paradise free from the pathologies troubling us today.[2]

So it is that we think every problem in our society can be solved if only an effective regime of knowledge can be devised and communicated to people, particularly impressionable children. The perceived epidemic of drug abuse by the young, for example, in 1983 led to the creation of DARE, the "Drug Abuse Resistance" program, which sends police officers to classrooms to "teach" students how to resist the peer pressure to take drugs, boosting their "self-esteem" in the bargain. This $750 million program is now in schools everywhere, its logo as familiar as Coke's or the Dallas Cowboys'. The only problem with the program is that every study of its effectiveness shows that it doesn't work. Kids who go through the program are not any less likely to take drugs than those who don't. Yet the program keeps steaming along, fueled by our shared assumptions that knowledge is virtue if only the "experts" are free to give that knowledge to people.[3]

Or take the problem of adolescent sexuality, the baneful effects of which include teen pregnancy, illegitimacy, venereal disease, and the general debasement and vulgarizing of human sexual experience that follows from pyromaniacal children playing with erotic matches. An article from *Time* magazine a few years ago illustrates the widespread assumption that a social pathology like teen sex demands some educational program for its solution. The author confidently asserts that "AIDS ended the debate over sex education." Forty-seven states mandate sex education, and all fifty support AIDS education. In other words, there is universal agreement that the perceived threat of a horrible disease resulting from careless sexual activity can be met only by an educational program. The problem, according to *Time* writer Mary Gibbs, is that the current "bloodless approach to learning about sex doesn't work." Sex ed, everyone Gibbs spoke with agreed, "has to be about more than sex. The anatomy lesson must come in the larger context of building relationships based on dignity and respect." The disagreement arises only over what role abstinence should play in the curriculum. The article ends with, and hence implicitly endorses, the advice of the popular sex-technician Dr. Ruth Westheimer: "'I think that a child knowing about his or her body will be able to deal with the pressure to have sex.'"[4]

Nor is this assumption—that enlightened reason can control the horses of passion—limited to popular journalism. A recent article in the technical journal *Adolescence* takes as its starting point the earlier recognition in *Time* that despite the "rapid proliferation" of educational programs, teenagers have failed to alter risky sexual behavior and hence slow their rate of HIV infection. And just as in the *Time* article, the problem is defined as one of curriculum. According to the authors, these AIDS-information programs don't work because they fail to include instruction in "moral reasoning," which "involves labor-intensive discussions of moral dilemmas that foster cognitive conflict or dissonance that is resolved through moving to a higher level of reasoning." The rest of the article "demonstrates," with a survey and statistical analysis, the truth of the assertion that "coupling moral development training programs with AIDS-information campaigns would be more effective than AIDS-information campaigns alone." The authors' research is grimly "scientific," replete with tables, charts, and forbidding-sounding phrases like "Factor Loadings for Rotated Factor Matrix" and "Hierarchical regression analysis."[5]

What neither the journalist nor the "scientists" question, however, is whether enlightened reason *can* control passion in all people in every instance, or whether something like "moral reasoning" even exists—or if it does, whether it can be the content of a curriculum or a science whose method and procedures ensure veracity, rather than being, say, part of a religious doctrine buttressed by divine authority and reinforced by fear, guilt, and shame. Both articles, in short, are founded on the Enlightenment ideal that knowledge is (or *should* be, if it isn't) virtue, that if one knows what is good for him, he will pursue it.

This ethical dimension of rationalism began, as did most everything else, with the Greeks. One Greek in particular, the fifth-century B.C. Athenian Socrates, eschewed the natural science of the earlier Ionian philosophers to concentrate on the human questions of what virtue might be, what the good for humans is, and how both might be acquired. But Socrates steadfastly refused to answer any of these questions. Rather, he satisfied himself with exposing the false opinions of those he examined who pretended to have knowledge of these matters. Nonetheless, he believed that the answer could come only through a rational procedure for discovering a rational truth. His procedure was the "Socratic dialectic," the rigorous questioning of assumptions and definitions to which he subjected his unfortunate interlocutors. Hence his belief that knowledge is virtue, that truly knowing the good, and the virtues partaking of it, would make one good and virtuous.

This fundamental assumption persisted through the subsequent epochs of Western rationalism. For all their differences, Platonists and Aristotelians, Stoics and Epicureans never doubted that man is a rational animal or that the key to his happiness as a human depended on the exercise of his reason. The great popularizer of the ancient world, the Roman politician and philosopher Cicero, in his *Tusculan Disputations* (45 B.C.) gives a convenient summary of this (by his time) commonplace belief: "Therefore if this soul has been so trained, if its power of vision has been so cared for that it is not blinded by error, the result is mind made perfect, that is, complete reason, and this means also virtue. And if everything is happy which has nothing wanting...and if this is the peculiar mark of virtue, assuredly all virtuous men are happy."[6]

Likewise, Christianity saw man's reason as the image of God breathed into him at the creation, a divine faculty wounded, to be sure, by the Fall and hence dependent on God's freely given revelation of its true nature and destiny. But once revealed, truth would be seen to be consistent with natural reason. As savants said in the Middle Ages, "Philosophy is the handmaid of theology"—reason serves revelation. So it is that in Dante's *Divine Comedy*, Virgil, the epitome of the Greco-Roman mind, the highest development of natural reason, escorts Dante to the top of Mount Purgatory, where the poet witnesses the revelation of Beatrice, the wisdom of salvation. Reason and revelation form one continuous spiritual and intellectual journey.

In the eighteenth-century Enlightenment, though, the rationalist ideal of Hellenism, whose rebirth began in the Renaissance, finally was liberated from the theological limitations of Christianity—there was, in social historian Peter Gay's terms, a "recovery of nerve," an optimistic belief in rational inquiry and its improving potential that had been lost with the triumph of Christian ascetic pessimism.[7] The rise of the New Science in the seventeenth century and its most spectacular triumph, the *Principia Mathematica* of Isaac Newton (1687), fired Enlightenment philosophers with the dream of human perfection achieved, not through the superstitions and mysteries of religion, but through the efforts of the human mind alone. Isaiah Berlin describes the hope that animated later thinkers dazzled by the achievement of Newton and other natural scientists:

The behaviour of human beings, both individually and in the aggregate, is in principle intelligible, if the facts are observed patiently and intelligently, hypotheses formulated and verified, laws established, with the same degree of genius and success—and why not?—

as had attended the great discoveries of physics, astronomy, and chemistry, and seemed likely soon to bring about similar triumphs in the realm of biology, physiology, and psychology. The success of physics seemed to give reason for optimism: once appropriate social laws were discovered, rational organisation would take the place of blind improvisation, and men's wishes, within the limits of the uniformities of nature, could in principle all be made to come true.[8]

Once this optimism took hold in the West, no amount of evidence of human depravity and imperfection could shake it. Through revolution, war, torture, cruelty, and the repeated bloody failures of all attempts rationally to reorganize human nature, Westerners have kept to their belief, again in Berlin's words, that "the rational reorganisation of society would put an end to spiritual and intellectual confusion, the reign of prejudice and superstition, blind obedience to unexamined dogmas, and the stupidities and cruelties of the oppressive regimes which such intellectual darkness bred and promoted."[9]

By the early twentieth century this faith had created *inter alia* the "human sciences" of psychology, sociology, and anthropology, those modern disciplines whose objective methods are supposed to lead us to the truth of the individual and his society. Just as the truths of physics had led to marvelous technologies radically altering and improving the material world, so too would these truths of the "human sciences" bring forth techniques and procedures for eliminating the evils from which mankind had suffered for millennia. Moreover, just as knowledge in the natural sciences was cumulative, leading to ever greater knowledge, so the knowledge of humanity would increase with every generation. Hence the birth of the powerful myth of progress: each generation will know more than the previous one, and this knowledge will lead necessarily to the material and spiritual improvement of our lives, the elimination of the moral and physical evils from which humanity has suffered for ages. In the words of nineteenth-century philosopher Herbert

Spenser at the end of that century: "Progress is not an accident, but a necessity. Surely must evil and immorality disappear; surely must men become perfect."[10]

Nowhere in the West has this optimism, this faith in a progressive improving knowledge, been more tenaciously clung to than in the United States. The reason can be found in the peculiar circumstances of American history. The American character saw its spiritual, economic, and political possibilities as unlimited as the land stretching westward. As Tocqueville put it, "The majority [of Americans] believe that a man by following his own interest, rightly understood, will be led to do what is just and good. They have all a lively faith in the perfectibility of man, they judge that the diffusion of knowledge must necessarily be advantageous, and the consequences of ignorance fatal."[11] So it was that the "human sciences" of sociology and psychology, with their promises of perpetual improvement, flourished in the United States as in no other Western country. And the result has been an entrenchment of these pseudo-sciences so firm that they have now become the sources of most of the received wisdom—and false knowledge—our politicians and social engineers depend upon when determining what steps they will take to solve our social problems. The difficulty, of course, is that both disciplines, despite wrapping themselves in the superficial procedures and jargon of real science, have about as much scientific legitimacy as mesmerism and phrenology, their nineteenth-century ancestors.

The inadequacies of psychology and its more well-known progeny, psychotherapy and analysis, as a scientific discipline have been repeatedly demonstrated.[12] As the scientist Peter Medawar has trenchantly put it, psychology "is an end-product,...like a dinosaur or seppelin; no better theory can ever be erected on its ruins, which will remain forever one of the saddest and strangest of all landmarks in the history of twentieth-century thought."[13] One has only to think of the silly excesses of the co-dependency movement, or the destructiveness spawned by the recovered memory fad, to realize how much

false knowledge circulates among us because of the drastic oversimplifications of human nature indulged in by psychology, which no
doubt would like to distance itself from its idiot offspring.

The co-dependency movement and its twelve-step recovery doctrine, despite its garb of scientific technique, have very little in
common with science. As culture critic Wendy Kaminer suggests,
the co-dependency movement is really nothing more than a secular
religion animated by "the ideology of salvation by grace. More than
they resemble group therapy, twelve-step groups are like revival
meetings, carrying on the pietistic tradition."[14] With its assumption
of universal addiction, and its bestowal of exculpating victim status
on just about everybody, the recovery movement appeals to anyone
and everyone—as the creation of the cable Recovery Network
demonstrates.[15] Though the erosion of personal responsibility, the
infantalization, and the vulnerability to con-artists, all of which are
products of the co-dependency movement, are socially harmful, they
are not as destructive to our civil liberties as the witch-hunts incited
by the unexamined assumptions and studied irrationalism of the
recovered-memory movement.[16]

Frederick Crews, one of the most trenchant critics of psychology,
has shown that despite mainstream psychology's decrying of the
excesses of this movement, its roots are in the fundamental assumptions about the human mind and its functioning that lie at the heart
of psychology.[17] Critical to both is the idea of repression, what Freud
called the "cornerstone" of psychoanalysis,[18] an idea that has passed
into the popular consciousness as a fact about the human mind, even
though, according to researcher David S. Holmes, "there is no controlled laboratory evidence supporting the concept of repression."[19]
Despite this lack of evidence, the recovered-memory adherents have
convinced courts and juries that a woman (rarely a man) can completely forget or "repress" a traumatizing childhood experience, usually sexual abuse by a male relative, but that it nonetheless maintains
the power adversely to affect the victim's personality and behavior.

Moreover, this buried memory can be unearthed by a therapist and remembered with amazing clarity of detail by the victim—who then proceeds to seek legal redress against her alleged abuser.[20]

The most famous court case incited by the recovered-memory superstition ended in 1989 in the conviction of George Franklin solely on the testimony of his daughter Eileen Lipsky. Ms. Lipsky, under the tutelage of a creative therapist, suddenly remembered with cinematic recall her father's murder of her eight-year-old childhood friend. Franklin's conviction was later overturned by a more sane court,[21] but the numerous convictions of other fathers and day-care workers based on memories fabricated by neurotics and therapists, or on the coaxed-out lurid fantasies of pre-rational children, testify to the destructive effects false knowledge can have, particularly when it cloaks itself in pseudoscientific jargon. So great is our faith in the power of science to discover the truth of our souls, that confronted with any quackery mantling itself in the language and methodology of hard science, we suspend judgment and common sense with all alacrity.

Perhaps the most pervasive example of how easily wanton speculation and oversimplifications dressed in the stolen garments of science dupe us into false knowledge, is the instant authority we grant to the "study," the *ipse dixit* of the modern world. Anytime a sentence is prefaced with the phrase "studies have shown," you can be sure to hear either some truism ponderously restated, or some half-baked oversimplification the authors of the study already believed to be true before they ever began. And when the "study" purports to prove some truth about that intricate, complex, quirky, unpredictable, unique creature that is a human being, then you can be equally sure that its conclusions add one more disease to the syndrome of false knowledge.

A good example of how a flawed study can create false knowledge that in turn becomes the basis of political action is the 1991 "Self-Esteem" study commissioned from Greenberg-Lake Associates

by the American Association of University Women. The results of
this "study" were proclaimed on the front pages of the most influential newspapers in the United States, and its dire conclusions can
be deduced from the *New York Times'* headline: "Gender Bias in
Schools Is Still Shortchanging Girls." Starting from the assumption
that girls are shortchanged in school, and hence wounded in their
self-esteem, because of the subtle gender biases of teachers, the study
went ahead and, *mirabile dictu*, discovered that little girls, between
the exact ages of eleven and seventeen, *are* short-changed in school
by the gender biases of their teachers, and so suffer from wounded
self-esteem, which in turn prevents them from excelling in traditional male pursuits. The study ultimately provided the intellectual
support for the $360 million Gender Equity in Education Act.

How did the self-esteem study reach this sweeping generalization
about millions of unique girls in millions of socio-economically
diverse home and school environments? By asking a few boys and girls
some questions, and then counting the answers. What sorts of questions? "I am happy the way I am," or "I am good at a lot of things"—
questions that asked of preteens would hardly elicit well thought-out
or consistent responses. Anyone with common sense can pick out the
other damning flaws of such a procedure through asking: first, does
something like self-esteem even exist; second, can it be "measured"
with any sort of accuracy, given that if it does exist, it must be a subjective state; third, do data acquired through "self-report," have much
value or accuracy; fourth, does the "quantity" of self-esteem have any
relationship to future achievement? Most importantly, though, the
study is fatally flawed by its gross oversimplification of human behavior, linking success, by a crude cause-and-effect mechanism, to some
phlogiston-like substance called "self-esteem." But even if we leave
aside these flaws, the study is condemned by its own data: the cohort
scoring highest on the self-esteem index was African-American boys,
the one group least likely not only to attend college, but also to survive past the age of thirty.[22]

This study, however, like most of its ilk, was delivered to a credulous press with all the phony objectivity conveyed by numbers with decimal points and an accompanying social science jargon.[23] Whether such studies tell us anything about "self-esteem" or the vagaries of teen sexual irresponsibility, they nonetheless win our acceptance of their intellectual chicanery by what we might call "Enlightenment arrogance," our hubristic refusal to admit that there are areas of human experience we are not likely to have much reliable *scientific* information about. We cannot accept that knowledge about humans may simply lie beyond the "complexity horizon," which the mathematician John Allen Paulos defines as "that limit or edge beyond which social laws, events, and regularities are so complex as to be unfathomable, seemingly random."[24]

The corollary of this arrogance is the "romance of science," our starry-eyed irrational faith in the power of research and technology to provide solutions to perennial human ills. What else explains our fascination with personal computers and the "information highway," our belief that they provide the magic solution to our educational woes, our faith that our fractured community will be electronically reconstituted through Internet chatter—even though the promise of computers to improve our lives or even increase productivity has so far not been met? Our problem is not that we lack information, but that we have too *much* trivial information crowding out the essential human questions. As Joseph Mitchell, the chronicler of the modern world's human detritus, put it, "The only information you get, when you're a child, is the information you're going to die. That's the information we're trying to hide. That's the information highway."[25]

Our bedazzlement by the romance of high-tech helps us to avoid the crucial question recently posed by essayist Barry Sanders: "Can we maintain a humanity that has been shaped by literacy in the face of a technology that threatens to transform, even to erase, identity and individuality?"[26] Moreover, our enchantment with technology fosters a dangerous "illusion of technique," as philosopher William

Barrett called it,[27] the assumption that knowledge of human nature, once discovered, will discover technologies of the soul which will morally improve us. This delusion has had, as we know, horrible consequences. It has created all the victims of the "terrible simplifiers," those, according to Isaiah Berlin, "whose intellectual lucidity and moral purity of heart seemed to make them all the readier to sacrifice mankind again and again in the name of vast abstractions upon altars served by imaginary sciences of human behaviour."[28] The desire to create new men through rational technique has usually ended up creating new corpses.

The "human sciences" spawned by the Enlightenment ideal ultimately founder on the sheer quirky uniqueness of every one of us, on the stubborn mystery of our hearts and wills. Dostoyevsky's prophetic Underground Man understood the dangers of these simplifications of human nature, for he was the spiteful, twisted creature of the world created by their nineteenth-century versions, particularly Utilitarianism. He knew that the attempts of the nineteenth-century "human sciences" to categorize and define human nature objectively would lead to dehumanization, that the essence of our identities was, not reason alone, but our power to express our freedom and individuality and humanity by *choosing*, even if we choose our own and others' destruction: "One's own free and unfettered volition, one's own caprice, however wild, one's own fancy, inflamed sometimes to the point of madness—that is the one best and greatest good, which is never taken into consideration because it will not fit into any classification, and the omission of which always sends all systems and theories to the devil."[29] And if we are thwarted in our desires, if we are reduced to mere "piano keys" played upon by the forces of nature or society, just to prove we are men and *not* piano keys we will hurl a brick through the glass of the Crystal Palace, Dostoyevsky's metaphor for all the brave new worlds promised by reason and technology.

We have seen this century the crash of many Crystal Palaces, yet we still stubbornly believe in the old ideal that knowledge is virtue, that we will be good if we rationally know the good, that the corruption and debasement of our society are not the expression of the fundamental mystery of good and evil in the human heart, but rather are merely the consequences of ignorance, problems for technicians to solve with the appropriate knowledge and technology. Meanwhile, the degradation of our lives continues even as the libraries are stuffed fuller with books and studies purporting to tell us the truth about our murky, dense selves. But this "truth" ultimately comprises nothing more than the ritualistic acts of those who worship the *idola quantitatis,* the "idols of quantification," and who stubbornly hold to their "faith in the efficacy of statistical formulae" as the way to tear the heart out of our mystery.[30] But all their works create little more than new viruses of false knowledge raising the fever of our discontent.

CHAPTER 2 ■ "FEELING IS ALL THERE IS"

Feeling is all there is.

— GOETHE[1]

The great object in life is sensation, to feel that we exist—even though in pain.

— BYRON[2]

We have seen how easily you can slip into a distrust of reason and science because of the excesses of scientism and the stress of technology. European civilization went through a somewhat similar collective reaction against the imperious rationalism of the eighteenth century, a varied and complex movement that we identify with the broad and imprecise label "Romanticism." In fact, long before the eighteenth century the pretensions of reason had been recognized, even before Christianity's subordination of it to the wisdom of revelation. The very birth of rationalism in fifth-century Greece was accompanied by a countermovement that, while not "romantic"

in the modern sense, nonetheless asserted the limitations of reason and the power of passion.

Athenian tragedy was the main venue for this assertion, presenting on its stage characters like Oedipus, the riddle-solver who did not even know his true name or his mother or father, hence marrying the one and murdering the other, his powerful mind incapable of reining in the eros and violence within him. Athenians could also watch the passion-ridden women of Euripides, characters like Medea, the spurned wife whose heroic wrath over her wounded honor drives her to murder her own children in order to punish her husband Jason. During her struggle with herself before she kills her sons, she voices the despair of all such victims of passion: "Passion is mightier than my counsels, and this is the greatest cause of evils for mortals."[3] With this anguished cry Euripides reproached his contemporary Socrates' belief that virtue is knowledge.

The Romantic reaction to rationalism, however, was different from that of Greek tragedy. The latter never idealized passion, and it criticized the rationalist, not for his denigration of the irrational, which Greek tragedy agreed was volatile and destructive, but for the rationalist's arrogant dismissal of a power he believed reason could control. No play shows us the inhuman destructiveness of the irrational as forcefully as Euripides' *Bacchae*. In this play, reason and social constraints are swept away by the terrible amoral power of the seductive Dionysus, god of the irrational and of the creative-destructive forces lurking beneath the bewitching beauties of nature. The Romantics, on the other hand, coupled their distrust of reason to a novel idealization of nature and the irrational, particularly feeling, which was transformed into a superior faculty for discovering truth. The significance of feeling for the Romantics, according to literary critic Walter Jackson Bate, was that it "transcends what is usually regarded as 'reason,' not only because it offers a more spontaneous vitality of realization, but also because it is aware of nuances of significance and of interrelationship to which the logical process is impervious."[4]

The chaotic diversity of Romanticism testifies to its heterogeneous origins. An early impetus came in the mid-eighteenth century from Germany, whose intellectuals and artists nursed a nationalist grudge against the arrogant cultural brilliance of the French. The *sturm und drang* or "storm and stress" movement attacked the "entire tidy ordering of life by the principles of reason and scientific knowledge."[5] They countered the bloodless French universal reason with a perfervid Teutonic passion rooted in the blood and soil of the fatherland, opposing the Classical marble of the city with the German oak of the Hyrcanian forest.[6] The poets and playwrights of this movement valued the unique individual and the intensity of his passions and sensibilities: hence their plays, Isaiah Berlin states, "celebrate passion, individuality, strength, genius, self-expression at whatever cost, against whatever odds, and usually end in blood and crime, their only form of protest against a grotesque and odious social order." Johann Gottfried von Herder, a leading light of the *sturm und drang*, repudiated the Gallic arch-rationalist Descartes's "I think, therefore I am" with a defiant, "I am not here to think, but to be, feel, live!"[7]

Another influence on Romanticism came from a conservative Christian reaction against the Enlightenment's ideal of human perfectibility, or at least improvement, through the development of reason, a belief which obviously repudiated the doctrine of original sin and man's dependence on the unearned grace of God for his salvation. Protestantism in general provided Romanticism with many of its assumptions: the importance, in the drama of salvation, of the individual's introspection of what historian of ideas Arthur Lovejoy called "the inexhaustible realm of the inner life of man"[8] rather than of the church and outward acts; the central place of passion rather than of reason; and an adversarial stance toward a corrupt world. German pietism in particular, at once highly emotional and obsessed with the individual's intense experience of his own conscience, had no use for the Enlightenment's program of improvement through cool ratiocination.

The Christian rejection of reason in favor of the heart characterized a strain of conservative Romanticism that to this day has continued to oppose the optimism of secular Enlightenment values. In
its most extreme forms, this contrary emphasis on man's irrational
depravity rather than his improvability would lead Joseph de
Maistre, an intellectual ancestor of fascism, to brood on the "dark
instincts" that govern our lives, the passionate forces made only more
volatile and dangerous by secular education and a critical sensibility,
forces ultimately controllable only by the fear of coercion: "All social
order depends on one man," de Maistre asserted, "the executioner."[9]

For all its different expressions and origins, however, the core of
Romanticism—and its legacy to our world—is its obsession with
man's emotional life and the intensity and value of feeling. One of
the most important exemplars of the Romantic sensibility's idoliz-
ing of the irrational is Goethe's Werther in the novel *The Sorrows of
Young Werther* (1774), an early-modern "best-seller" whose influence
could be seen in the scores of melancholy young men sporting their
hero's canary-yellow waistcoats and, in some instances, even emulat-
ing his suicide. Werther's character, adventures, and fate provide a
catalogue of the Romantic ideals, whose full flowering would come
in the nineteenth century in France and England, and whose
assumptions persist to this day, influencing the way we understand—and misunderstand—human nature and values.

The center of Werther's character is his heart—"this wildly fluc-
tuating heart of mine," as he calls it, "of which I am so proud, for it
is the source of all things—all strength, all bliss, all misery."[10] The
heart is the organ of "feeling": intense, immediate, frequent, and
overwhelmingly vivid responses, first, to beauty and sentiment,
whether these be found in art, nature or other people, particularly an
adored loved one, or, second, to one's life-experiences, whether these
be happy or sad, joyful or tragic. The only evil is boredom and
apathy, the poisoned fruit of a critical consciousness that withers at
the roots the heart's spontaneous expression. Moreover, this obses-

sion with one's subjective experience promotes a radical individualism pitting the sensitive soul against the strictures of a philistine,
insensitive, and grasping social order.

One of the most enduring Romantic legacies to us moderns is
our view of nature and its beauty as phenomena charged with significance for our private emotional states. Werther is an important
ancestor of this idea. He is a lover of nature, responding to its beauties with that eighteenth-century fervor new to the Western consciousness: "The solitude in these blissful surroundings is balm to
my soul, and with its abundance, the youthful season of spring
cheers my heart, which is still inclined to shudder. Every tree, every
hedgerow is a bouquet. It makes me wish I were a ladybug and
could fly in and out of this sea of wondrous scents and find all my
nourishment there" (24). However, the value of nature's beauty lies,
not in itself, but in its power to express the emotional state of the
sensitive soul, as Werther himself confesses: "When I used to look at
the far-off hills across the river from the crags that give me a full
view of the fruitful valley below and saw all things burgeoning
around me…how warmly I used to be able to embrace all this and
feel like a god in its abundance!" (62). Yet the suffering occasioned
by his doomed passion for the inaccessible Lotte transforms nature
into "an eternally devouring, eternally regurgitating monster" (63).
Either way, what is significant in these two very different passages is
that nature's beauty or its cruelty becomes an extension of the sensitive consciousness, a projection of the egocentric's fascination with
his own emotional life.

Just as scenic beauty arouses intense feeling, so do other people,
especially if they are touching or poignant or quaint—children are
for Werther, as they are still for us, a source of sentimental
response—a modern phenomenon, by the way, rarely found in the
medieval or ancient world. The lower classes, too, afford the slumming man of sentiment occasions for a patronizing emotional hedonism, since the undeveloped intellect of the masses does not get in

the way of their intense enjoyment of life. "Oh," Werther enthuses, "how thankful I am that my heart can feel the simple, harmless joys of the man who brings to the table a head of cabbage he has grown himself, and in a single moment enjoys, not only the vegetable, but all the fine days and fresh mornings since he planted it..." (43). One wonders what the cabbage-grower thought of the back-breaking labor he underwent to win some scant nutrition—or what he thought of providing food for lounging esthetes. One has only to think of our modern poets and intellectuals hanging out among pro-letarians, third-worlders, and ethnic minorities to see the persistence of this Romantic ideal.

Finally, art as a source of beauty and sentiment here embarks as well on its long journey as a secular religion: in the scene where Lotte and Werther, watching a thunderstorm pass over the landscape, both think of the same poem by the German Romantic Klopstock and start to weep, is an archetype of sentimental art-worship, the bran-dishing of art as the sign of a sensitive and superior soul, that today still determines many people's experience and valuation of art. Witness the on-going flap over attempts to limit or eliminate the subsidies provided by the National Endowment for the Arts. Supporters of the NEA trot out every tired cliché about the lone artist daring to tweak the stuffy noses of the "boobsoisie" as he plumbs the depths of human experience to bring back truths those philistines are too timid, but need, to confront. All this despite the fact that the successful artist today is comfortably subsidized by the government, the universities, and corporate largess—that is, by the boobsoisie.[11]

But more than all these venues of emotional response, love and sexual passion afford the Romantic his most intense opportunities for feeling. Werther's great, fatal love is Lotte, who during the course of the novel is first engaged and then married to the dull rationalist Albert. Poor Albert, Werther sneers, is "sensible" and "respectable" (58), hence clearly not good enough for Lotte.

Werther's doomed love for Lotte establishes one of the fundamental paradigms of the Romantic sensibility, and the one still prevalent today—the idealization of, and the obsession with, the *subjective experience* of sexual passion. Werther shows us that Romantic love is not about sex but about *desire*, the individual's solipsistic wallowing in the emotional disturbances occasioned by unfulfilled sexual attraction. Lotte herself understands this about Werther's attraction to her when she admonishes, "I fear that it is just the impossibility of possessing me that makes your desire for me so fascinating" (108). Werther is not in love with Lotte but with his own experience of being in love, with the passionate charge, the drama and significance unfulfilled sexual desire gives to everyday life. In other words, Werther is actually in love with *himself*; his experience represents the snake of radical individualism devouring its own erotic tail.[12] If Werther actually had sex with Lotte, his desire would begin its slow death at the hands of familiarity and the hard mundane work of maintaining an adult relationship. Hence he blows his brains out, finding in suffering and death the ultimate intense feeling.

All of these expressions of the Romantic sensibility—individualism, nature-love, primacy of feeling, and the obsession with the experience of sexual passion—are alive and flourishing in our own mental universe. Two historical developments explain why. The more remote in time but the most important was the creation of consumer capitalism, an economic system that depends on the creation of new products to gratify, not needs, but wants conjured up out of chaotic human desire by the new technology of mass advertising. The creation of wants in turn depends on fostering a dissatisfaction with reality, an obsession with the self and its pleasures, and a distrust of traditional values and authority—all of which found first validation in Romanticism.[13]

A debased and trivialized Romanticism is thus today kept alive in advertising and popular culture, the vehicle both for engendering a dissatisfaction with everyday life when compared to the exotic idealized worlds of the ad or movie, and for promising the means for gratifying, through the product, the desire for a more highly charged and intense life. This link of generalized desire to particular product explains the prevalence of sexual love in advertising and popular culture: the consumer ideal gains in attractiveness and intensity the more it is sexualized.

This link between consumerism and sexual idealism was prophetically recognized by Gustave Flaubert in his *Madame Bovary* (1856). Emma Bovary, dissatisfied first with her father's farm and then with her husband, the dull doctor Charles Bovary, her active, passionate, selfish imagination fired by the engravings in mass circulation magazines and by the lurid novels she consumes, finds in adultery and in spending beyond her means a temporary intensity of feeling and meaning. But the humdrum imperfect reality of each product and each sexual encounter quickly strips away the flimsy gauze of passionate idealism with which she had wrapped them, until both her spending and adultery destroy her. Flaubert makes clear that her suicide is ultimately precipitated by financial as well as moral bankruptcy, each reinforcing the other, each the expression of a debased romantic dissatisfaction with what the poet Wallace Stevens called the "malady of the quotidian" that necessarily characterizes most of our lives. We can easily recognize this style of love, for it is our own. Like Madame Bovary we use sexual feeling and the consumer products it sells to ward off our dissatisfaction with the necessary tedium of human life and the hard work of human relationships. Thus we never grow up, our unrealistic expectations of love and life kept at a fever pitch by the sophisticated imagery of advertising and popular culture. Considered objectively, our notions of love are not just immature but downright creepy, as the nineteenth-century gothic sensibility understood. Gothic takes the Romantic obsession with sexual desire and death to its logical conclusion in the virtual necrophilia of *Wuthering Heights*'s Heathcliff or the sexualized terror of Count Dracula.

A more recent explanation for the currency of Romantic ideals than the rise of consumer capitalism is that great outbreak of anti-nomian irrationalism—and hedonistic consumerism—we call the sixties. Anyone who came of age then remembers that great outburst of Romantic idealism among the children of privilege: the attack on an oppressive reason, the valuation of imagination liberated by drugs, the idealization of sex as politically liberating, and the whole anti-urban, anti-technology, anti-authority, anti-social, radically hedonistic atomism dressed in a thin camouflage of leftist politics—all subsidized by an expanding economy. How quaint, now, sound the pronouncements of pedants-turned-guru like Herbert Marcuse: "The civilized morality is reversed by harmonizing instinctual free-dom and order: liberated from the tyranny of repressive reason, the instincts tend toward free and lasting existential relations—they generate a *new* reality principle."[14] We have seen the results of this particular brand of false knowledge, the price paid for "reversing civilized morality": the *un*civilized *im*morality that debases our lives: sexual disease, sexual degradation in the media and popular culture, unwed teen mothers, feral children raised by moral idiots, and the emotional wreckage left behind by rampant divorce—our new "real-ity principle."

Nourished, then, by consumerism and the institutionalized sixties-style idealization of the irrational, Romanticism is alive and well, the Tweedledum of the Enlightenment Tweedledee.

A ready example of debased Romantic ideals comes to mind in the largest grossing film of 1994, *Forrest Gump*, that "feel-good tragedy for the Prozac generation," as Philip Lapote calls it.[13] The central character is, literally a dummy unencumbered with a rational consciousness or intelligence. Hence nothing interferes with the direct and sincere expression of his feelings, which the movie pres-ents to us as a self-evident absolute good: the redemptive power of his uncritical love, after all, salvages at least two damaged souls. Contrary to everything we know to be true about our human existence, Gump becomes the nice guy who finishes first in spectacular fashion. If only we could disburden ourselves of our cynical inhibiting reason, the movie seems to say, and like Gump innocently trust our feelings and their spontaneous expression, we could make the world a nicer place and end up rich and famous to boot. The simplistic sentimentalism of the film is on a par with those bumper-stickers that ask us to "Practice Random Acts of Kindness." Unfortunately, everything in history—that "frightful monument of sin," as Lord Acton called it—tells us that human misery and suffering and cruelty are the result, not of reason itself, but of its lack; not of a paucity of feeling but of an excess of destructive passions.

In such a state as we find ourselves in, it is hard for us to know what it true or what is possible, or what we can reasonably expect from our lives and relationships. But just perhaps the excesses of a worn-out sentimental romanticism have now driven us back towards the *terra firma* of reason. We can only hope.

CHAPTER 3 ▪ DISCONTENTED WITH CIVILIZATION

When we start considering this possibility, we come upon a contention which is so astonishing that we must dwell upon it. This contention holds that what we call our civilization is largely responsible for our misery, and that we should be much happier if we gave it up and returned to primitive conditions.

— FREUD[1]

In addition to romantic love and to the cult of feeling, Romanticism has given us four potent myths about human life and history that permeate our consciousness and provide a fertile soil for false knowledge: the idealization of Nature, the belief in a past Golden Age superior to the present, the myth of the Noble Savage, and a distrust of Reason. All four reflect a profound dissatisfaction with civilized life, and though developed most highly during the eighteenth and nineteenth centuries, all have roots in earlier societies.

As soon as culturally and politically sophisticated civilizations arise, the demanding complexity of life creates a yearning for an imagined time when men lived in harmony with nature, unburdened by the restless mind and its frenetic activity. The increasing technological sophistication and inhuman scale of material life in the twentieth century—the monstrous size of our cities, the dizzying speed of our lives, the artificiality of life cut off from nature, the sheer complexity of psychically managing ourselves in an intricate, high-tech world clotted with ephemeral information and contrived electronic images—all have given an urgent attractiveness to certain ancient myths.

NATURE'S SWEET LORE

> *One impulse from a vernal wood*
> *May teach you more of man,*
> *Of moral evil and of good,*
> *Than all the sages can.*
>
> *Sweet is the lore which Nature brings;*
> *Our murdering intellect*
> *Mis-shapes the beauteous forms of things—*
> *We murder to dissect.*
>
> — WORDSWORTH, "THE TABLES TURNED"

There never was a time, as Harvard historian Simon Schama notes, when humans did not experience nature without a frame of "myths, memories, and obsessions."[2] With their hypertrophied brains and freakish power of speech, humans are literally *un*natural, and can perceive the rest of creation only through the lenses of culture and thought. They are what French social critic Luc Ferry calls the "antinaturalist beings par excellence."[3] Hence alienation from nature is built into the human condition, and those today who decry the destruction an exiling civilization has wrought on the natural world are not, as they think, arguing for a return to some pristine harmonious life with nature, but are recycling myths and longings as old as civilization itself.

What *is* relatively recent, though, is the *idealization* of nature as a realm of peace, harmony, freedom, and beauty, a space where human desire is free, like Dante's in the Garden of Eden on the top of Mount Purgatory, to follow its bliss without artificial, inhibiting cultural restraints. That idealization is possible only in a complex urban culture in which poets and philosophers are liberated from the daily struggle with nature's recalcitrance that farmers perforce experience.

The experience of agriculture in premodern societies, what historian Victor Davis Hanson calls its daily "boring, filthy, and physically exhausting"[4] struggle with a stubborn nature, acted as a check on wholesale idealizations of nature. For example, a look at ancient Greek literature elicits descriptions of natural beauty, but time and time again a lovely natural pleasance is the backdrop for some manifestation of one or more of nature's violent forces. In the *Homeric Hymn to Demeter* (700 B.C.) a beautiful meadow filled with flowers suddenly gapes open to allow Hades, king of the dead, to carry off the maiden Persephone. In the *Odyssey* (700 B.C.) Calypso's Edenic island is nothing more than a narcotic limbo, a life-in-death existence Odysseus burns to escape. And in the *Bacchae* (405 B.C.) the lovely tableau of meanads awaking in the forest, new mothers nursing gazelles, the earth flowing with wine and milk and honey, dissolves into horror when the aroused devotees of Dionysus attack the men sent to capture them, the crazed women killing and burning, pillaging and destroying cities.[5]

For the Greeks, then, a people of small farmers, nature is something to be controlled and exploited, its chaotic energies harnessed for the work of civilization. In the Hellenistic period, those few centuries between Alexander's conquests and Rome's hegemony (300-100 B.C.), the rise of large metropolitan centers like Alexandria in Egypt presumably fostered in poetry a greater appreciation of natural beauty and of the urban sophisticate's longing for a lost rural paradise. This complex of motifs constitutes the long-lived literary genre called pastoral. Yet the poems of Theocritus, the third-century B.C. "inventor" of pastoral, for all their appreciation of nature's beauty, still recognize the inhuman brutal power of nature and pas-sion lurking within the pleasance. Hence in the first *Idyll*, one shep-herd warns another to beware disturbing Pan, the goat-footed god of panic and lust who haunts the forest, for he is "spiteful" and "bitter wrath sits on his nostrils."[6] Nature is still something dangerous and volatile, riven with forces demanding the limiting controls of culture and the mind. So too did the Romans view nature—those dour farm-ers who saw all order as predicated on duty and hard work, values made necessary by a hostile natural world that hides its sustenance from men and constantly attacks his fragile order. "Toil mastered everything," Virgil wrote in the *Georgics* (37-30 B.C.), "relentless toil/And the pressure of pinching poverty."[7]

This adversarial stance toward nature, this need to dominate and control its forces, is often attributed to Christianity and its fear of the material world, the playground of Satan destined for the apoc-alyptic fire.[8] But in actual fact, its origins are as much Greek and Roman as Judaeo-Christian. According to Genesis, the world and its creatures were given to man's dominion and use (Genesis 9.2-3). But orthodox Christianity also saw the world as God's creation and hence good, its evil occasioned by our first parents' disobedience. Nature's order and beauty still signified their Creator's intention for man, the salvation history conceived in God's eternal mind and shining through the order and beauty of the world. Psalms such as 8, 19, 33, and 148 praised the beauty and order of nature as reflecting and sig-nifying the goodness of God. Hence man is to be the steward of this natural bounty, not its mere exploiter.[9] However, the beauty of nature was not its own end, but rather a sign of some spiritual real-ity. Dante, witnessing the appearance of Beatrice in the Garden of Eden, remembers a dawn sun rising through a rosy veil of cloud: not for the sake of its beauty and the pleasure attending the contempla-tion of that beauty, but because it signifies the imminent revelation of divine love and wisdom that literally recreates his soul, confirm-ing that it has been healed of the wound inflicted on it by the Fall.[10]

With the eighteenth century, however, we begin to see the appreciation of nature and its beauty as reflective of some *immanent* meaning that also expresses the human observer's passionate sensibility. Now in nature one finds not, as did the Greeks and Romans, a congeries of destructive forces that necessitate the limits imposed by the mind and its techniques; not, as did Christianity, a flawed but still accurate representation of God's divine goodness; but rather an inherent spiritual reality more intense and true than, and a wisdom superior to, the dry bloodless dissections of the rational mind, especially for the sensitive soul whose nerves are like the string of an Aeolian harp. Werther, we have seen, responds to nature this way. Other German romantics used the numinous primal beauty of the German forest as a stick with which to beat Gallic urban artificiality.

But nature-love flourished among the French as well. The eighteenth-century French expounder of many of Romanticism's key assumptions, Jean-Jacques Rousseau, in his influential novel *Julie ou La Nouvelle Héloïse* (1761) describes Saint Preux, lover of Julie, bewailing the "fatal gift from Heaven" that is the "sensitive soul." He is the "plaything of the air and seasons. His fate is determined by sunlight or mists, cloudy or clear weather, and he will be content or sad as the winds blow."[11] Nature's beauty provides fodder for the sensitive soul, expressing, expanding, and ultimately validating its various shifts of feeling. So we see that the Romantic idealization of nature is as human-centered and exploitative as the utilitarian's view of it as comprising destructive forces to be controlled or raw material to be exploited.

This idealization reached perhaps its most enduring expression in England, where the contrast between the black soot and smoke of growing cities and industries and the shrinking green forests and meadows intensified nature's vulnerability to the "Satanic mills."[12] Wordsworth's "Tintern Abbey" shows us nature's "beauteous forms" linked to the speaker's sensibility unfulfilled by the noisy complexity of modern urban life: "But oft, in lonely rooms, and 'mid the din/Of towns and cities, I have owed to them/In hours of weariness, sensations sweet,/Felt in the blood, and felt along the heart;/And passing even into my purer mind,/With tranquil restoration."[13] The value of nature lies in its restorative beauty that gives meaning to a life stunted by the "fretful stir/Unprofitable, and the fever of the world" (52-53). Modern life and the critical mind are both diseases that alienate the soul from its origins and true reality, the harmony with a natural paradise lost now except to the pre-rational child and the sensitive artist whose imagination can liberate him from the "shades of the prison-house,"[14] the dreary inhibiting fetters of reason and society.

By the mid-nineteenth century, these attitudes, once fresh, had hardened into the dullest of clichés. Flaubert shows us the banality of the provincial mind by having Emma Bovary and her future lover Léon expatiate tritely on the beauty of nature: "'Oh, I love the sea!' said Monsieur Léon. 'And doesn't it seem to you,' continued Madame Bovary, 'that the mind travels more freely on this limitless expanse, of which the contemplation elevates the soul, gives ideas of the infinite, the ideal?'"[15] The art critic Ruskin would complain about the "pathetic fallacy," the attribution of human emotion to nature, and in the early twentieth century writer Gertrude Stein would deny most emphatically any connection between human emotion and nature when she snorted, "A rose is a rose is a rose." But the protests of intellectuals and artists could not stop the incorporation of nature-love into the larger culture. Like the other Romantic ideals, nature-love was too useful for the growing consumer economy and its exploitation, through advertising, of our escapist fantasies, our need to find relief from the increased complexity and anxiety of modern urban life.

Nature-love permeates the consciousness of the West. Popular culture is saturated with it, national parks are enduring monuments to it, and as Simon Schama points out, even our suburban front lawns, the "phantom suburban meadow," are testimonies to how thoroughly nature-love has been ensconced in our cultural universe.[16] Even corporate polluters like oil companies tout in glossy full-color advertisements their love of nature and the environment, and tobacco companies give money to environmental movements to deflect scrutiny from the cost in human suffering of their products.[17] But the most obvious evidence is in your grocery store, where food-products try to get the phrase "all natural" on the label as many times as possible. The "natural," what comes from nature, is immediately recognized as good, whereas the "artificial," what derives from human skill and technology, is bad—precisely the reverse of how an ancient Greek or Roman would view things.

As we will see in Part II, though, it is the environmental movement that today keeps alive Romantic idealizations of nature. Consider the following from environmentalist Thomas Berry:

> Just now one of the significant historical roles of the primal people of the world is not simply to sustain their own traditions, but to call the entire civilized world back to a more authentic mode of being. Our only hope is in a renewal of those primordial experiences out of which the shaping of our more sublime human qualities could take place. While our own experiences can never again have the immediacy or the compelling quality that characterized this earlier period, we are experiencing postcritical naiveté, a type of presence to the earth and all its inhabitants that includes, and also transcends, the scientific understanding that now is available to us from these long years of observation and reflection.[18]

With its assumption of an immanent harmony between nature and humans, its portentous vagueness (what exactly is a "type of presence"?), and its dash of the noble savage, this passage hearkens back to the long tradition of nature-love satirized over a hundred years ago by Flaubert. Indeed, this statement echoes the pompous banalities of Léon and Emma.

And this assertion of human and natural interconnectedness does not just characterize the meditations of the Sierra Club elite. It is also in the films of Disney, always the best place to encounter the most widespread and attractive received ideas. The mega-hit *The Lion King* offers up the old Romantic nature-love wine in new ecological bottles. The Lion King Mufasa explains the "circle of life" to his son and heir Simba: "Everything you see exists together in delicate balance...," the elder Lion King explains. Sure, lions eat antelope, he admits, but "when we die our bodies become the grass and the antelope eat the grass. And so we are all connected in the great circle of life." The harmony of humans—and *The Lion King*, of course, is about humans—with the natural world, including its beasts, is a central assumption of the idealization of nature.

The problem with the "circle of life" metaphor, however, is obvious from Mustafa's own explanation. It's easier to wax lyrical about the circle when one is a predatory lion rather than its prey, whose unpleasant fate is to be hunted, torn apart, and devoured raw. Nature and its creatures are not a "circle" but a food-chain, a "fierce, eternal destruction," as Keats put it.

The old dream of harmony with nature, when coupled with the legitimate concerns of resource conservation, is a species of false knowledge that sentimentalizes and distorts the human experience, as we will explore in more detail in Part II. And the idealization of nature can lead to decisions that, in the long run, are harmful both to the environment and to people. The high value placed on "natural," for example, has made cotton very fashionable these days, no doubt because it is an "all-natural," hence more environmentally correct, fiber than high-prole polyester. But as geographer Martin W. Lewis points out about this thirsty plant, "To supply the world's growing demand for this 'natural' fiber, tropical forests are being cleared in Central America, the Aral Sea in Central Asia is being reduced to a salt-encrusted wasteland, the sudd marshland of southern Sudan is threatened with drainage, and the Ogalla aquifer of the central United States is being steadily sucked dry."[19] Or consider BST, bovine somatotropin, a hormone that occurs naturally in milk. Some dairymen began injecting it into their cows to increase production. Despite no known negative effects, an outcry arose against this "artificial" chemical in milk. The politically correct ice-cream company Ben and Jerry's bragged that its products were free of BST—all the while, of course, they were chock-full of one of the deadliest natural substances, fat.[20] Because of this irrational distinction between natural and artificial, we spend millions regulating chemicals with even a hint of carcinogenic potential, yet ignore the much greater number of naturally occurring carcinogens.

The worst example, however, of a misplaced idealization of the natural leading to serious consequences for human beings is the prejudice against inorganic fertilizers that has slowed the implementation of high-yield agricultural techniques in Africa. Because of this attitude on the part of Western ecological activists, who take their own superior nutrition for granted, Norman Borlaug, who pioneered high-yield agriculture and has saved literally millions of lives in countries like Pakistan and India once prey to famine, has seen his funding from the Ford and Rockefeller Foundations and the World Bank dry up. While well-fed European and American romantic ecologists indulge their fashionable technophobia, millions of human beings in Africa are starving to death.[21]

Just as the idealization of nature leads to irrational choices that do more harm than good, our next example of Romantic nonsense, the myth of the noble savage, distorts our understanding of history and human nature by idealizing primitivism and denigrating civilization, thus suggesting false solutions to our problems.

THE NOBLE SAVAGE

> {Man} runs eagerly after all the miseries to which he is prone, and from which beneficent nature has taken care to protect him...man is naturally good. What, then, can have depraved him to this extent, if not the changes that have arisen in his con-

stitution, the progress he has made, and the knowledge he has acquired?

— ROUSSEAU[22]

Just as the complexity of civilized life creates in its denizens the yearning for the simpler world of nature, so too the artificiality of civilization can lead to an idealization of those more primitive folk who still live in harmony with the natural world free from the constraints and crimes of civilization. Hence the myth of the noble savage, that staple of the Romantic sensibility whose roots also lie in ancient societies.

Like nature-love, the idea of the noble savage depends on an advanced civilization perceived to be the source of unnatural crimes and evils. As such it appears at the beginning of complex civilizations. The Sumerians had Enkidu, the "wild man" of the epic *Gilgamesh*. The Greeks too had various primitives who could function as foils to a degenerate civilization. The Scythians, Homer's "mare-milkers, most righteous of men," by the fourth century B.C. had become for the Greeks exemplars of the noble primitive life free from the corruptions of advanced societies.[23] The Roman Cicero approvingly tells the story of Anacharsis, a philosophical Scythian who refused a gift of money because his "shoes are the thick skin of the soles of [his] feet, [his] bed is the earth, hunger [his] relish."[24] The Romans themselves had the Germans, those fierce, forest-dwelling wild men troubling the empire's northern borders. Not even the calamity of losing a couple of legions in the Teutoburg Forest could diminish the first-century A.D. historian Tacitus's admiration for these simple-living sturdy primitives, freed from the effeminate luxuries corrupting the Romans both physically and morally.[25] And in the Middle Ages, the Wild Man, a forest-dwelling primitive who is brought back to civilization from the wilderness, possessed "exceptional strength, ferocity, and hardiness combined with innocence and an innate nobility."[26]

The idea of the noble savage, though, became much more potent after the European discovery of the Americas provided apparently real-life incarnations of primitive societies living in harmony with a beneficent nature.[27] The late-seventeenth-century poet Dryden, who first used the phrase "noble savage,"[28] described "guiltless men, that danced away their time/Fresh as their groves and happy as their climes," for they were untroubled by the corrupt complexities of a decrepit European civilization. Hence the new world natives enjoyed a life similar to that Rousseau posited for the "celestial and majestic simplicity of man before corruption by society."[29]

The characterization of American Indians in these idealized terms started with the first European who encountered them in the Caribbean, Christopher Columbus. His catalogue of the Carib's qualities could serve as a definition of the mythical noble savage: "open-hearted and liberal," "guiltless and unwarlike," "very gentle, not knowing what is evil, nor the sins of murder and theft," "a loving people, without covetousness," "the best people in the world, and the gentlest." And the reason for these qualities was the absence of the accoutrements and evils of civilization, especially private property and war. As we will see in Part II, these same assumptions can be found in the books of other writers who described the New World, including Las Casas, Hakluyt, John of Holywood, Walter Raleigh, Amadas and Barlow, and many others.[30]

Montaigne's essay "Of Cannibals" (1580) is perhaps the classic example of how the myth of the noble savage provided a cultural template with which to understand the Indians of the New World. The key to this myth is, as we have seen, the contrast with a corrupt "modern" European civilization artificially divorced from nature. Thus Montaigne counters the charge of barbarism or savagery leveled against the Brazilian Indians with an assertion of their superiority due to their closeness to nature: "Those people are wild, just as we call wild the fruits that Nature has produced herself and in her normal course; whereas really it is those that we have changed arti-

ficially and led astray from the common order, that we should rather
call wild."[31] Because of that natural "wildness" the Indians live in a
"state of purity" with a "naturalness so pure and simple" (153).
Montaigne makes it clear that the absence of a technologically complex civilization frees these happy primitives from the moral corruption afflicting Europeans:

> This is a nation, I should say to Plato, in which there is no sort of
> traffic, no knowledge of letters, no science of numbers, no name for
> a magistrate or for political superiority, no custom of servitude, no
> riches or poverty, no contracts, no successions, no partitions, no occu-
> pations but leisure ones, no care for any but common kinship, no
> clothes, no agriculture, no metal, no use of wine or wheat. The very
> words that signify lying, treachery, dissimulation, avarice, envy,
> belittling, pardon—unheard of. [153]

Montaigne's catalogue makes it obvious that intellectual activity,
and the cultural institutions and technologies it creates, are the bane
of civilized man's existence.

The New World Indian as noble savage, as we will see, is one of
the most widespread and influential of modern myths, capable still
of fostering false knowledge. One could argue that the founders of
cultural anthropology in the early part of this century such as Franz
Boas were motivated in part by the myth of the noble savage, which
led them to reject the claims of European racial supremacy based on
cultural and technological superiority. Surely the long tradition of
describing the Polynesians as sexually liberated noble savages, as
evidenced in the eighteenth-century philosophe Diderot's *Supplément
au Voyage de Bougainville*, facilitated Boas's student Margaret Meade's
idealized but erroneous description of Samoa as a sexual paradise free
of the guilt and repression presumably suffusing a decrepit modern
European civilization.[32] Since Mead's time other ethnic minorities,
marginal groups such as criminals and sexual deviants, and suppos-

edly oppressed third-world victims of modern capitalist civilization have all become prime candidates for a noble savage status promoted by patronizing writers and intellectuals who enjoy all the benefits in security, nutrition, and comfort that the same civilization affords.[33] Although not idealized to nearly the same extent as Indians,[34] Africans occasionally were transformed by Europeans into noble savages, as early as Aphra Behn's romance *Oroonoko. A History of the Royal Slave* (1688). Three hundred years later in America, African-Americans have become nearly as popular as Indians to the left, which is always in search of "primitives" with which to scourge a repressive complex society.

An influential example of black Americans as noble savages appears in Norman Mailer's influential and incredibly silly essay, "The White Negro."[35] All the elements of the myth can be found in this exercise in existential angst tarted up with romantic banalities. First there is the dissatisfaction with modern civilized life and its "stench of fear" exuded by the twin spectres of Hiroshima and Auschwitz (338). America, with its bourgeois "conformity and depression" (338), is particularly horrible, and only the Negro, or his white epigone the hipster, can escape this nightmare and find a meaningful and authentic existence as a "rebel..., a frontiersman in the Wild West of American night life" (339).

Why the Negro? Quite simply, because he is compelled by a racist society to be irrational and uncivilized—the very same rationale, by the way, that racists have always used to restrict the rights of African-Americans. The following passage combines these racist stereotypes with the romantic idealization of primitivism, all in order to gratify vicariously the jaded middle-class recusant's need for authenticity:

> The Negro...[must] live a life of constant humility or ever-threatening danger. In such a pass, where paranoia is as vital to survival as blood, the Negro had stayed alive and begun to grow by following the

need of his body where he could. Knowing in the cells of his existence
that life was war, nothing but war, the Negro (all exceptions admitted [!]) could rarely afford the sophisticated inhibitions of civilization,
and so he kept for his survival the art of the primitive, he lived in an
enormous present, he subsisted for his Saturday night kicks, relin-
quishing the pleasures of the mind for the more obligatory pleasures
of the body.... [340-41]

The hipster attempts to imitate the Negro, for he realizes that "hip
is the sophistication of the wise primitive in a giant jungle, and so
its appeal is still beyond the civilized man" (343). Twenty-five years
later Mailer's interest in the prison writings of another "primitive"
rebel against a square repressive society, the petty thug Jack Abbot,
contributed to the felon's early release—and to the murder of an
unfortunate waiter who graphically experienced the effects of a lack
of "the sophisticated inhibitions of civilization."

Even if you consider the murder of Mr. Adan as an untypical
consequence of intellectual slumming, one has only to think of the
pernicious effects of noble savage stereotypes on young African-
American men today—their depiction in films and popular music as
"gangsta niggas" ready to kill and maim and rape because they lack
the "inhibitions" of reason and civilization.

But the myth of the noble savage nourishes even more widespread intellectual disorder by providing an imagined goal of social
and political restructuring, an end so desirable and noble that any
sacrifice is justified, as Isaiah Berlin has noted:

The concept of the noble savage was part of the myth of the unsul-
lied purity of human nature, innocent, at peace with its surroundings
and itself, ruined only by contact with the vices of the corrupt culture of western cities. The notion that somewhere, whether in a real
or a imagined society, man dwells in his natural state, to which all
men should return, is at the heart of primitivist theories; it is found

in various guises in every anarchist and populist programme of the last hundred years, and has deeply affected Marxism and the vast variety of youth movements with radical or revolutionary goals.[36]

Every such attempt, of course—from the Nazi dream of recreating the pristine purity of the ancient Germans, to Mao and Pol Pot and the numerous other Marxists creating "new men" who, purged of the evils of false consciousness, would live free of nature's necessity—has ended in violence and savagery.

As burdensome as its complexities are, civilization is not our bane but our salvation—as Aristotle famously put it, we are social animals, and to live otherwise is to be an animal or a god. Nor does there exist *anywhere* on the planet *any* human being free of potential or actual evil and cruelty. As Kant said, "From the crooked timber of humanity nothing straight can be made." By denigrating Western civilization—the imperfect but still best hope for controlling humanity's penchant for evil and for providing the greatest freedom for the greatest number of people—the myth of the noble savage nurtures the false hope that human perfection and freedom are possible *without* civilization.

THE GOLDEN AGE

Who does not know of the Golden Age?

— AETNA 9[37]

The attitudes towards nature and primitives we have been examining presuppose a theory of history in which the simple past, consisting of life lived in harmony with nature, is morally superior to the corrupt and complex civilized present. Hence the idea of history as increasing degeneration is as old as the myths of the noble savage and a maternally benign natural world, both of which are subsumed in the myth of the Golden Age. That many of us today hold to this view of history, while simultaneously believing in the

Enlightenment myth of progress through knowledge, testifies to the human ability to hold at the same time two mutually exclusive beliefs, as long as they serve a psychic need.[38]

In fact, both views of history appear in Greek culture, at the very beginning of Western self-conscious historicizing.[39] The myth of progress is expressed in the story of Prometheus, the Titan who defied Zeus and saved the human race from extinction by giving them technology and fire: "All of mankind's skills [*technai*] come from Prometheus."[40] The natural world is not a friendly home for humans; it is rather a brutally indifferent collection of destructive forces and fierce predators. Only the mind and its projections out into the hostile natural world, the techniques that reshape that world and exploit its energy, can ensure our survival. This view of history as intellectual progress from primitive origins recurs throughout Western thought, and finds its highest expression in scientific optimism, the idea touched on earlier—that increasing knowledge of the natural and human worlds will ultimately eliminate all evils and create a utopia in which we all live like gods, beautiful and ageless, immortal and eternally happy.

A quite different interpretation of history sees the simple past as a paradise free from work and pain, because, the myth goes, back then nature took care of humans like a fond mother. The Golden Age myth obviously derives from some older Near Eastern source, a variant of which appears in Genesis. There the "noble savages" Adam and Eve, innocent of good and evil, are sustained by a nurturing garden that provides for all their wants, making both technology and self-consciousness unnecessary. The earliest extant Greek version, and the source of the rubric "Golden Race," is found in the didactic poet Hesiod's *Works and Days* (c. 700 B.C.):

> First of all the deathless gods who dwell on Olympus made a golden
> race of mortal men.... And they lived like gods without sorrow of
> heart, remote and free from toil and grief: miserable age rested not

on them; but with legs and arms never failing they made merry with feasting beyond the reach of all evils. When they died, it was as though they were overcome with sleep, and they had all good things; for the fruitful earth unforced bare them fruit abundantly and without stint. They dwelt in ease and peace upon their lands and with many good things, rich in flocks and loved by the blessed gods.[41]

Hesiod combines the key elements of the myth that will accompany its long journey through the Western imagination: the absence of crime, sickness, and misery; and a friendly earth that "on its own" provides sustenance and makes technology and life in cities unnecessary. These two elements are in fact linked, for the implication is that the more complex existence of urban life that follows from agriculture is responsible for human unhappiness.

Hesiod goes on to describe the progressive degeneration of the human race through the Silver, Bronze, and Heroic Ages. More to the point here is his description of the Iron Age, the present in which we live, the age of wickedness, depravity, labor, bad women, and disease: "For now truly is a race of iron, and men never rest from labour and sorrow by day, and from perishing by night; and the gods shall lay sore trouble upon them" (176-780). Later elaborations of the Iron Age explicitly link its miseries to urban civilization and technology: private property, sea-faring, trade, mining and metalworking, and agriculture. Greed, what the Roman poet Ovid calls the "cursed love of having,"[42] is particularly linked to all these inventions and their necessary outcome, war. Thus civilization is the source of all evil, for it has alienated humans from their once harmonious life with nature and subjected them to unnatural crimes and miseries.

The myths of the Golden and Iron Ages have recurred throughout Western history. In times of stress they provide a conceptual framework for understanding present misery and for promising a future renewal of the lost paradise. Often the myth of the Golden Age fed political propaganda designed to link a regime with this regenerating power. The Roman emperor Augustus, Charlemagne, and Elizabeth I all exploited Golden Age imagery to validate their rule.

More generally, these myths provided powerful psychic compensations for the difficulties of the human predicament. And as society in the modern world became even more technologically complex, these myths, along with a related ideal like the pastoral, survived as attractive refuges from the contingencies and stress of living. At least psychic release can be had by dreaming of noble primitives, freed of the anxiety and complexity of modern civilization, dancing the time away in gardens of nature, whether these primitives be the shepherds of pastoral or the New World Indians of the Renaissance. As we will see in more detail later, the myth of the Golden Age retains today this wish-fulfilling allure, whether it is located in a lost Atlantis, pre-slavery Africa, a matriarchal paleolithic Europe, or pre-Columbian America.[43]

Unfortunately, these modern simplistic idealizations of the past, apart from being contrary to the facts, allow us to avoid the central problem of human evil. They locate evil, not in ourselves and our choices, but in mysterious external forces of change that exiled us from paradise, and in the evil instruments of that change, usually these days white European males. And in linking our evils to reason and its creations, the Golden Age myth fosters a dangerous antirationalism that helps to obscure the solutions to our problems and holds out the false hope that paradise can be recovered and technological progress can be reversed. But as Isaiah Berlin has eloquently argued, the irreconcilability of human values means that all utopias are simply unattainable: "If some ends recognized as fully human are at the same time ultimate and mutually incompatible, then the idea of a golden age, a perfect society compounded of a synthesis of all the correct solutions to all the central problems of human life, is shown to be incoherent in principle."[44] Unfortunately, these days a fashionable antirationalism inherited from Romanticism makes "incoherent" a badge of honor.

THE FLIGHT FROM REASON

> *For not obeying the dictates of reason, and neglecting the cryes of*
> *truth, we faile not onely in the trust of our undertakings, but in*
> *the intention of man it selfe, which although more veniall in ordi-*
> *nary constitutions, and such as are not framed beyond the capac-*
> *ity of beaten notions, yet will it inexcusably condemne some men,*
> *who having received excellent endowments, have yet sat downe by*
> *the way, and frustrated the intention of their habilities.*
>
> — *PSEUDODOXIA EPIDEMICA* 1.5

In chapter 2 we saw that a distrust of reason and a suspicion of
its more grandiose claims have both developed alongside rationalist
idealism ever since the Greeks. Oedipus is the mythic paradigm of
the dangers of intellectual hubris, for he is the riddle-solver par
excellence, the one who knows the answer to a profound question—
What is a human being?—yet who is still arrogantly ignorant of
another, perhaps even more important question—Who am I? We
saw too how Romanticism married antirationalism to an idealization of the irrational, a union made more attractive by the relentless
triumphs of the modern sciences and the destructive effects of technology on humans and nature. Rousseau reflects this distrust of
reason and its development as the highest good for humanity, when
he claims that "the state of reflection is contrary to nature, and that
the man who meditates is a depraved animal." And despite his con-
cession that some benefits accrue to humans from reason, Rousseau
later asserts that man's natural goodness has been depraved by "the
changes that have arisen in his constitution, the progress he has
made, and the knowledge that he has acquired."[45] Walter Jackson
Bate summarizes this antirationalist assumption shared by most
strains of Romanticism as their "conviction that the essential nature
of man was not reason—whether it be the ethical insight into the
ideal or even the sheer mathematicism of the Cartesians—but that
it consisted, in effect, either of a conglomeration of instincts, habits,

and feelings, or else, as German subjectivism was beginning to illustrate, of an ego which creates and projects its own world, and which has little real hope of knowing anything else."[46]

But the Romantics, though, were making a necessary claim for the value of the individual's heart and feeling in the face of an imperialistic universal rationalism. In its most extreme forms, rationalism denied much that is truly valuable about both the spiritual dimensions of our humanity and the truths of the heart and imagination; and rationalism also dangerously evaded or simplified the central problem of good and evil by reducing it to a material phenomenon solvable by scientific procedures. As Dostoyevky's Underground Man put it, "Reason is a good thing, that can't be disputed, but reason is only reason and satisfies only man's intellectual faculties"; and though much of our life that lies beyond reason is chaotic and sordid, "all the same it is life and not merely the extraction of a square root."[47]

In the late twentieth century, however, the antirationalism of the educated elite does not champion, like the Romantics, a respectful recognition of the mystery of human identity. Contemporary antirationalism scorns the idea of the human person as obfuscatory nonsense. The new antirationalism is really a species of nihilistic skepticism. As scientists Paul R. Gross and Norman Levitt put it, this attack on reason and science "seems to represent a rejection of the strongest heritage of the Enlightenment," and takes a stance in which "irrationality is courted and proclaimed with pride."[48] When it provides the underpinnings of the attack on science, this intellectual freak is dangerous, for it both short-circuits the pursuit of the necessarily rational solutions to our problems and perpetuates one of the more toxic strains of false knowledge.

The "postmodern" or "poststructuralist" antirationalism in vogue these days lurks mainly in the university English, social sciences, and philosophy departments. In those subsidized groves, cleverness with language is highly valued, and reality is more easily kept at bay than it is in science laboratories, corporate boardrooms, or even the corner garage. Antirationalism reflects as well some intellectual fads of the past thirty years, academic fashions whose origins lie, as most fashions do, in Paris, that Graceland of the humanities professoriate.[49] I offer a typical statement of this rodomontade: "All facts, data, structure, and laws are assembled descriptions, formulations, constructions—interpretations. There are no facts as such, only assemblages. There is always only interpretation.... The concepts 'being,' 'consciousness,' 'identity,' 'presence,' and 'self' are creations, fabrications, patchworks—interpretations. Functions not facts. Effects of language, not causes. The same goes for 'meaning.'"[50] Nor is this radical scepticism about the possibility of rationally discovering truth the property of a few eccentric academics. What critic Reed Way Dasenbrock has said about literary theorists is true for all the so-called "human sciences": "Theorists who agree on little if anything else unite to view the word and the concept [truth] with suspicion."[51]

Boiled down to its essentials, this antirationalism is obviously part of a larger nihilism that asserts the impossibility of *any* meaning or knowledge—except, of course, its own—since meaning or knowledge are the epiphenomena of "discourses," linguistic practices that pretend to give transparent access to a meaning or truth about a reality existing apart from language. According to postmodern theorists, linguistic signs, whether of literary or scientific "discourse," can only refer back to themselves or other signs, and so are reflective of their formative rules and the sign-systems that bring them forth. These rules and systems in turn reflect repressive social structures whose intent is to consolidate and validate their own privileged positions based on exclusion and oppression, not to reveal truth. Thus rather than being the human capacity to manipulate a coherent method for discovering truth about the world, reason is a sort of parlor trick, a historically situated "discourse" that cannot reveal the truth of the world because that "truth" and that "world" are only linguistic signs made possible by an arbitrarily determined system of signification. All of what we naively call "reality" is like Gertrude Stein's Oakland—there's no "there" there. What we have instead is "interpretation," an endless dance of signifiers over the abyss that the ignorant masses stupidly believe is still occupied by "reason," "reality," "self," "truth," or "God." Thus the postmodern philosopher's work is engaged in the process of a liberating "demystification" of these systems that serve an oppressive power-structure.

As it has become increasingly tedious to have to point out over and over, all those who really believe this stuff have no basis for making these statements, since they're all "Cretan liars" ("All Cretans are liars: A Cretan said this"). If the professors *really* believed it, they'd just keep quiet. As well as suffering from fatal internal contradictions, poststructuralism has very little basis for touting itself as a challenge to any institution, let alone the university, where it has firmly and comfortably ensconced itself. An ideology so universally orthodox and subordinated to professional preferment and advancement can hardly be politically subversive. Most of the time the promulgation of these ideas, when not advancing careers, instead serves a sort of jejune impishness, a desire on the part of timid, politically ineffectual professors safely to tweak the noses of the bourgeois parents whose tuition payments and taxes foot the bill. If poststructuralist ideas were confined to the humanities or social science departments, little harm would be done, since most students have enough residual common sense to ignore such silliness.

Yet we should beware of the inclination to dismiss poststructuralism as an academic fad of concern only to marginal professors talking to themselves in books and journals nobody else reads. At heart, the constellation of ideas that make up poststructuralism is essentially anti-humanist, and anti-humanism has been the intellectual starting point for most of the horrors of this century. Literary critic David Hirsch asks, "Can literary theories based on an ideology that disdains all the institutions of democracy and disparages the individual as an inexorable self also safeguard human rights and freedom of the integral person?"[52] The answer is no, they can't. To say that the self is a "construct" or that "human rights" are nothing but camouflage for bourgeois hegemony is to pave the way for the alteration of those constructed "selves" and the abrogation of those "rights" that do not serve the interests of those in power, or for their outright elimination. After all, what's so bad about eliminating a "construct"? As Hirsch eloquently argues, "It is misleading to disengage contemporary antihumanism from Nazi dehumanization, for they share philosophical and cultural origins."[53]

This is not to say that contemporary poststructuralists are incipient mass murderers. But the connection between their ideas and the dehumanization that makes mass murder possible must be acknowledged, and the hypocrisy of their concern for social justice—or should we say "social justice," since aren't those "signifiers" a mere "arbitrary construct of bourgeois hegemony"?—must be exposed. Moreover, these ideas have also provided the intellectual support for an attack on science that potentially can do more immediate damage outside the groves of academe. Gross and Levitt's description of the poststructuralist view of science shows its connections to the epistemic nihilism described above: "[S]cience is not a body of knowledge; it is, rather, a parable, an allegory, that inscribes a set of social norms and encodes, however subtly, a mythic structure justifying the dominance of one class, one race, one gender over another."[54]

Unfortunately, these ideas are not limited to the professional arcana of esoteric humanities research based on hearsay misreadings of Thomas Kuhn's *The Structure of Scientific Revolutions*.[55] They seep out into the popular consciousness, becoming part of received wisdom. Pasadena's Jet Propulsion Laboratory (JPL) is the one place where you would think that the efficacy of modern science has repeatedly been demonstrated. After all, the space orbiter Galileo for several years has been beaming back to earth *factual* information about the more distant regions of our solar system, most lately the atmosphere of Jupiter. The Galileo works because its inventors and manipulators have discovered truths about the physical world available only through the methods and techniques of Western science. Yet even at the JPL, the current anti-science voodoo forms part of the lab's educational outreach programs. Its booklet, "Teaching That is Out of This World," repeats some of the zanier feminist anti-science nonsense, such as Sandra Harding's assertion that Isaac Newton's *Principia Mathematica* is a "rape manual" encoding the self-serving constructs of bourgeois patriarchy.[56] Even more frightening, this constructivist view of science permeating the JPL booklet very nearly made it into the National Science Education Standards for grades K-12. The May 1994 draft displayed, according to physicist Gerald Holton, a "constructivist bias throughout," one reduced only after a vociferous protest on the part of some members of the scientific community.[57]

One can't help thinking that it must take an enormous effort at willful blindness to repeat these ideas. If the successes of NASA and the JPL are too remote, just switching on the television or picking up the phone should quickly dispel such hallucinations. Those gadgets work because the natural world behaves the way science tells us it does. As Alan Chalmers succinctly puts it, "In spite of the social character of all scientific practice, methods and strategies for constructing objective, albeit fallible and improvable, knowledge of the natural world have been developed in practice and have met with success."[58] No doubt those who endorse these petulant complaints against science have numerous reasons for doing so, though sheer ignorance about science and its methodology must be the most significant.[59] The more understandable reasons are occasioned by the nefarious and destructive ends to which science has been put this century. In other words, the attack on science partly reflects the old Romantic protest against what William Blake called "single vision and Newton's sleep" without being redeemed by the concomitant Romantic valuation of the "holiness of the heart's affections and the truth of the imagination," as Keats memorably put it.

But whatever the drawbacks and deficiencies of science—and these obviously should be acknowledged and exposed—it nonetheless, as Ernest Gellner points out, is a style of knowledge that "has proved so overwhelmingly powerful, economically, militarily, administratively, that all societies have had to make their peace with it and adopt it."[60] As such, it remains the human race's best hope for alleviating the material, if not the spiritual, problems facing it. The jury is still out on whether science has been a good or a bad thing for the human race. Who can say whether vaccines and antibiotics and agricultural technology have saved more lives than have been destroyed by high-tech weaponry and industrial pollution?[61] Yet who can honestly say he would trade our spiritually empty but materially prosperous modern world for the spiritually rich but materially miserable medieval world? Nostalgia for spiritual fulfillment is always easy on a full stomach. The problem is not with science per se but with *ourselves*, with the way we misuse science to gratify our irrational passions and appetites or to give us "truths" about ourselves beyond science's reach; as literary critic and historian Roger Shattuck puts it, "Science is neither a sin nor a grail. Not our child but our invention, science as a discipline will never grow up to think for itself and to take responsibility for itself. Only individuals can do those things."[62] But for scientifically illiterate humanities professors to demonize science and reduce it to just one "discourse" or "practice" among many others that are just as (or more!) valuable, ultimately serves to validate much New-Age claptrap whose credo—"in nonsense lies salvation," Wendy Kaminer defines it—[63] carries serious potential for harm.

In fact, these silly ideas about science and reason are possible only in advanced societies whose intellectuals are pampered by the inventions and technologies science has discovered. I never cease to be amazed at sleek professors, the beneficiaries of high-tech nutrition and health-care, who present anti-rationalist ideas in linear arguments based on appeals to evidence cited copiously in footnotes, or who tap out anti-science fulminations on laptop computers and then jet off to read them at an international conference, while they use a cellular phone to refill their Prozac prescriptions. None of these people, when ill or threatened by disease, call on the services of shamans or witches so that they can take advantage of those other non-Western "discursive practices" whose value is presumably equal to that of Western science. Rather, they hustle down to the hospital like the rest of us, where they demand the latest in medical technology and chemical painkillers. The anti-science stance of some feminists is particularly ungrateful, since most of women's "liberation" has been underwritten by technologies like birth-control pills and abortion, not to mention Enlightenment ideals of innate human rights and equality.[64] Clitoridectomies, foot-binding, and joining the pyre of the deceased husband are not the cargo of the West.

But as the Underground Man points out, humans are "monstrously ungrateful."[65] There's no reason why professors should be any less so than normal people. Yet they *should* know better: aren't they blessed with what Browne called "excellent endowments," not just of brains but of leisure and pelf? That they should endorse such silliness constitutes a betrayal of the "trust of our undertakings," and one that hastens the spread of false knowledge.

CHAPTER 4 ▪ TRAGEDY AND THERAPY

To suffer is necessity for mortals.

— EURIPIDES[1]

Love, power, riches, success, a good marriage, exciting sex, fulfillment
are not impossible dreams. They can be yours if you want them.

— JOYCE BROTHERS[2]

The two complexes of ideas we have been describing—the
Enlightenment faith in the power of reason and the Romantic
attachment to feeling—have coalesced into a strange hybrid vision
we can call the "therapeutic." To call the twentieth century the "Age
of Therapy" is by now an oft-repeated truism. "The contemporary
climate is therapeutic, not religious," Christopher Lasch asserted in
The Culture of Narcissism, an influential analysis of the destructive
effects of the therapeutic sensibility. "People today hunger not for
personal salvation, let alone for restoration of an earlier golden age,
but for the feeling, the momentary illusion, of personal well-being,
health, and psychic security."[3]

Most people want to lay this shift to the therapeutic at the feet of Freud, for he developed and popularized the psychological and psychotherapeutic interpretations of the human predicament, interpretations in which, as culture critic Charles Sykes puts it, "many of the theological and existential issues of human life [are translated] into therapeutic terms."[4] This Enlightenment faith in the power of reason to describe with scientific precision the mysteries of human identity was buttressed as well by the belief that "techniques" could be invented for changing it.[5] Thus the therapeutic view is based on the assumption that people are "not as competent or as good or as happy as they could be; that there are few limits to the alterations they can make; and that change is relatively easy to effect. If only the right methods are used and the right attitudes are held, people can make significant changes and become almost whatever they want."[6] What Bernie Zilbergeld describes here results from the combination of an obsession with happiness (defined as certain kinds of desired emotional states and feelings measured against ever-escalating standards of happiness) with a faith in the power of technique wielded by experts to achieve those states—the unholy alliance of Enlightenment and Romantic assumptions.

The therapeutic vision, however, has spread beyond psychology and psychotherapy to dominate our whole society's sense of what is desirable and possible for humans and their relations with one another. It has created expectations for human life that are totally unrealistic and doomed to disappointment. As such, it encourages false knowledge: it creates not just unattainable expectations of happiness, but also the various pseudo-scientific techniques and procedures supposed to deliver on these promises.

In short, the therapeutic vision entails a rejection of the tragic vision that dominated the Western intellectual tradition until modern science and its success promised to eliminate the necessary limits of human existence and aspiration. Now, as Charles Sykes puts it, "In place of a recognition that human life is marked by disappointment and limitation, we have enshrined the infinite expectation—for psychological gratification, self-actualization, self-realization, and happiness—not as a goal to be won but as an entitlement."[7] Quite simply, we have embraced a lie, a distortion of human life that blinds us to what is realistically possible for human beings. We can see just how much the human condition has been distorted by the therapeutic vision by brushing up on the tragic view of life.

THE GENERATION OF LEAVES

> *Earth-shaker, you would not consider me to be sensible, if I should fight with you because of wretched mortals, who like leaves now flourish full of fire, eating the fruit of the earth, and now wither and perish.*
>
> — HOMER[8]

The god Apollo's famous assessment of the human condition is one of the earliest expressions of the tragic vision in Western literature. Like all other life in the natural world, mortals are defined by absolute limits imposed by their material bodies. They are subject to hunger, sex, anger, and fear, as well as to other desires conjured out of their imaginations. They are made to suffer from injury and disease. They grow old and feeble and ultimately die. They are at the whim of natural forces that weaken and destroy the fragile orders of civilization, the victims of predators and plagues that worsen the struggle for survival. And they are the toys of time, Heracleitus's "child playing checkers," a relentless process of chance and change that brings new suffering, that wrecks plans and schemes with unexpected contingencies, and that culminates in the bleak democracy of death.

This vision of human life was so central to the ancient Greeks that they invented tragedy as a public, civic expression of humanity's subjection to the non-negotiable necessities described above. Again and again in Greek tragedy brilliant, overachieving mortals are wrecked by the unforeseen consequences of their own passions or by the whims of the gods or by the absurd permutations of chance and time. Klytaimestra, Oedipus, Ajax, Antigone, Kreon—all soar against the limits of human aspiration, only to crash in spectacles of terror and pity. Yet the tragic vision does not consist just of this recognition of our self-destructive weakness and failure. The tragic vision recognizes as well that those very necessities limiting us are also what give our aspirations dignity and value. That we struggle for self-knowledge and achievement, in the teeth of such powerful limits to both, is what makes us admirable. "Break out what will!" Oedipus cries on the brink of horrifying revelations, and we admire his mania for self-knowledge, even as we shudder at the crimes he must learn he has committed, the terrible price of his knowledge.[9] We have worth because we risk losing, and we are *conscious* of that risk, of how much we have to lose. In this we are better than the gods, the Greeks thought, because they risk nothing and are therefore envious of our heroic struggle.

The tragic vision, then, does what the English poet and critic Matthew Arnold said the Greek tragedian Sophocles did—see life steadily and see it whole. The tragic hero looks into the grim limits of human life, and rather than turn away or cower before them, strives to achieve something worthwhile—despite those limits, despite the certainty of failure, despite the unforeseen consequences of success. After all, humans are tragic, not because they fail, but because they *succeed* in transcending, if only for one brief dazzling moment, those limits. Their aspirations create brilliance at the same time as they create the conditions for degradation and suffering. Yet in that very struggle we find our dignity and worth as human beings.

Yet even among the Greeks, some were dissatisfied with this view of human existence. Plato's is the best example of a different understanding of what we are. Positing an immaterial, rational, immortal soul, Plato saw in the rational apprehension of *true* reality— not material nature, what Yeats's Plato called "a spume that plays/Upon a ghostly paradigm of things," but the eternal world of immaterial ideas—a way out of the tragic predicament, at least for those whose intellects could be developed enough to ascend from the material shadow-world of the cave to the sunlight of true reality. And the soul's process of escaping the tragic material world was a *rational* one, a process of the mind. Here we see the beginning of the West's on-going love affair with reason, its faith in the mind and its techniques as the way out of the tragedy of the human condition, at least for the philosophical soul that could escape the prison-house of the body transfixed by space and time.

This dialogue, begun by the Greeks, between the tragic and what we can call the philosophical vision, is the central story of Western thought. Christianity was in many ways a reconciliation of these two visions. Life was tragic, yes, because of the Fall, which brought suffering and death and sin into our world. Yet that tragedy was only one episode in the larger drama of salvation, a "comedy," in Dante's terms, because the play ends not in death but in "life"—the saved soul's escape from death and sin, and its eternal reconciliation with the God it desires. But salvation was not won by the techniques of the rational mind, and getting saved did not alter the fallen condition of the material world, which remained the arena of sin and death. No matter how reconcilable with natural reason, salvation ultimately was a "mystery": the mystery of God's redeeming love, of his grace, of his revealed wisdom. It was his gift to us, revealed in the unfolding of His providential plan, the result neither of our progressive knowledge of the world, nor of our technologies for manipulating that world.

The dominance in the West of the Christian worldview ensured that this fallen earthly life, at least, would continue to be understood in tragic terms. But along with Christianity, the tragic vision began to retreat before the spectacular success of science and the technologies it created. Now the ancient limits of human life seemed not so absolute. Disease, hunger, the vagaries of the natural world gradually succumbed to an ever-increasing knowledge. And the myth of progress suggested that *all* the old necessary limits of human life would eventually fall to the technologies and techniques forged in the human mind—not merely suffering or hunger or violence or the other consequences of our passions, but also old age and even death itself. Rather than finding our human identity and dignity in those limits, as tragedy did, we would leap beyond them. Rather than finding our paradise in the eternity beyond this world, we would create paradise here and now.

Needless to say, the tragic view of human life is nowhere to be found any longer in our popular culture and discourse. It is too bleak, too "defeatist," too counter to the cheery myth of unending progress and instant gratification dominating our worldview. Our therapeutic vision tells us all is possible. We can live without risk, without loss, without suffering. Every desire can be gratified, every pain can be alleviated, every limit can be transcended, and every happiness can be achieved by everybody. As Satan promised Eve— and as Joyce Brothers also promised—we can become gods.

FROM BENEVOLENCE TO THERAPY

As well as believing that psychological techniques will overcome the tragic conditions of human life, the therapeutic vision endorses an obsessive concern with the emotional states those conditions arouse in people and with the happiness obtainable once those conditions disappear. The obsession with feeling is, as we saw, a central tenet of Romanticism, but the high valuation put upon emotional reactions to the spectacle of personal suffering and that of others has other forebearers.

Developments within Christianity account for modernity's greater interest in the individual's emotional capacity.[10] In the seventeenth century, philosophers and theologians like the Cambridge Platonists revolted against the grim predestination of the Calvinists and their characterization of most humans as irredeemably damned. This rejection of a pessimistic assessment of human nature lead to a contrary emphasis on God's love and benevolence and on the analogous human emotions of pity and sorrow. This "Christian sentimentalism" idealized, as social historian Colin Campbell put it, the "benevolent, empathizing man who, moved by pity and compassion to perform acts of charity towards his fellows, exemplified the idea of holiness as goodness."[11] Rather than innately wicked, man was now considered to have a divinely granted capacity for sympathy with and love for his fellows. These benevolent feelings arose from having been created in God's image, and so presumably spurred to acts of kindness and charity. They were "the best means at once of actualizing the beneficent designs of God for man and of realizing the aim of religion to perfect human nature," wrote R. S. Crane.[12] In this view, humans are naturally gentle and sympathetic and sociable because of the benevolent feelings they all share, especially what the late seventeenth-century divine Samuel Parker called a "vehement tendency to acts of love and good will."[13] An immediate emotional response to human suffering became the sign of moral goodness.

In the late eighteenth century, the third Earl of Shaftesbury (1671-1713) and Francis Hutcheson (1694-1746) preached that man had an innate moral sense expressed through his feelings. Moreover, this emotionally apprehended goodness, they taught, was related to harmony and beauty. The pleasure aroused by contemplating beauty was linked to goodness and virtue and hence validated the pleasures of emotionalism, for "whatever aroused feelings of pleasure was both beautiful and good."[14] An "emotional hedonism" was born, a "curious type of hedonism—the often frankly avowed pursuit of altruistic emotions for egoistic ends," said R. S.

Crane.[15] The Scotsman David Fordyce, in *The Elements of Moral Philosophy* (1754), described this pleasure in suspiciously sexual terms: it is a "kind of agreeable Discharge," a "pleasing anguish," and a "Self-approving Joy."[16]

The individual who embodied all these ideals was the "man of feeling," characterized by "sensibility": "an ideal sensitivity to—and spontaneous display of—virtuous feelings, especially those of pity, sympathy, benevolence, of the open heart as opposed to the prudent mind."[17] The new genre of the novel was soon filled with sensibility and sentimentalism, and facilitated the popularization of both. Oliver Goldsmith's *The Vicar of Wakefield* (1766), Laurence Sterne's *A Sentimental Journey* (1768), and Henry Mackenzie's *The Man of Feeling* (1771), with its hero Harley's outbursts of weeping every ten or so pages, allowed readers vicariously to experience the self-satisfying pleasure that came from responding emotionally to the characters' suffering and sensitivity. In sensual language similar to that of Fordyce, this pleasure was repeatedly called a "luxury" in late eighteenth-century novels, which are filled with expressions such as "luxurious woe," "luxurious pity," and "the voluptuousness of sorrow."[18] Moreover, these emotional "luxuries," unlike the mere appetitive, were not just pleasurable, but also legitimized as signs of moral superiority as well.

The assertion of innate human goodness and display of emotion by early sentimental humanitarians received an echo in Romanticism and indeed influenced that movement. Both sets of ideals asserted that humans are naturally good, and that their goodness is expressed, not through their reason, but through their emotional responses, particularly their reactions to the suffering of their fellows and to beauty of any sort. Indeed, moral goodness and superiority would now be measured by the intensity and frequency of such displays of sensitivity. We have already seen these ideals in Goethe's Werther, with his frequent public emotional displays of sorrow or joy condemned by an unfeeling society. Later, Rousseau's

Saint Preux, from *La Nouvelle Héloïse*, displays the same petulance that his superior sensibility is not recognized by the rest of the world, which "will punish him for having sincere sentiments in every affair and for passing judgment on it according to that which is true rather than that which is conventional."[19]

Such an emphasis on extravagant public displays of emotion coupled, as it frequently was, with a smug assertion of moral superiority, did not convince everyone of the value of sensibility and emotional hedonism. Even Sterne's widely popular *A Sentimental Journey* caused at least one eighteenth-century reader to complain, "[W]hen a man chooses to walk about the world with a cambrick handkerchief always in his hand, that he may always be ready to weep, either with man or beast,—he only turns me sick."[20] By the end of the eighteenth century the counterclaims of rational moralists were being openly aired. Novels such as Mrs. West's *The Advantages of Education* (1793), or stories like Maria Edgeworth's "Madamemoiselle Panache" (1795) showed the dangers of an excessive sensibility unchecked by sense.[21] The conflict between sense and sensibility was most famously explored by Jane Austen in her novel *Sense and Sensibility* (1811), in which Marianne Dashwood's impetuous emotionalism nearly brings disaster on herself and her family after she falls for the unstable Willoughby.[22] Just how thoroughly our culture endorses the assumptions of sensibility can be seen in the 1995 film version of *Sense and Sensibility*. In it the beautiful actress portraying Marianne, the mise-en-scéne, the lighting, the cinematography all combine to endorse and approve Marianne's romantic sensibility that Austen's novel satirizes.

Despite its histrionic self-indulgence, however, this new respect for the ability to respond emotionally to the spectacle of others' suffering did have many beneficial effects. It led to a heightened sensitivity to the plight of the less fortunate, and it fostered an antipathy to cruelty.[23] And it eventually provided the Victorians with the emotional impetus for improving the lot of orphans, the poor, prisoners, even animals, and did away with barbaric spectacles such as public executions. No doubt it had a role to play in the growing revulsion in the early nineteenth century to American slavery, if only through the sentimentalism of Harriet Beecher Stowe's *Uncle Tom's Cabin*.

Yet as Goethe's Werther shows, sensibility can also lead to an emotional solipsism that does little for the suffering of people other than use that suffering for the emotional delectation of the superior soul. Certainly reading Dickens's heart-wrenching descriptions of human suffering often is its own end, doing nothing more than affording the reader an irrational pleasure that testifies to his moral superiority. "It is pleasant to perceive the evils you yourself are free from," as the Epicurean Lucretius said.[24] The self-serving hedonism characterizing the man of sensibility gives force to Oscar Wilde's quip that one must have a heart of stone to read about the death of *The Old Curiosity Shops*'s Little Nell and not burst out laughing. After all, hedonistic taste is no more disputable than any other. But effecting genuine change in this world requires hard work and rational solutions more than a ready lachrymose response to suffering. Moreover, sensibility too often turns inward to the spectacle of one's *own* suffering or unhappiness, making of them a pleasurable fetish. This is the legacy of the cult of sensibility to our own therapeutic vision—a masochistic obsession with our perceived unhappiness or mental suffering. And in that private psycho-melodrama, the suffering of others ultimately has importance only because it is an external representation and reinforcement of our own.

The creation of our modern therapeutic vision, however, depended on the fusion of sensibility with the rational technique that the new "science" of psychology would provide. This process was given urgency by the profound sense of cultural and historical dislocation created by the rapid changes of the late nineteenth and early twentieth centuries, the dislocation captured in modernist works like T. S. Eliot's *The Wasteland* (1922). The increased complexity of life in huge impersonal cities where, as Wordsworth said,

"getting and spending we lay waste our powers"; the loss of traditional values occasioned by a rapidly changing, highly mobile society; the impact of industrialization and technology on the
conditions of daily life and work; the waning tide of the "sea of
faith," the decline of religion before the forces of secularization and
the "cash nexus"—these are the usual suspects that turned the world
into the modern "wasteland." Many of these changes, moreover,
were accelerated in American society, with its even greater social
mobility, its transience, its cult of self-creation and advancement, its
frantic optimism, and its radical individualism.[25] These conditions
contributed to the American unease and anxiety captured by George
Beard in his influential book *American Nervousness* (1881), and could
be seen as well in the late nineteenth-century predecessor of the
therapeutic vision, "New Thought." This was a combination of
"Christian theology, spiritualism, suggestion, Transcendentalism,
and smatterings of Hindu and Buddhist esotericism" that provided
techniques for escaping suffering and gratifying desire by tapping
into the powers of the subconscious.[26] The American psychic soil was
ready for the flowering of psychotherapy.

But still other attributes peculiar to American culture and character made Americans uniquely susceptible to the promise of psychotherapy: the belief in the obligation and possibility of
self-improvement, the faith in progress, the assumption that happiness is a right, the reliance on solutions generated by experts—in
short, all the attributes brilliantly captured by F. Scott Fitzgerald in
his portrait of the self-created dreamer Jay Gatsby in *The Great
Gatsby* (1925).[27] But whereas Fitzgerald's recognition of the tragic
limits to human desire left Gatsby floating dead in his pool, his
dreams crashed in ruins, the disciples of Freud crossed the Atlantic
to assure us that, if we but followed their techniques, we could realize Gatsby's dream of unchanging happiness and gratified desire—
for a price, of course, for a price.

But like the green light at the end of Daisy's dock, the fulfillment promised by therapy has continued to beckon just beyond our reach. The vicissitudes of the twentieth century have only intensified the unease and dissatisfaction in which the therapeutic vision continues to flourish. The fabulous wealth of the postwar industrialized nations has eliminated for vast numbers of their citizens material suffering and deprivation. Yet at the same time it has created expectations of happiness that only gods could fulfill and has elevated to the status of "suffering" the once-normal responses to the slings and arrows of an imperfect world. The attempt to find human meaning in the acquisition and consumption of ever more gaudy consumer goods has failed as well, trapping us instead in the never-ending pursuit of the ever-illusive Product, the Holy Grail glittering, we are sure, behind the glass of the next shopping mall chapel or in the glossy vulgarity of the next advertisement. Finally, the trivial hedonism celebrated in popular culture and magnified by the high-tech transmission of unreal images merely degrades our humanity, and renders us unfit for the hard work of building any lasting and meaningful relations with imperfect people in an imperfect world.

Late social historian and critic Christopher Lasch is worth quoting at length on the relation of our debased culture to the therapeutic sensibility:

Plagued by anxiety, depression, vague discontents, a sense of inner emptiness, the "psychological man" of the twentieth century seeks neither individual self-aggrandizement nor spiritual transcendence but peace of mind, under conditions that increasingly militate against it. Therapists...become his principal allies in the struggle for composure; he turns to them in the hope of achieving the modern equivalent of salvation, "mental health." Therapy constitutes an antireligion...because modern society "has no future" and therefore gives no thought to anything beyond its immediate needs. Even when therapists speak of the need for "meaning" and "love," they define love and meaning simply as the fulfillment of the patient's emotional requirements.... "Love" as self-sacrifice or self-abasement, "meaning" as submission to a higher loyalty—these sublimations strike the therapeutic sensibility as intolerably oppressive, offensive to common sense and injurious to personal health and well-being.... Mental health means the overthrow of inhibitions and the immediate gratification of every impulse.[28]

In short, the Man of Feeling has become a neurotic victim. He is a childlike figure[29] obsessed with his mental unhappiness, these days occasioned by ever-more nuanced slights to his fragile self-esteem. He chafes at the tragic limits of human existence and is driven by expectations of psychic and material happiness that he demands the experts fulfill with their techniques and products. In the late twentieth century, these expectations for happiness, this obsession with personal "suffering," and the old Benevolent Man's moral superiority purchased merely by the display of pity for and sympathy with the suffering of others, can all be seen in two new men that have evolved from the Man of Feeling: Sensitive Man and Compassionate Man.

SENSITIVE MAN

For all his emotional hedonism, the Man of Feeling's displays of excessive emotion had a spiritual significance beyond the individual, for God implanted sympathy and empathy in humans in order to ensure charitable and philanthropic behavior. Modern Sensitive Man, however, has lost that spiritual context. Instead we have Robert Frost's "the tenderer-than-thou/Collectivistic regimenting love." Sensitive Man is sensitive both because of the self-gratifying pleasure of moral superiority that follows displays of his sympathy with others' suffering, and because he feels he too is an innocent victim of unjust social or psychological forces and deserves the same consideration. Hence he demands a recognition and validation of his suffering similar to that he extends to others, a self-indulgence often hidden behind the virtue of "tolerance."[30] As Charles Sykes says of Sensitive Man, "[O]ne must be *attuned* to the feelings of others and adapt oneself to the kaleidoscopic shades of grievance, injury, and ego that make up the subjective sensibilities of the 'victim.' Everyone must now accommodate themselves [sic] to the sensitivities of the self, whose power is based not on force or even shared ideology but on changeable and perhaps arbitrary and exaggerated 'feelings.'"[31]

Evidence of Sensitive Man's ubiquity abound; indeed, Bill Clinton was twice elected president partly because he convincingly projected the persona of the modern Man of Feeling who could "feel our pain," and has remained the master of manipulating therapeutic sensibility for his own benefit.[32] These days every subgroup that can establish its bona fides as a victim is entitled to exaggerated deference to its members' fine-tuned receptiveness to psychic injury. Now "insensitive" and "hurtful" have become insults as deadly as "racist" and "sexist," epithets denoting those who do not display the required sensitivity to suffering. The long-anointed official victims—women, ethnic minorities, homosexuals, and the handicapped—are no longer the only ones to voice their demands for ever more nuanced sensitivity to their feelings. New cadres of victims crop up every day. Transsexuals, the fat, the ugly, males traumatized by the "masculine mystique," "co-dependents," anyone victimized by a dysfunctional family or some compulsive "disease": all claim our painstaking consideration of their hypersensitive reactions to the unfairness of human existence. Now we have not only "ageism," but "middle ageism," an intolerance that "viciously curtails the American dream and embitters our image of the life course."[33] Another new addition to the conga-line of victimhood comprises those suffering from Multiple Chemical Sensitivity—a "disease" that makes one vulnerable to odors, particularly perfume. A whole industry of activists and nuisance-suit lawyers has sprung up to champion the rights of these new "victims," and to force the rest of us to be sensitive (or else) to their disability.[34]

But the triumph of Sensitive Man is most obviously seen in the creation of the Sensitivity Training industry. Nothing captures the strange alliance of Enlightenment faith in technique with the cult of sensibility's proto-Romantic obsession with feeling than these "workshops" in which people will be rationally "taught" by "consultants" and "experts" how to achieve the highly subjective and amorphous condition of "sensitivity." Corporations, churches, and particularly universities—whose freshmen provide eager "progressive" administrators with a captive audience—are all purchasing the expensive programs of sensitivity consultants: in 1981, seventeen articles appeared in the media with the phrase "sensitivity training"; by 1992, the number had increased to over five hundred.[35] A lot of money can be made by dispensing false knowledge.

The purpose of these programs is to create what the Greeks knew to be the impossible: the therapeutic nirvana, the paradise in which no one will feel badly because everyone—especially those wicked Masters of the Universe, white males—is attuned to everyone else's feelings about various disadvantages and slights to self-esteem.[36] Hence those found guilty of "racial insensitivity" or "sexual harassment"—crimes often defined by the shadowy subjective responses of their "victims"—are condemned to sitting in "sensitivity seminars" and being lectured about their depravity. Unfortunately, trying to teach people to be tolerant often has the opposite effect. This has been the case with institutional attempts to inculcate racial tolerance, one of the most popular species of sensitivity training in universities. In many cases such training has *worsened* race-relations on campus: racial incidents are most frequent in those universities that are the most aggressive in attempting to teach students racial sensitivity.[37]

The cult of sensitivity that is increasingly being institutionalized on university campuses and in the sensitivity training industry promotes several varieties of pernicious false knowledge. It made infants of people, particularly college students, who are led to believe that the world should be a place where they will never feel bad or suffer disappointment, where they will be coddled and indulged and mothered, and where their already overinflated estimation of themselves will be continually reinforced. This is precisely what is happening on many campuses. For years grade inflation and the debasement of standards have increased partly because of professors' reluctance to wound the delicate self-esteem of students. Lately, new courses designed to ease the anxiety and stroke the self-esteem of freshmen have been proliferating. Eighteen-year-olds who can work, vote, drive, pay taxes, fornicate, procreate, and otherwise act as adults, get their hands held by phalanxes of counselors, facilitators, consultants, tutors, and even faculty. No one seems concerned about what will happen to these adults when they have to enter the real world and discover that it can be a cold, uncaring place where their anxieties and psychic fears are not the prime order of business.[38]

Another byproduct of the sensitivity obsession is the linguistic anxiety permeating academe and the media. More and more feel-good euphemisms—what historian Russell Jacoby calls "linguistic smile buttons"[39]—sacrifice plain speaking and accuracy on the altar of sensitivity. People who were once "crippled," and then "handicapped," are now "differently abled." Such euphemisms perpetuate the lie that being blind or deaf or unable to walk is a sort of "alternative lifestyle" rather than a condition that seriously limits, while not devaluing, one's life. Feminism, of course, has thrown out of the language all sorts of useful words like "craftsman" or "spokesman" or "man-made," since presumably some female somewhere will be traumatized by the verbal implication that women cannot "craft" or "speak" or "make" something. I have given up trying to explain to people the absurdity of calling someone a "chair" instead of "chairman." "Far East" is out, as is "New World" to describe the Americas.

Too Eurocentric. Don't say some statement "fell on deaf ears"—that would be "hurtful" to the deaf, or should I say, to the "auricularly challenged."[40]

The problem, of course, is not just that linguistic concern is selective and hence hypocritical: white males, fundamentalist Christians, and conservatives are still fair game for insult and epithet. Rather it is that euphemism and linguistic cosmetics do not alter reality, only mask it. They are lies. Moreover, the attempt to protect people from subjectively calibrated or presumed verbal slights to their self-esteem inexorably leads to an attempt to curtail free speech, as the numerous "speech codes" that have sprung up on many college campuses attest. And the history of crimes perpetrated under cover of verbal camouflage, the mass-murders called "Final Solution" or "Ethnic Cleansing," should make us wary of trying to change reality by changing words.

Another offshoot of the cult of sensitivity is the so-called New Puritanism. This is a form of self-righteous intolerance that, as historian and social critic Elizabeth Fox-Genovese notes, "more closely resembles the image created by the critics of Puritanism than it resembles the original Puritanism."[41] That is, the New Puritanism intensifies to obnoxious extremes the old cult of sensibility's assertion of moral superiority based on finely nuanced responses to suffering, and then adds Puritanism's intolerance of those who do not belong to the elect of true believers.[42]

The New Puritans are, for example, those feminists who believe all men are incipient rapists and as such need to be shackled with courtship restrictions and sanctions intended to minimize the chance that their depraved sexuality will inflict suffering on some innocent woman. So we have the "date-rape" hysteria, in which *adult* women college students transform errors of judgment—once the stuff of domestic tragedy—into innocent victimization that necessitates the therapeutic intervention of counselors, facilitators, and sensitivity-trainers who will empathize with the victim's suffering and instruct the male beast in his innate depravity. Or we get the melodrama of "sexual harassment," in which moustache-twirling males tie innocent females onto the railroad tracks of boorish innuendo and suggestive gesture—where the ladies await rescue by those same doughty sensitivity-trainers and facilitators, not to mention salivating lawyers.[43]

The point is not that rape and sexual harassment do not occur, or that when they *do* occur should not be punished severely. They should. The point rather is that the obsession with the subjective feelings of people makes it difficult to define accurately which behaviors are crimes deserving of legal redress, and which are the necessarily painful byproducts of interacting with imperfect people in an imperfect world. Perhaps even worse, the New Puritanism, like linguistic sensitivity, legitimizes restrictions on personal freedom; it fosters intolerance against the perceived inflictors of suffering, often in the absence of evidence of their guilt; and it makes infants of the victims, who then become the cowed clients of the sensitivity industry and its therapeutic techniques.

The net result is the spread of false knowledge about human relations and expectations and about the validity of the techniques proposed to correct the unfair impediments to universal happiness. As Marilynne Robinson asks, "Where did the idea come from that society should be without strain and conflict, that it could be satisfying, stable and harmonious? This is the assumption that has made most of the barbarity of our century seem to a great many people a higher philanthropy."[44] We have seen whence the idea sprang: from the alliance of Enlightenment faith in technique with the cult of sensibility's high value placed on the recognition of suffering. This same combination of a sentimentalized concern for suffering victims, with a willingness to use psychological techniques for correcting the perpetrators of that suffering and create "New Men," also characterizes the New Puritanism.

Then there is that other offspring of sensitivity we have met already, self-esteem, the mysterious psychological philosopher's stone whose touch can turn the dross of life into the gold of happiness. Even though no correlation between achievement and self-esteem has ever been established,[45] and even though nothing like self-esteem can even be adequately defined or measured, the educational establishment is permeated with the doctrine that *nothing*, not even abysmal ignorance, can be worse than wounding the tender sensibilities of students. Such a view fosters what the late William Henry III calls the "Big Lie": that nobody fails, that everybody can be a winner, that everybody is equal in talent and achievement.[46] The result has been a lowering of standards and expectations from kindergarten to university in order to ensure that indeed nobody fails, for the simple reason that nobody *succeeds* at anything worthwhile. It's like improving everybody's tennis game by removing the net. So we have legions of American students lacking fundamental knowledge, yet who nonetheless purportedly have the highest self-esteem on the planet.[47]

Finally, and most important, the obsession with sensitivity, particularly in the universities, poses a threat to the pursuit of truth, which requires a nurturing soil of freedom in order to flower. As Charles Sykes puts it, "Once feelings are established as the barometer of acceptable behavior, speech (and, by extension, thought) becomes only as free as the most sensitive group will permit."[48] Truth hurts, as we all learn early on. And as we noted in the Introduction, many people dearly hold onto bad ideas because such false knowledge makes them *feel* good, makes them *feel* secure, or makes them *feel* as if their lives have meaning. Lies bolster self-esteem—that's why we tell so many of them. The myth of racial superiority is one such bad idea, and the attack on it no doubt made many people feel bad and wounded their self-esteem. Nonetheless, it was and is a lie that needed exposing.

Truth is painful, but it is liberating: this is the wisdom of Sophocles's *Oedipus Turannos*, in which the lie of Oedipus's identity festers as a destroying plague, and the truth must be revealed, no matter who suffers. Only after cathartic suffering can wisdom be won and the healing begin.

COMPASSIONATE MAN

In *Bleak House* (1853), Charles Dickens created the quintessential "compassionate" person, Mrs. Jellyby. This practitioner of "telescopic philanthropy" as Dickens describes her has "devoted herself to an extensive variety of public subjects." Her current project is directed toward enlightening heathen Africans and ameliorating the lot of unfortunate Londoners by settling the latter among the former. Yet as she furiously dictates her letters promoting her philanthropic scheme, her shabby household and neglected children continue to fall into ruin. One child has his head stuck in the area railings, one falls down the stairs, his head audibly bumping the whole way, and the oldest girl is filled with vehement hatred both for her mother and for the unfortunate heathens in Africa.

Mrs. Jellyby's combination of misplaced compassion for distant suffering with indifference to the suffering right below her nose— her "telescopic philanthropy"—characterizes as well modern Compassionate Man, the public persona of Sensitive Man.

Compassion is as much in vogue these days as sensitivity, especially what Alan Bloom called "conspicuous compassion," the ostentatious, competitive display of grief at the suffering of the various fashionable victims sanctioned by the media and universities.[49] In the election year of 1996, *Time* magazine reported that "the notion of compassion is at the heart of both the national political debate and the presidential campaign." Even the Republicans were parading their "compassion" in order to head off the usual charge that they are hard-hearted monitors of the corporate bottom line.[50] Both parties' conventions were filled with "human ailment and affliction thrown down as trump cards in political advocacy."[51] We experience so much compassion that every so often we hear about "compassion fatigue," our inability to react to suffering because we have been bombarded with so many demands on our sensitivity.

Like sensitivity, displays of compassion are desirable because they cheaply endow a person with moral superiority. They show that he is a lover of humanity, a foe of unfairness, and an enemy of those benighted villains who cause this suffering. It is, in short, a moral status symbol, a white hat and halo all rolled into one.[52] Conspicuous compassion permeates our society, but it especially can be found whenever people who fancy themselves sensitive "liberals" start to talk about the "poor" and the "homeless," usually in Dickensian terms of heart-rending pathos. One of the most annoying examples of conspicuous compassion is the smug, promiscuous wearing of red ribbons at public functions like the Academy Awards in order to show off concern for AIDS victims. This practice has now spawned a veritable rainbow of ribbons that can be paraded to demonstrate how sensitive you are to various subspecies of suffering.

What's wrong with conspicuous compassion? Absent any *action*, it is fairly useless, a congeries of superficial gestures and verbal pieties indulged at a distance—hence "telescopic philanthropy." Ultimately it is a self-indulgent luxury, more accessible, as Revel points out, than active critical thought.[53] Any value this display of compassion may have for increasing awareness of social problems is quickly trivialized by repetition. And when television is the source of images of suffering, the medium's notorious penchant not only for trivializing, but also for rendering what it televises unreal, desensitizes us to suffering, which becomes indistinguishable from soap operas and beer commercials.[54] All we are left with is a superficial emotional response that can become dangerous if it drives government policy, as we saw happen in the United States's recent forays into Somalia, Haiti, and Rwanda.

Worse, though, indiscriminate compassion begs the question of who is responsible for suffering—and so confuses the issue of where our social intervention should begin. Indiscriminate compassion ignores the central role character and moral choice play in our behavior. Hence "red-ribbon" compassion obscures the simple truth that most AIDS victims have contracted their disease through avoidable, unhealthy habits like frequent receptive anal intercourse or the sharing of hypodermic needles. Likewise the problem of the "homeless" is often presented in the media as one affecting out-of-work middle-class families, luckless victims of a cold-hearted capitalism. As everyone knows, however, the majority of the homeless are young men. Some are substance abusers, some are crazy people turned out into the street when the state mental hospitals closed up shop.[55] And some are just born to lose, as any tattoo parlor knows. But many of us cannot confront this reality of human failure and imperfection because it violates our therapeutic vision, and because we, as social critic Marvin Olasky says, "rely on the mediated compassion offered by journalists philosophically committed to social universalism and professionally involved with the production of sentimentality."[56]

I am not advocating heartless indifference in the case of AIDS victims or bums. We should do what we can to aid our fellows in their need—but with action, not with ostentatious ribbons and pious words. At the same time as we act to reduce human misery, we need to recognize that one of the tragic limits of humans is their own self-destructive choices for which they often have to pay the price of suffering in this world. Conspicuous compassion ignores the issue of personal responsibility and accountability, and hence evades this tragic truth. The crazy person turned out into the street is not distinguished from the drug addict or alcoholic, the homosexual bath-house habitué from the breast-cancer victim. All get their ribbons. Moreover, conspicuous compassion implies that suffering *always* results from some unfair and correctable condition that therapists and social technicians could fix if the bad guys (the "insensitive," who usually vote Republican) didn't get in the way. It reinforces, ultimately, the erroneous vision of human life as perfectible, and suffering as an aberration to be eliminated rather than a defining and potentially ennobling necessity of life, and a source of wisdom about the tragic limits of human identity. As Aeschylus said, "We learn by suffering."

Finally, compassion may do its objects more harm than good in the long run, as Lasch notes: "A misplaced compassion degrades both the victims, who are reduced to objects of pity, and their would-be benefactors, who find it easier to pity their fellow citizens than to hold them up to impersonal standards, attainment of which would entitle them to respect."[57] Jean Bethke Elshtain puts it thus: victims require not sentimentality, "but politics, relief animated by a moral calculus."[58] Even the social psychologists, who have advanced the cause of compassion in the universities and social-welfare bureaucracies, are beginning to see the baleful effects a patronizing compassion can have on its recipients' sense of self.[59] This damage to self-image occurs because those who we decide deserve our compassion are kept perpetual victims, and a victim is by definition inferior to his victimizer. Victims are passive, helpless, in need of patronizing care from the more fortunate who can afford pity at a distance, particularly when it is not accompanied by the cost of action. Compassion has become, as Lasch put it, "the human face of contempt."[60]

THE CONSEQUENCES OF THE THERAPEUTIC

The therapeutic vision attempts to turn the techniques of the head to the creation of certain desirable feelings in the heart. The problem is that the heart—both our subjective feelings and the mysterious springs of our actions—is too complex and various and mutable to be the object of scientific description and technological intervention and correction. Only by radically oversimplifying human nature and experience, by "tearing the heart out of our mystery," as Hamlet put it, can the illusion of therapeutic technique be maintained. That illusion has perhaps been responsible for most of the false knowledge that troubles us today.

By maintaining the spurious hope that the tragic limitations of human life can be avoided and that human unhappiness can be eliminated, the therapeutic vision has been responsible for the wildly unrealistic expectations to which we in the industrialized West cling. The average American today enjoys a level of material comfort earlier peoples would have imagined only for gods. Whereas most of humanity before the late twentieth century spent its time and labor and psychic energy on acquiring nourishment through back-breaking labor, we take for granted not just a steady supply of sanitary food but an incredible variety of choices unavailable to even the richest of people in earlier times. We are the healthiest people who ever existed, living longer and more vigorous lives, and freed from everyday pain; most of our diseases and injuries are self-inflicted. We decry our violent society, but the odds that a middle-class American will fall victim to murder are still much lower than the chance that he will die in an auto accident or from heart disease caused by high-fat diets. By every criterion we are the most fortunate human beings ever to walk the face of the earth.

Yet despite this god-like comfort, we are unhappy. And we are unhappy because our expectations have been stoked to a level unthinkable for most of humanity before the twentieth century. Over thirty years ago historian Daniel Boorstin described these expectations and their contradictory nature:

> We expect anything and everything. We expect the contradictory and the impossible. We expect compact cars which are spacious; luxurious cars which are economical. We expect to be rich and charitable; powerful and merciful, active and reflective, kind and competitive. We expect to be inspired by mediocre appeals for

"excellence," to be made literate by illiterate appeals for literacy. We expect to eat and stay thin, to be constantly on the move and ever more neighborly, to go to a "church of our choice" and yet feel its guiding power over us, to revere God and to be God.[61]

Boorstin traced these expectations to the new media that could rapidly transmit images and information and create illusions for our consumption. I would add another obvious reason—the sheer wealth that in the West was created after the devastation of World War II and that raised more people to a higher standard of material existence than had ever been experienced.

Certainly the middle-class malaise currently occupying our social commentators derives from economic insecurity, the suspicion that the material lifestyle to which we have become accustomed is slipping away from us. A whole slew of books has recently been published, documenting our discontents. These days the "anxious middle"—as journalist E. J. Dionne, Jr., recently called the middle class[62]—is in a funk, worried about slipping below that standard of living to which it was lead to believe it was entitled. Agitated by corporate "downsizing" and disappearing middle-management jobs, pinched by stagnant wages, fretting over the costs of the global economy, the middle class feels threatened because it may not be able to afford a new car every year, or because home-ownership—a rare luxury for most of human history—may be out of reach for its children.[63]

In the midst of this anxiety—much of which is generated by half-truths and dubious statistics treated as scientific facts—we lose sight of just how good most of us still have it.[64] We work fewer hours, take more paid vacation days, live in bigger homes, have them filled with more gadgets, own more cars, and live five years longer than we did twenty years ago.[65] Our problem is not that the quality of our lives has declined but that our *expectations* about what constitutes the good life are overinflated by the historical anomaly of unusual affluence enjoyed by masses of people as a consequence of

World War II. Robert Samuelson has recently pointed out that, "Having first convinced ourselves that we were going to create the final American utopia—an extravagant act of optimism—we are now dismayed that we haven't—a burst of unwarranted pessimism."[66] Conditioned by the myth of progress, we cannot confront the possibility that the last fifty years may have been an atypical spike in economic history. We don't want to accept that we may have reached the highest possible level of affluence for the greatest number of people; worse, we find unthinkable the possibility that we all someday may have to return to a material lifestyle more typical of what the rest of humanity has settled for in its history. Yet these contingencies are more probable than the rosy scenario of an ever-increasing wealth more widely distributed to an ever-increasing number of people.

Because of this malaise born of false knowledge about what the good life reasonably entails for a human, we demand unworkable economic and social policies. And we punish those rare politicians who try to tell us that we can't have our cake and eat it. Hence the political impasse, say, over balancing the budget and reducing the deficit: we want somebody else graciously to give up his unearned "entitlement" while we stubbornly hold on to our "earned" one. Hence our refusal to confront the impending bankruptcy of Social Security and Medicare—a financial crisis partly precipitated by our desire to circumvent the tragic limits of time and old age through expensive medical technology.[67] We never stop to consider that what we call "entitlements"—most of which were intended not to give us a comfortable retirement but to afford minimum protections against economic misfortune—would have been a luxury to most of humanity existing before the late twentieth century, and *are* luxuries to the bulk of humans living today. Yet we consider them bare necessities.

But what about those Americans living in what we call "poverty"? Aren't they worthy of our sympathy and compassion for their suffering? By any measurement, the standard of life we statistically define as "poor" today would have been considered well off in earlier ages, when poverty meant continual physical suffering and exhausting labor and early death by disease and starvation.[68] In contrast, the American "poor" today enjoy a remarkable level of material comfort: 93 percent own color televisions, 60 percent own microwaves and VCRs, and 72 percent own washing machines— figures higher than those for *all* economic classes in Europe. And *our* poor people's economic consumption is more than twice *their* actual income.[69] Clearly the "suffering" of the statistical poor, like that of the middle class, must be understood in psychological, not material, terms, a consequence of their not achieving the wildly unrealistic standard of happiness and the good life promulgated by advertisements and television. And much of the material suffering that does indeed exist—the squalor and sordid neglect visible in our cities—can be traced to bad choices with unpleasant consequences that only oppressive state interference in personal freedom could eliminate.

The therapeutic vision, in sum, has destroyed the age-old concept of sin and moral responsibility, and has replaced it with "sickness." Marvin Olasky has traced this development in America back to the nineteenth century and the Rousseauist "social universalists" who believed that people were bad because a heartless environment gave them no choice. Change the environment with the new techniques of scientific knowledge, and human nature would follow suit: "Man's basic nature was not corrupt, but good; there were sins but not sin, evil acts but not evil. Problems arose from social conditions rather than inherent moral corruption."[70] As early as 1846 Horace Greeley was arguing that "the heart of man is not depraved: that his passions do not prompt to wrong doing, and do not therefore by their action, produce evil."[71] Some half a century later Clarence Darrow argued that "there is no such thing as a crime as the word is generally understood," and he asserted that people were in jail "simply because they cannot avoid it on account of the circumstances which are entirely beyond their control and for which they are in no way responsible."[72]

Psychotherapy, of course, reinforced this move away from issues of moral choice and failure to the "scientific" identification of the origins of destructive behaviors and their correction with therapeutic technique. Isn't "free will" just a fiction to which our consciousness attributes our behavior? Doesn't the real origins of our actions lie in subconscious forces that only the trained psychologist can map and define?

Nowhere is the therapeutic concept of "sin as sickness" more egregiously obvious than in the "co-dependency" movement. As described by Wendy Kaminer, the co-dependency and twelve-step movements have as their central assumption the same impatience with the idea of innate human wickedness, and with the tragic consequences for human choices, that we have been discussing: "Inner children are always good—innocent and pure—like the most sentimentalized Dickens characters, which means that people are essentially good, and, most of all, redeemable.... Evil is merely a mask—a dysfunction. The therapeutic view of evil as sickness, not sin, is strong in codependency theory."[73] Since we are all victims of some compulsion or other whose roots lie in the traumatizing of our innocent "inner child" by our demonic families, we are none of us responsible for our various addictions. We shop, fornicate, commit adultery, drink, snort coke, smoke, steal, overeat, and act like jerks all because we are "sick," not because we choose to sin. Thus we deserve compassion and sympathy, not "hurtful" criticism or shame or guilt. And we must turn (wallet in hand) to the various "techniques" of "experts" who will cure us of our disease and escort us into the brave new world of perpetual psychic happiness.

The "sin as sickness" idea is harmful not just for individuals, but for civic society as well, for we no longer have a "moral common ground and therefore no public relevance of morality."[74] Without that moral common ground predicated on personal responsibility, there is no way we can collectively hold *any* of us responsible for *any* of our actions. And without personal responsibility, a democratic, free, open society cannot begin to solve its social problems, for the solutions ultimately depend on the collective efforts of those free individuals who must take moral responsibility for their actions and mistakes. Otherwise, social problems will become the domain of therapeutic "experts," who will need more and more coercive power—and less and less freedom on the part of recalcitrant individuals—to make their "solutions" work. The net result, of course, will be the *end* of a democratic, free, open society—as we have seen repeatedly in this bloody century.[75]

And there is an economic price to pay as well for indulging in what medical critic G. E. Zuriff recently called "medicalizing character." The Americans with Disabilities Act, which forces businesses and public facilities to make "reasonable" accommodations for those with disabilities, includes in its definition of disabilities what once would have been called character flaws but are now classified by the American Psychiatric Association as "mental disorders." The person who lacks empathy is full of envy and takes advantage of others—once traits that would earn somebody a niche in Dante's Inferno or a terrace in Purgatory—now may be diagnosed as suffering from "narcissistic personality disorder," and so deserving of special consideration by his boss and co-workers. Zuriff estimates perhaps ten to twenty million workers may be classified as "disabled" by one of the many so-called "mental disorders" catalogued in the ponderous *Diagnostic and Statistical Manual of Mental Disorders* (*DSM*), the American Psychiatric Association handbook that most of the time provides the categories of mental disabilities for those administering the Americans with Disabilities Act, and whose pages "are replete with mental illnesses that have been hitherto regarded as perfectly normal behavior."[76] Since the *DSM* categorizes just about all of human behavior as indicative of some mental disorder or other, this dependence on the *DSM* means that *all* of us can be considered "disabled" and hence entitled to special treatment under the Americans with Disabilities Act.[77]

The most baleful result of this loss of sin and moral responsibility, however, is the abandonment of the idea of evil. Critic Andrew Delbanco writes, "[T]he work of the devil is everywhere, but no one knows where to find him. We live in the most brutal century in human history, but instead of stepping forward to take the credit, he has rendered himself invisible. Although the names by which he was once designated...have been discredited to one degree or another, nothing has come to take their place."[78] But even those like Delbanco who worry over the "death of Satan" still approach the issue from the point of view of Enlightenment rationalism. Rather than seeing evil, as Dostoyevsky did, as part of the mystery of the human heart and its freedom, explicable only in terms of the contrasting mystery of redemptive love, our modern thinkers see it as a necessary metaphor for some as yet undiscovered physiological process in the human mind. "There is reason to hope," Delbanco writes with an almost touching naiveté, "for a cooperative intellectual venture between religion and science that may lead to a revival of serious moral thinking, in which the category of evil might once again have meaning."[79] Perhaps evil is just the name we give to certain drives once selected by evolution for their survival value but that now must give way to other instincts such as altruism, which "may turn out to be not just a religious ideal but an evolutionary advantage."[80]

Likewise the editors of the British medical journal *Lancet* castigate those who assert that evil does not exist—only to voice the hope that "a scientist...will come across evil, maybe from the preserved brains of those afflicted.... Should that happen, evil will be classifiable and may even prove reversible."[81] So too *The Humanist*, in which Paul Shore calls for "evil studies" and speculates, "Perhaps with greater understanding of [evil's] origins and limits, our children will have better luck than we have had."[82] So too Lyall Watson, who wants to analyze evil as "a force of nature, a biological reality" to be explicated using the techniques and insights of "evolutionary biology, anthropology, and psychology," since it is a "part of the ecology" that like the rest of nature "makes sense in its own terms."[83]

In other words, more research, more knowledge, more "studies" will penetrate the heart of our mystery. But that faith in reason and in the power of knowledge is what is ultimately responsible for destroying the idea of evil in the first place. Evil, after all, to the Enlightenment rationalist was just a fiction created by the ignorant and superstitious to account for human actions that actually could be accounted for in scientific terms and to justify an oppressive priestly power. But if Satan can convince us that he is a mere metaphor for some physical process that the progress of scientific knowledge some-day will uncover, then he has pulled off a trick as effective as the one Baudelaire noted—convincing us that he doesn't exist.

The idea that evil doesn't exist, or that it is a metaphor for some as yet unknown material phenomenon, is the most dangerous piece of false knowledge circulating in the modern world—for the simple reason that inexplicable evil *does* exist, not just in the atrocities of monsters but in every one of our own hearts. We have the photo-graphs to prove it, from Auschwitz, from Nanking, from My Lai, from Rwanda, from the streets of our cities and suburbs where every day, ordinary people look into the heart of darkness, like what they see, and then step over the line. And often they do so for no expli-cable reason other than that they can *choose* to do so. But because we cannot confront this tragic reality of the human heart and the mys-tery of its free will, we hide behind the false knowledge of the ther-apeutic vision, which tells us that we are not responsible, for free will is a chimera;[84] that our parents or environment or our genes made us do it; that we can forget about shame and guilt, those dis-carded traditional checks on destructive behavior, and simply seek treatment from the technicians of the soul who will guide us into the paradise beyond good and evil, beyond guilt and shame.

But how can the therapeutic vision explain to us something like the following scene from Bosnia, site of this insane century's latest refinement of pointless evil as described by Rezak Hukanovic?

Never in all his life was Djemo to see a more horrifying sight. The poor man stood up a little, or tried to stand up, continuing to let out the excruciating screams. He had blood all over him. One of the guards took a water hose from a nearby hydrant and directed the strong jet at the poor prisoner. A mixture of blood and water was flowing down his exhausted, gaunt, naked body as he bent down repeatedly, like a wounded Cyclops, raising his arms above his head, then lowering them toward the jet of water to fend it off, while his throat issued forth the sound of someone driven to insanity by pain. And then Djemo saw, he saw what had happened clearly, everybody saw it: they had cut off the man's sexual organ and half of his behind.[85]

This is no mere "sickness," no mere metaphor. The men perpetrating this atrocity do not do so because of bad genes or a bad upbringing or wounded self-esteem or an evolutionary genetic mechanism no longer suited for a changed environment. Nor are these men deformed monsters whose ilk will be eliminated someday by knowledge or psychological technique or genetic manipulation. They are just like us: given the right circumstances, capable of anything. Which is the sheer, horrifying mystery of evil lurking in every human heart, the reality from which both the Enlightenment and Romantic visions turn their eyes—the former because it believes knowledge is virtue, the latter because it believes that humans are naturally good.

The reality of evil, either ignored or trivialized by the therapeutic vision, was no stranger to the old tragic vision. Sophocles recognized it—it was the same force that wrecked his brilliant heroes Oedipus and Ajax. Oedipus, remember, is willing to torture a herdsman for information, and the crazed Ajax tortures a ram, thinking that it is his old enemy Odysseus. Dante too knew evil's face—he journeyed through all its manifestations, saw the torment of the soul who chooses not love but hate; not wisdom but ignorance; not God but Satan. Dostoevsky knew evil, too; saw it incarnated in the political devils and atheists of his own age willing to slaughter millions for a utopia and the "new man." It is only we smug "postmoderns" who can't see evil.

THE LANTERN ON THE STERN

The study of history is the best medicine for a sick mind; for in history you have a record of the infinite variety of human experience plainly set out for all to see; and in that record you can find for yourself and your country both examples and warnings; fine things to take as models, base things, rotten through and through, to avoid.

— LIVY[86]

If men could learn from history, what lessons it might teach us! But passion and party blind our eyes, and light which experience gives is a lantern on the stern, which shines only on the waves behind us.

— COLERIDGE[87]

The common theme of this first section is that historically shaped ideas about human nature and its possibilities lie behind many of the assumptions and beliefs that generate false knowledge. The therapeutic vision—that strange alliance of the rationalist dream of perfection via technique, with the Romantic valuation of individual emotional states and sensitivity—permeates our mental universe and the institutions on which we depend for public information. The result is false knowledge: about what humans can expect from their lives, and about what does and does not lie within our power to know and change. Since we pursue false goals predicated on erroneous assumptions about what we are, it is no wonder that we are in such a muddle, constantly frustrated by our inability to transcend our tragic limitations, by our failure to bend the stubborn timber of ourselves and the world to our will.

Of all the causes for our embrace of Satan's tempting lie that we can be as gods, an ignorance of history is perhaps one of the most important. History is crucial to our self-understanding, but not because of Santayana's by now trite warning that those who forget history are condemned to repeat it. History does not repeat itself, either as tragedy or as farce. The importance of history lies rather in its ability to give a sort of visual depth to our expectations and ideas, to place them in the only context that matters—the dense, intricate record of what humans have thought and attempted and experienced, their successes and failures, their nobility and pettiness. As Livy suggests, history gives us ideals to strive for and failures, both practical and moral, to avoid. By familiarizing ourselves with the record of humanity's deeds and crimes we achieve a critical distance from the manifold passions and interests of the present, and we win a calm space in which we can judge with a cooler eye the hectic novelties and temptations bombarding us from every television and newspaper and wolfish huckster whether of things or ideas.

Without that contextualizing distance we fall into the trap of what Gary Saul Morson calls "chronocentrism," the arrogant "temporal egotism" that judges everything by the standards and "knowledge" of the present, as though our accidental lateness confers on us greater wisdom instead of knowledge of a greater number of facts.[88] But just as objects nearer to us appear bigger than they actually are, and we obliterate the sun with a thumb, so the ideas of the present take on an importance and heft they might not deserve. Forgetting the wisdom of the Preacher that there is nothing new under the sun, we continually cry out like Shakespeare's Miranda "O brave new world!" and seldom hear the older, wiser Prospero snort, "'Tis new to thee."

We need history now more than ever. The lure of a distorting and self-flattering chronocentrism is sweetened by the technology of the image, with all its vivid immediacy and imperious novelty and rapid-fire turn-over. Yet perhaps more than at any other time we are increasingly ignorant of the past. Little history is taught in the schools, and that "little" is nothing more than a strange sort of apologetic melodrama combined with special-interest puffery. It puts me in mind of Jane Austen's comic *The History of England*, in which she declares her aim to be "to vent my Spleen *against*, & shew my Hatred *to* all those people whose parties or principles do not suit with mine, & not to give information."[89] Nor can we expect any help from the professional historians in the universities, for most of them have gone a-whoring after the false god of history as socially constructed fiction, as the romance penned by power-structures to serve their own ends and justify their privileges.[90] Nor is the media much interested, their technological limitations and constraints favoring the new and the "relevant."

Finally, the driving force behind both the schools and the media, the therapeutic vision, can have no use for history. Indeed, it must abhor history's grim record of human limitations and disregard for individual "feelings." The recorded past of the human race is, as Voltaire called it, a "tableau of crimes and misfortunes." Nowhere does it give us *any* evidence that humans can achieve what the therapeutic vision promises: liberation from the tragic limitations created by our passions and aspirations, escape into the paradise of gratified desire and perpetual happiness. Rather, history testifies to the wreckage of such arrogance and the failure of good intentions and the ruin of utopia after utopia. History humbles us, like the old philosopher who stood behind the triumphing Roman general and muttered over and over, "Remember you are mortal." Better for those genial optimists Compassionate Man and Sensitive Man that they enjoy popular culture's gratifying fantasies of sentiment and perfection.

In the next section we will examine some present-day popular errors that shape opinion and policy. They will appear inadequate for many of the reasons detailed in this section. But one consistent feature they all will share is a historical blindness inflicted by "passion and party," one so complete that those who embrace such errors cannot even look behind themselves to see the monitory wreckage in their wake, let alone look ahead to chart our course for the future.

PART TWO

Of Three Popular and Received Ideas

CHAPTER 5 ■ ROMANTIC ENVIRONMENTALISM

Socrates. Forgive me, my dear friend. You see, I am fond of learning. Now the country places and the trees won't teach me anything, and the people in the city do.[1]

— PLATO[1]

I n September of 1995 the *New York Times* and the *Washington Post* published the 35,000 word manifesto of the Unabomber, a terrorist who, with package-bombs, maimed twenty-three and killed three people for facilitating the modern industrialized world's assault on nature. Although the murders were condemned with varying degrees of enthusiasm by most environmental groups, the Unabomber's assumptions and arguments reflect the same Romantic myths and idealizations of nature that inform most of modern environmentalism, whether moderate or radical.[2] This popular and influential species of false knowledge has an impact on our society far beyond the unfortunate people mangled and killed by the Unabomber.

The Unabomber manifesto is a compendium of old Romantic complaints against modern civilization and technology. "The Industrial Revolution and its consequences have been a disaster for the human race," FC (the Unabomber's pen-name) declares. Society has been "destabilized," life made "unfulfilling," and much "psychological suffering" inflicted on people in industrialized nations, physical suffering on those in the Third World, as well as "severe damage" visited on nature.[3] The culprit is a high-tech industrial society that isolates man from nature and forces "people to behave in ways that are increasingly remote from the natural pattern of human behavior" (37). "Technology has gotten the human race into a fix from which there is not likely to be any easy escape," FC warns (58). The solution? "WILD nature; those aspects of the functioning of the Earth and its living things that are independent of human management and free of human interference and control. And with wild nature we include human nature, by which we mean those aspects of the functioning of the human individual that are not subject to regulation by organized society" (63).

Despite his banal rehashing of the Golden Age myth and Romanticism's protest against industrialism's "Satanic mills," the Unabomber's manifesto was explicitly endorsed by some radical environmentalists who do not risk their comfortable lives by displaying the Unabomber's consistency, his willingness to play out to their logical end the antihumanist assumptions underlying even the less radical forms of environmentalism—the murder of humans responsible for the threat to nature. Kirkpatrick Sale, one of the most vocal and well-remunerated recyclers of debased Romanticism, wrote of the manifesto that it "is absolutely crucial for the American public to understand" and that it "ought to be on the forefront of the nation's political agenda." Sale announced that "the Unabomber and I share a great many views about the pernicious effect of the Industrial Revolution, the evils of modern technologies, the stifling effect of mass society, the vast extent of suffering in a machine-dominated world and the inevitability of social and environmental catastrophe if the industrial system goes on unchecked." The Unabomber is a "rational and serious man, deeply committed to his cause." Sale mainly faults this "rational" murderer, who maimed and killed the innocent, for taking a "utilitarian" anthropocentric view of nature—that is, for not being antihumanist enough.[4]

Sale agrees with the Unabomber—and misses the manifesto's patent absurdities—because the ideas of both are animated by the same myths that form a continuum of assumptions shared by the terrorist and the well-heeled environmentalist alike.[5] Basic to both is the old myth of the Golden Age, which, as seen, rejects Iron Age civilization and technology for an imagined time when humans and nature lived in harmony, when a benevolent earth provided, like a kind mother, everything necessary for humans to survive without work or effort, and when the evils of war, slavery, and private property didn't exist—a way of life enjoyed by Noble Savages, primitive societies past and present.[6] Added to the Golden Age myth are certain Romantic assumptions, particularly an idealization of nature that ignores its inhuman destructiveness and emphasizes instead its beauty and spiritual significance and harmony with humans—an idealization made possible only by technology's liberation of people from the harsh realities of wresting sustenance from a recalcitrant and destructive natural world.[7]

The therapeutic value of natural beauty for those oppressed by artificial civilization has been asserted in America for two hundred years. Toward the end of the eighteenth century, men who had the leisure and money to explore the shrinking wilderness—that is, who were not obliged to make their living from cultivating nature— began to find in it the opportunity for experiencing the raptures of sublimity that, they thought, characterized the man of superior sensibility. Philip Freneau's "The Philosopher of the Forest," from 1781 and 1782, "contrasted his simple, moral life in the woods of Pennsylvania with the distorted existences of city-dwellers." Twenty years later Benjamin Rush asserted that "man is naturally a wild animal" that is "never happy...'till he returns" to the woods. Estwick Evans in 1818 anticipated the modern romantic ecologist's therapeutic nature-religion when he enthused, "How sublime is the silence of nature's ever-active energies! There is something in the very name of wilderness, which charms the ear, and soothes the spirit of man. There is religion in it."[8] And James Fenimore Cooper's Leatherstocking more than anyone else popularized the religion of nature.

This romantic disgust with society and civilization and the idealization of nature as therapy recurs throughout the nineteenth century, but most famously in the work of Henry David Thoreau, who believed that "from the forest and wilderness come the tonics and barks which brace mankind"—as long as civilization and its amenities are nearby, as they were for Thoreau. And both the disgust and the idealization have characterized modern American environmentalism from the start. In the writings of John Muir, godfather of romantic ecology and founder of the Sierra Club, can be found the idealization of nature as a therapeutic force powerful enough to counteract the miseries of Iron Age civilization. "Wild nature," Roderick Nash summarizes Muir, "was replete with 'Divine beauty' and 'harmony.' Especially to 'lovers of the wild,' its 'spiritual power' emanated from the landscape. If civilized man would only seek the wilderness, he could purge himself of the 'sediments of society' and become a 'new creature.'"[9] The Golden Age distrust of civilization is here coupled with the Romantic idealization of nature as therapy for the disaffected man of sensibility.[10]

However, this long tradition of American romantic nature love, which Muir unabashedly wore on his rhetorical sleeve, is disguised in contemporary environmentalism by an overlay of studies, numerical data, computer models, and statistics that give a veneer of authority to the movement's pronouncements. The ozone layer, the greenhouse effect, the loss of the rainforest can all be presented in a scientific form that obscures the fundamental philosophical issues of human identity and its relationship to the natural world, issues that cannot be cast into scientific terms and that involve messier conflicts of values and competing goods.[11] Moreover, most of us lack the requisite training that would enable us to weigh and evaluate the various apocalyptic claims usually presented with a barrage of numbers and formulae. My purpose here is not to dispute the various assertions of environmental degradation and destruction, which has been done by others more qualified for the task.[12] Greg Easterbrook and others have shown that the "apocalyptic naturism"[13] that characterizes the environmental movement overstates humanity's destruction of the planet and underplays the very real advances that have been made in slowing down pollution and cleaning up what mess we have made, as well as improving human life on the planet.[14] Indeed, what is striking about modern environmentalism has been the spectacular failure of its predictions, from Paul Erlich's prophecy of global mass starvation by 1975 brought on by overpopulation, to Rachel Carson's vision of a birdless world. Rather than dispute environmentalist claims, however, my concern is with the old myths that continue to drive much environmental thought, even as it is dressed up in the procedures and terminology of science. This unholy alliance of scientific authority with Romantic therapeutic irrationalism is one of our most potent sources of false knowledge.

The central fallacy of environmentalism is its distortion of the relationship of humans to nature, and its projection of human values and concerns onto an amoral material world. Environmentalists speak as though we were "natural" creatures somehow fallen from our once happy home into an artificial exile of civilization. The ancient Greeks knew better: they understood that humans are *not* completely natural but rather are the site of a collision of nature and culture which uniquely defines them as humans. Humans possess a natural body with appetites and passions, but they have as well rational minds that can think up unnatural devices that alter the material world—everything from language to tools to social practices like marriage. In the myth of Prometheus, humans without minds and culture are pitiful creatures, their feeble bodies no match for a much more powerful nature. In order to help humans survive, Prometheus gives them not just an energy source, fire, but the *mind*, which can use fire to alter the environment through technology and so overcome the greater force of nature. Thus the chorus of Sophocles' *Antigone* sings, "Nothing is more awesome/terrible/wonderful than a human being," nothing stranger or more terrible than man, for man defies with his crafty mind the power of nature, creating his identity in the teeth of nature's indifference and hostility.[15]

What makes us recognizably human, then, is *not* what is natural about us but what is *un*natural: reason and its projections in language, culture, ritual, and technology; self-awareness, conscious memory, imagination, and the higher emotions; and, most important, values, ethics, morals, and the freedom from nature's determinism that allows us to choose, whether for good or ill. Nothing else in nature possesses *any* of these attributes, despite the wishful thinking of those who believe they are teaching chimps to "talk," or who consider a monkey digging up termites with a stick to be "using tools," or who label baboon rump-submission a "social practice," or who subjectively interpret the behavior of animals to indicate the presence of "self-awareness" or higher human emotions such as love, grief, regret, guilt, shame, or loyalty. For every dog that howls over the body of its dead master there is another that, if necessary, will happily eat his corpse.

Three attributes of humans in particular mark their difference from every other creature on the planet: culture, free will, and consciousness. Every human community, no matter how technologically primitive, possesses kinship relations; rituals mediating marriage, birth, and death; various artistic forms that shape experience according to aesthetic values; taboos regarding food and sex; and social relations light years in complexity beyond the most intelligent primate's. That's why Aristotle famously defined humans as social animals: they are the only creatures collectively to share and consciously to recognize customs and habits and skills and laws that mediate and regulate their behavior and relations with one another. No chimp buries its dead, or marries its mate in a communal ritual, or cooks its food, or worships a divine power, or writes a sonnet, or loves unconditionally. The crude behaviors that to some human observers *resemble* these activities are so remote from even the most primitive human community's social practices that they can be called "cultural" only metaphorically. And when one considers more advanced civilizations and their incredible alteration of the material world, the distance between ourselves and our primate cousins grows astronomical to the point that any resemblances become meaningless.

In most environmentalism, however, the assumption is that humans are natural creatures who somehow have been alienated from their true identity because of an artificial technology and civilization[16]—precisely the assumption of the Golden Age myth, which traces Iron Age evil to the invention of technology, especially agriculture, and cities.[17] As we have seen above, civilization is the villain in environmental thought, which is why the radical Earth First! battle cry is "Back to the Pleistocene," that is, back to a time before agriculture and cities—in short, before Iron Age civilization began, when the earth, as Ovid puts it in his version of the Golden Age myth, "unplowed bore fruit, and the field unfallowed grew white with heavy grain, the rivers flowed now with milk, now with nectar, and golden honey dripped from the green oak."[18] John A. Livingstone, in his hysterical attack on humanity and civilization, is very explicit about the evil of civilization arising from the invention of agriculture: "It has been suggested that the Fall from Grace was the agricultural revolution. The expulsion from the Garden was the consequence of our having taken up gardening."[19] So too Otto and Dorothy Solbrig, who write, "The hunter-gatherer life was as close to life in the Garden of Eden as humans have come."[20] Paul Shepard's

The Tender Carnivore is at once a sustained celebration of the hunting-and-gathering existence and a denigration of everything that has happened since agriculture was invented: "The collapse of an ecology that kept men scarce and attuned to the mystery and diversity of all life led as though by some devilish Fall to the hunting and herding of man by man, to the hoarding of grain and the secularizing of all space."[21] Given this belief, it is only predictable that the environmentalists idealize pre-agricultural hunting-and-gathering peoples, both contemporary and prehistorical as, in the words of historian Lawrence Keeley, "lambs in Eden, spouting ecological mysticism and disdain for the material conditions of life,"[22] even though there is very little evidence about what prehistoric hunting/gathering existence was really like.[23] Actually, what kept hunters and gatherers "scarce," of course, were unpleasant experiences like food shortages and infanticide and a chronic deficiency of calories, not to mention diseases that kept their life expectancies low and infant mortality high.[24] And the evidence shows that such societies were and are far from peaceful, warfare being frequent and involving a higher percentage of available manpower than war in modern societies.[25] But Shephard is concerned with myth, not fact.

In Ovid's mythic Golden Age, the earth, "untouched by the hoe and unwounded by the plow herself gave all things."[26] And Shepard's description of contemporary hunters could come straight from Ovid: "Cynegetic [hunting] people are leisured, generous, hospitable. They do not stockpile possessions or children. Their only private property is personality.... Group aggression, plunder, slavery, do not exist. There is no political machinery, little feuding, and no war.... Because he is a hunter, he is the most deeply loving and profoundly compassionate animal. Generally he is free of communicable disease and famine."[27] Once more we are reminded of Ovid's Golden Age when, "without law," men kept faith and did the right, there were no cities, and "without soldiers the secure tribes passed their days in soft ease."[28] The need to escape reality through wish-fulfilling fantasy apparently was as great in Imperial Rome as it is in modern America.

This reworking of the Golden Age and Noble Savage myths give the disaffected modern intellectual a gratifying fantasy about a simpler life, as did Jamie Uys's charming film *The Gods Must Be Crazy*, which contrasts the Golden Age innocence of the Bushmen with the harried violent Iron Age existence of South African city-dwellers.[29] But in the long run the Golden Age myth offers nothing of value in solving the problems humans face. In fact, complaining about civilization is ultimately a sterile exercise in wishful thinking. As long as we're inventing prehistoric ecotopias, why stop with hunters and gatherers? Why not complain about upright posture and the opposable thumb? Wouldn't we all be happier swinging in trees like our chimp cousins? But several thousand years of civilization made possible by agriculture, with all its glories and tragedies, not to mention the development of a mental life Livingstone and Shephard exemplify, *happened*, whether we like it or not. And civilization has made us what we are. To reject it in favor of some vague sentimentalized and sanitized notion of the hunting-and-gathering life culled from public television nature shows and the pages of *National Geographic* is as senseless as rejecting our oversized brains or power of speech. We may as well wish, like Eliot's Prufrock, to be "ragged claws/Scuttling across the floors of silent seas."

Humanity's freedom from nature's laws and processes is even more important than civilization in making us what we are. Unlike any other creature in nature, humans can *choose* their behaviors. Go down to your zoo and watch the flamingos. They will stand in their pool and mechanically scrape the concrete bottom with their feet, and then strain the water through their beaks. What they are doing is stirring up mud that isn't there and straining for shrimp that aren't there. But that behavior is hard-wired into their brains, and so they continue to do it even though they get their food out of a dish. The bird that diverts a predator from her nestlings, and the

mother rat that eats its supernumerary offspring are likewise following genetic instructions that they cannot choose to disobey. All
animals do what they do because they are genetically programmed
to do it, and the few behaviors that appear to be local adaptations to
new circumstances are ultimately insignificant and transitory anom-
alies compared to the behaviors that are determined by genes.

Humans, though, can resist nature's determinism and choose to
behave in ways that run counter to her most insistent genetic instructions. As French critic Luc Ferry says, man "is indetermination par
excellence: he is so oblivious to nature it can cost him his life. Man is
free enough to die of freedom.... His *humanitas* resides in his freedom, in the fact that he is undefined, that his nature is to have no
nature but to possess the capacity to distance himself from any code
within which one may seek to imprison him."[30] Because we are free,
we are creative in a way no other creature is: we can bring into the
world something new and unexpected, like culture, something that
nature's laws could never foresee or determine. And we can hand that
something new down to our offspring, initiating a chain of actions
and alterations that change us irrevocably. We are self-creating and
self-determining, and so we are *moral*—able to choose in full awareness of the consequences of our choices, in full awareness of how those
consequences will affect our fellow creatures. No other animal, no
matter how intelligent, can do this. The chimp that has been conditioned to connect manual signs with objects cannot signal, like
Melville's Bartleby, that it "prefers not to," that it refuses to play
along with the humans who have imprisoned and trained it.

Finally, humans possess consciousness—an awareness of their
uniqueness and its necessary end, of the consequences of their
choices—that does not burden any other creature. Thus we experience guilt and shame and grief and anxiety, we mourn the past and
dread the future, we dream and imagine alternative worlds, we grow
bored and disappointed with ourselves for no environmental or
genetic reason whatsoever. Not so our dogs or cats, who live in the

blissful eternity of the moment, with only that moment's experience, its genetic impulse of hunger or copulation or fear or sleep.
Like Keats's nightingale, they know nothing of "the weariness, the
fever, and the fret" of the human world "where but to think is to be
full of sorrow/And leaden-eyed despairs." We humans, burdened
with the "disease of consciousness," are all Hamlets, "thinking too
precisely on the event." We live in a vast world of potentiality, a possible universe comprising our own devices and unforeseen chance, a
cosmos the chimp gazing in the mirror never sees.

Humans, in sum, are not natural; nature is a necessary, but not
sufficient, part of human identity. Nor is the natural world with
which we are most intimate completely "natural." Thousands of years
of human culture and agricultural technology have altered nature's
raw material into an artificial "nature" more conducive to human survival. As historian Simon Schama points out, the human-driven
change in nature "is coeval with writing, with the entirety of our
social existence. And it is this irreversibly modified world, from the
polar caps to the equatorial forests, that is all the nature we know."[31]
Yet the modern world has lost its familiarity with that human-cre-
ated nature, simply because most of us now don't have to grow our
own food, and we live in technology-mediated environments. The
most important factor in shaping sentimental modern attitudes
toward nature is the unfamiliarity with farming that now characterizes the vast majority of urban-dwelling moderns. Cut off from the
reality of growing the food that they take for granted, urban nature-
lovers idealize a "wild" nature that no longer poses a threat to them.[32]
But the very food they eat is "unnatural": it is the creation of thousands of years of human skill and technology altering that "wild"
nature so that it can be compelled to provide food for humans. The
grain and fruit and vegetables we eat simply did not exist ten thousand years ago, nor did the cattle, horses, sheep, pigs, dogs, and other
creatures selectively bred and cross-bred to be what they are today.[33]

In other words, the dichotomy is not, as in sentimental envi-

ronmentalist writings, between a pristine "wild" nature and an artificial civilization, but between wild nature and *domesticated* nature,
nature altered by human skill to serve human needs. During those
many centuries when food was *not* taken for granted and 99 percent
of the people worked hard, sometimes unsuccessfully, to grow it,
"wild" nature represented the cruel predatory forces that cared nothing for human suffering and deprivation, and that actively, it
seemed, tried to thwart humanity's attempts to survive. Hence in
Dante the "dark wood" can symbolize evil, sin, and death because a
fourteenth-century traveler faced very real danger from the wolves
and other predators that inhabited the "wild." But that "wild" has
been defanged by technology, and so we well-fed, air-conditioned
urban-dwellers can sentimentalize it with impunity, secure in our
knowledge that the rescue helicopters and high-tech hospitals are
available in case Mother Nature cares to remind us just how dangerous she can be.

NATURE IS NOT HUMAN

> We receive but what we give,
> And in our life alone does Nature live:
> Ours is her wedding garment, ours her shroud!
>
> — COLERIDGE, "DEJECTION: AN ODE"

This great divide between the human and natural worlds is more
often than not ignored in environmentalism, with the result that
human values are projected onto nature, and nature is spoken of in
terms irrelevant to it. This is a paradox of environmentalism: it
indulges a thoroughgoing anthropocentrism and anthropomorphis-
ing even as it claims that it wants to "decenter" humans from its ideology and to consider nature in its own terms. But nature *has* no
values, no ethics, no morality. The lack of these, along with its sheer

vast scale in space and time, makes it literally inhuman, and thus an inadequate source or model for any ethics or values; for, in the words of Luc Ferry, "all valorization, including that of nature, is the deed of man and...consequently, all normative ethic is in some sense humanist and anthropocentric."[34]

Just how inhuman and meaningless nature is can be seen by considering the Earth in its own terms and scale. Take nature's time-scale, as described by Easterbrook: "The cosmos is thought to be eight to 20 billion years old; Earth and its companion sun 4.5 billion years old; simple microbial life 3.8 billion years old; complex microorganisms perhaps 2.8 billion years old; animal life perhaps 600 million years old; mammalian life around 200 million years old."[35] Our species, however, is about 350,000 years old—an eye-blink in terms of cosmic history. Now think of a single human being fortunate enough to live the biblical three-score and ten years. Obviously, in *nature's* scale, this individual is literally meaningless. His suffering and death are invisible, lost in a cosmic ocean of living things, an infinitesimal speck that doesn't count in the relentless march of the aeons. But for *us*, who know that each of us is unique, who know that when we die something passes from the earth that will never return, individuals count very much. And when they *haven't* counted is when we have seen the most horrifying atrocities, particularly in this century when about 100 million individual men and women were absorbed into various categories of dehumanized "enemy" whose liquidation was then required. This is what is forgotten by the critics of "bourgeois individualism," who, unlike unfortunate millions in this century, are not numbered as members of a group but as *individuals* possessing inalienable rights.

In the vast expanse of nature's time, then, death is a matter of complete indifference, even as it is one of the great engines of natural processes. Not just the death of any individual member of any given species, but the deaths of whole species is shrugged away by Dame Nature. We are much concerned these days with species

going extinct, yet extinction has been the norm for life on earth
ever since life appeared 3.8 billion years ago—according to one
estimate, 99.9 percent of all species of life that ever existed are
extinct, the vast majority of them at the hands of nature, not
humans.[36] One of the most devastating of extinctions, the end-
Permian 225 million years ago, destroyed as much as 96 percent of
marine life. If we look just at the extinctions that have occurred
since the rise of animal life nearly 600 million years ago, there have
been 5 major extinctions that destroyed at least 65 percent of existing species.[37] Humans are around only because of the last mass
extinction, the one 65 million years ago at the end of the
Cretaceous that wiped out the dinosaurs and so cleared an environmental space in which mammals could flourish. Clearly, the irrev-
ocable loss of animal and plant life that troubles modern
environmentalists bothers nature not a bit. Indeed, extinction has
been the engine of change and the spur to greater biodiversity. Like
Dante's Fortuna, relentless brutal change seems to be the only value
nature respects; as Easterbrook puts it, change is nature's "most
powerful ally."[38] And this change entails the destruction of vast
numbers of living things. In that context, the loss of millions of
humans, let alone one, is again literally meaningless.

It is obvious that, given nature's unconcern with the experience
of any transient individual member of a species, nature cannot provide any values for humans. Only human social practices and culture
provide the ethics and moral life that recognize obligations among
individual humans and that foster a concern with individuals, their
choices, and their fates. Hence most environmentalists, as the books
below testify, are necessarily consistent anthropocentrists: they must
project human values and concerns onto a nature to which such
things are irrelevant. No matter how presumed anti-anthropocen-
trists try to run away from what they are, every corridor ends in a
mirror reflecting their humanity.

Take, for example, the most egregious case of environmentalist anthropocentrism, the oft-repeated claim that industrial civilization is "destroying the planet," as when McKibben says that "in a sense we turn out to be God's equal—or at least, his rival—able to destroy creation."[39] This apocalyptic—and hubristic—claim assumes a grossly inflated estimation of human power, and an equally severe underestimation of nature's power and resiliency. As Easterbrook points out in his thorough documentation of nature's destructive power and ability to withstand those assaults, "Human assaults on the environment, though mischievous, are pinprinks [sic] compared to forces of the magnitude nature is accustomed to resisting."[40] Consider just one example: the ten-mile-wide comet that struck Mexico sixty-five million years ago and perhaps precipitated the demise of the dinosaurs. The impact had the force of 300 million hydrogen bombs—compare that to the 60,000 bombs in place at the peak of the Cold War. After the comet struck, something like 60 percent of the species then alive became extinct.[41] The impact perhaps weakened the earth's crust and initiated volcanic activity that created its own forms of destruction. Yet the earth survived "the unimaginable multiple whammy of the atmosphere set on fire by a killer rock strike; followed by years of summer frost, megasmog, and acid rain from hell; followed by decades or centuries of continuous global volcanism set loose by the rock's effect on the crust."[42]

And that is just one of numerous natural catastrophes that periodically have struck the planet and destroyed much of its life. Throw in bombardment by meteors and asteroids, the "greenhouse" effect caused by volcanic activity, ice ages, tectonic plate movements, periodic changes in the earth's orbit, and polarity reversal in the earth's magnetic field—and the few centuries of human environmental depredation are a mere brief rash. Wholesale destruction is nature's *modus operandi*. The world around us today came into being by destruction and death, and will pass away eventually by the same processes, whether humans are around or not. And from *nature's* perspective, what difference does it make if humans make some small contribution to this process? Whether global warming is caused by volcanic activity or industrial pollutants, the net effect is the same as far as nature is concerned. As Leakey and Lewin point out, "From nature's point of view the distinction between us and a comet is negligible."[43] Our destructiveness is an issue, then, only because we run the risk of making our environment uninhabitable for *ourselves*.

Another environmental projection of human values onto nature is the respect demanded for "biodiversity," the beautiful variety and complex interdependence of all life on Earth, both of which are threatened when species are driven to extinction. But does nature really care about diversity? Again, the diversity of life forms that has developed during the last 600 million years during the "Cambrian" explosion of diverse life-forms—a mere moment in cosmic time— is, like everything else in nature, an accident, not some intended culmination of a progressive development.[44] For billions of years nature did very well without biodiversity. For a couple of billion years the only life form was prokaryotes (cells without organelles like nuclei, chromosomes, and so on), and nature didn't seem to mind.[45] Indeed, the most successful life form in the earth's history has been bacteria, which by every criterion still dominate the planet, dwarfing the relatively scanty number of species that create our much valued "biodiversity."[46] And bacteria are virtually immune to our destructive habits. How, then, from *nature's* perspective, could the brief 600 million years of biodiversity be more valuable than the 2 billion years during which the prokaryotes were the only life on the planet? Biodiversity is of value only to *humans*, because it characterizes the natural world in which humans happen to live: it provides benefits for humans; it sustains the environment in which humans live; and humans can appreciate it aesthetically. When Leakey and Lewin write that "we may value biodiversity because it nurtures the human psyche, the human spirit, the human soul,"[47] we must ask: What can these possibly mean in *nature's* terms? The answer is nothing. There is no "psyche" in nature, no "soul," no "spirit," only matter and force, blind and indifferent. Only *humans* give nature a spirit and a soul, because we find in it a beauty and a meaning that, we feel, connect to or express our own experience—"passions of rain, or moods in falling snow," as Wallace Stevens put it. But without humans, all that beauty and mystery mean nothing, for they simply don't exist without us. As the *philosophe* Diderot said, "If we banish man, the thinking or contemplating being, from the face of the earth, this moving and sublime spectacle of nature will be nothing more than a sad and mute scene."[48]

From nature's perspective, then, humans and their activity are a mere millisecond of a hectic fever soon to be cured one way or another, either by the human species' own self-destructiveness, or by some natural "antibody"—some ebola-like superdisease, or a comet, or some geologic event we can't foresee. It is the strength of one of the more fascinating strains of environmentalism, J. E. Lovelock's Gaia hypothesis, that it at least acknowledges nature's power and humanity's minuscule role in the earth's cosmic drama. Lovelock defines Gaia as "a complex entity involving the Earth's biosphere, atmosphere, oceans, and soil; the totality constituting a feedback or cybernetic system which seeks an optimal physical and chemical environment for life on this planet."[49] Thus whatever humans may do, ultimately Gaia will adjust and go on, surviving the minor "disease" of humanity just as it has survived the numerous other vastly more powerful assaults on it. *We* won't be around, of course, but Gaia won't miss us any more than we miss a bacterium or virus our bodies have successfully warded off.[50]

As with biodiversity, so with all the values that environmentalists, including Al Gore, celebrate in their books—they are *none* of them created by nature or of concern to nature, and so none of them is "natural." Likewise with the causes of social justice most environmentalists espouse along with their concern for nature: racism, sexism, poverty, inequality: all are meaningless in nature's terms.[51] There is no equality in nature, no justice, "no covenants between

wolves and sheep," as Homer said. All of these ideas and qualities—
beauty, harmony, awe, reverence, justice, equality—have their origins and meaning *only* in the human mind and in human culture.
This means that our relationship to the natural world must be
defined, not in natural, but in *human* terms—of what will promote
human values and well-being, of what will ensure a sustaining environment for those to come after us. Thus we should avoid degrading
our environment *not* because of nature, but because of the humans
who need clean air to breathe and water to drink, fertile soil to grow
food, and natural beauty to nourish their souls. How best to provide
an environment conducive to human flourishing and well-being will
depend, not on a false knowledge whose origins lie in cultural myth
and garbled science, but on the best scientific information and technology available, and on a philosophical discussion about what the
human good is, how we should accomplish it, what our responsibilities are to ourselves and the environment, and so on. That is, the
rational activity of the scientist must be subordinated to an ethical
and moral framework.[52]

For clearly, we do face serious problems arising from our degradation of the environment. My intent in criticizing Romantic environmentalism is not to say that everything is fine and so we can
continue to waste and pollute and develop all we want. I feel quite
the opposite, if for no other reason than my own anger at seeing the
rural San Joaquin Valley in which I grew up—a garden of small
farms and towns where every day through the clear air the Sierra
could be seen to the east, and where, every night, the Milky Way
glowed in the sky above—systematically destroyed by city-folks and
their overdevelopment and urbanization, so that now the mountains
can be seen only after the rain has scoured the sky clean of smog, and
the Milky Way is never seen at all, and the small farms are being
paved over into strip-malls and cookie-cutter housing tracts. My
point rather is that clear-headed evaluations of risk, benefit, and
human well-being must be the basis for our actions, not emotionally

gratifying myths. In other words, *humans* and their flourishing and their good must be at the center of all the solutions we invent for our problems, not nature.

After all, if we fail to stop our assaults on our environment, we will be culpable, not from the perspective of nature, to whom we are a minor irritant, but from our own moral perspective, and it is we humans who will suffer the consequences, not nature, who has survived much more serious attacks than our few seconds of dirt and waste. And finally, we will be wrong because we are free to choose *not* to destroy senselessly, not to pollute in unreasonable ways, not to kill for no advantage. That we choose to do all these things will be a betrayal of ourselves and our better natures, not a betrayal of the Earth.

DEEP ECOLOGY

"Deep ecology" is a phrase coined by the Norwegian philosopher Arne Naess in 1972, and has since come to signify a species of environmentalism that goes beyond mere concerns for resource management. Some may want to dismiss the deep ecology movement as a fringe element of environmentalism, especially when it is associated with the radical group Earth First! and its anti-human founder, David Foreman, who thinks "man is no more important than any other species."[53] But as a recent history of environmentalism points out, the secure place of deep ecology in the academy "means that deep ecology is being disseminated to the next generation of those who, as citizens or policymakers, will be deciding about environmental issues."[54] Though the "ecotage" and terrorism of the more radical proponents of deep ecology are decried by the mainstream, the flawed assumptions of the fringe are the same as some of those found in more moderate environmentalist thought.

The influential statement of the principles of deep ecology is found in the book *Deep Ecology: Living as if Nature Mattered,* by Bill

Devall and George Sessions.[55] In it we find a farrago of old myths,
New Age mysticism, and vaporous Romantic nature-love leavened
with radical therapeutic individualism—in a work that supposedly
wants nature to "matter" more than humans. Consider the authors'
initial definition of deep ecology:

> Deep Ecology is emerging as a way of developing a new balance and
> harmony between individuals, communities and all of Nature. It can
> potentially satisfy our deepest yearnings: faith and trust in our most
> basic institutions; courage to take direct action; joyous confidence to
> dance with the sensuous harmonies discovered through spontaneous,
> playful intercourse with the rhythms of our bodies, the rhythms of
> flowing water, changes in the weather and seasons, and the overall
> processes of life on Earth. We invite you to explore the vision that
> deep ecology offers [7].

Revealing here is the rhetoric of New-Age narcissism—"satisfy our
deepest yearnings"—connected to a portentously vague celebration
of the "rhythms of flowing water," whatever those are. Along with
the assertion of a harmony between humans and the natural world,
this rhetoric reflects the old subordination of nature to the psychic
requirements of the sensitive individual that we saw earlier in
Goethe and Rousseau, and that Flaubert mercilessly satirized. This
therapeutic thrust continues throughout Devall and Sessions's book,
as when the authors endorse "lifestyles that promote personhood and
self-realization" (28), or when they note with approval Naess's concern for "a more sensitive openness to ourselves and nonhuman life
around us" (65). Obviously, none of this has anything to do with the
natural world, which cares nothing about the human issues of "self-
realization" or "openness," let alone the unnatural idea of "personhood." There are no "persons" in nature. Nature here is being
reduced to a screen on which is projected the dissaffected modern's
psycho-melodrama.

As well as the therapeutic imperative, Sessions and Devall indulge in other Romantic idealizations. The old assertion of harmony between humanity and nature appears in references to "Earth wisdom" and to the self as an "inseparable aspect of the whole system wherein there are no sharp breaks between self and the *other*," (65) and in a definition of "maturity and growth" as an "identification which goes beyond humanity to include the nonhuman world." This "nonhuman world" includes perforce cockroaches, lymphomas, and HIV, "nonhuman" life forms that I presume the authors also have in mind when they assert that "all things in the biosphere have an equal right to live and blossom and reach their own individual forms of unfolding and self-realization with the larger Self-realization" (67).

We are treated as well to the myth's distrust of technology, which in Romanticism was put to the service of a critique of industrial civilization and science, and these days serves the antirationalist attack on Western culture as a whole. In terms redolent of the Unabomber, we hear that "technological society not only alienates humans from the rest of Nature but also alienates humans from themselves and from each other. It necessarily promotes destructive values and goals which often destroy the basis for stable viable human communities interacting with the natural world" (48).

As in Hesiod and Ovid, here the development of technology marks the fall from the Golden Age of harmony with a maternal nature that once freely provided sustenance for humans. And, of course, our self-loathing Western authors see this alienation from nature as the peculiar fault of the wicked West, which "has become increasingly obsessed with the idea of *dominance*: with dominance of humans over nonhuman Nature, masculine over the feminine, wealthy and powerful over the poor, with the dominance of the West over non-Western cultures" (66, emphasis in original). If the West is the source of all evil, then non-Western primitive cultures logically represent our salvation, those noble savages who still live a Golden-Age existence: "Ecotopian visions…can be drawn from the anthropological literature on hunters/gatherers, small-scale agricultural communities, and contemporary primal cultures"[56] (162). These cultures are not "hierarchical and centralized," just like Ovid's denizens of the Golden Age who lived without law or property[57] (19), and so, like Montaigne's cannibals, they serve convenient sticks with which to beat a jaded civilization.

Clearly, Devall and Sessions are presenting psychologically gratifying myths rather than workable rational solutions to environmental problems. The angst-ridden urban-dweller, assailed by the complexity and noise of modern high-tech life, finds a therapeutic gratification in daydreams of harmony with nature and simple primitivism, all the while he continues to enjoy the benefits of nutrition, health care, and sanitation which that same high-tech society provides. As a variant of the myth of nature-love, deep ecology can perhaps satisfy the yearning for meaning felt by many anxious moderns who no longer find in traditional religion a sustaining narrative that can make sense of their lives.[58] But considered as a practical program for negotiating the impact of humanity on the environment, deep ecology offers nothing but useless and destructive false knowledge.

THE END OF NATURE

Bill McKibben's *The End of Nature*[59] brought many of the ideas, and thus many of the false assumptions, of deep ecology to a larger audience than that reached by Devall and Sessions. McKibben's argument is more nuanced and eloquent than Devall and Sessions's: he is concerned with "a certain set of human ideas about the world and our place in it" (8), a certain way that he thinks humans once related to the natural world that is now coming to an end because of the relentless depredations of industrial society. By nature he means "the separate and wild province, the world apart from man to which he adapted, under whose rules he was born and died" (48). But it is the meaning of this nature, "of the wind, the sun, the rain" that he claims has changed, leaving us in a "postnatural world" (60).

What these "ideas" and "meaning" are remain somewhat vague, but whatever they are, they reflect *human*, not natural, values projected onto the morally neutral material world of deterministic laws and processes. Herein lies the central confusion of McKibben's book. The nature he mourns is "the separate and wild province," everything that is *not* human and social: "Nature's independence *is* its meaning; without it there is nothing but us" (58). Nature's "separation from human society" (64, emphases deleted) is what, to McKibben's regret, we have ended. Now "there's nothing there except us. There's no such thing as nature anymore—that other world that isn't business and art and breakfast is now not another world, and there is nothing except us alone...and so there is no escaping other people" (89). But that nature totally separate from us is, as McKibben forgets, without values or morality—it is sheer existence and amoral processes, none of which are beautiful or ugly, or good or evil, unless there are people to judge them so.

But when McKibben speaks of that natural world whose loss he mourns, he repeatedly attributes to it *human* values utterly irrelevant to that supposedly "separate" natural world. Consider the following: "As long as some places remained free and wild, the idea of the free and wild could live" (66). But nothing in nature is either "free" or "wild"—these are *human* categories and values. What in nature, a sphere of biological determinism, can be truly said to be "free"? Is the lion "free" *not* to kill and eat the antelope? Is the baboon "free" *not* to submit its rump to the alpha baboon? Is the ibis "free" *not* to feast on the helpless crocodile hatchlings? "Wild" and "free" presuppose their respective conceptual opposites, the tame or civilized and the not-free; hence *both* "wild" and "tame" are *un*natural, man-made states. Paradoxically, then, McKibben attacks civilization and its assault on nature with values that derive from that same civilization.

McKibben's ultimate project, as with all the practitioners of long tradition of nature-love, is therapeutic, the creation of a religious sensibility that can make sense of the human condition in a complex civilization. McKibben is surprisingly frank about this intent: "Many people, including me, have overcome [the decline of religion] to a greater or a lesser degree by locating God in nature. Most of the glimpses of immortality, design, and benevolence that I see come from the natural world—from the seasons, from the beauty, from the intermeshed fabric of decay and life, and so on" (71). This flaccid pantheism is redolent of James Fenimore Cooper's *The Prairie* (1827). There the "man of nature" Leatherstocking proclaims that he "has lived for seventy years in the very bosom of natur'...where he could at any instant open his heart to God without having to strip it of the cares and wickednesses of the settlements." But nature is neither benevolent nor malevolent. Nature's order is actually quite inhuman, not at all "lovely" (73), for it is an order in which the suffering and deaths of not just individuals but whole species are matters of utter indifference.

Ultimately, McKibben, like Devall and Sessions—and like the Unabomber—is unhappy with the consciousness, the rationalism, and the civilization that make humans what they are. As such, McKibben is rehashing, in much less interesting terms, the old Romantic use of wild nature as the backdrop for the individualistic search for self-validation apart from a repressive society. Byron wrote "my joy was in the Wilderness" or "I love not man the less, but nature more," and McKibben would agree.

But McKibben also manifests the antihumanism lurking beneath both Romantic individualism and our forms of environmentalism, as when he says that "the comfort we need is inhuman" (217). In fact, a dislike of people and society, the hallmark of Romantic radical individualism, recurs throughout McKibben's book, as we saw above where he frets because "there's nothing there [in the world] except us." Getting rid of "people"—that is, humans understood as Aristotle's social animals—appears to be the way to recover that "separate" nature McKibben values so highly. Thus he wonders what would happen "if we began to truly and viscerally think of ourselves as just one species among many" (172), if we considered ourselves as a mere "part of the world, just like bears" (174). Well, the answer is we would cease to be human, and so we would behave like the rest of nature—amorally, indifferent to cruelty and suffering, capable of *anything*. In other words, we would cease to exist—and along with us everything we have created as solaces for our supposedly unnatural lives: compassion, pity, art, altruism, nobility, all the good we choose and risk and lose—and all the goods I daresay McKibben values.

McKibben's book is simply another form of therapeutic myth. It does not address the fundamental philosophical issue of what exactly we are, nor does it confront the profound differences separating humanity and nature, which must be taken into account whenever we start to talk about values or ethics or morality. Like the Golden Age or the Noble Savage myths, or like the Romantic idealization of nature, *The End of Nature* offers not solutions to our problems but escapist compensations for the burden of being what we are—Sir Thomas Browne's "great amphibium," neither beast nor angel, neither natural nor unnatural, neither at home in the world nor exiled from it.

EARTH IN THE BALANCE

With Albert Gore's *Earth in the Balance*[60] the flawed assumptions and ideas associated with deep ecology[61] reached its largest audience yet. Over half a million copies of the book have been sold, testifying to the general acceptance this species of false knowledge has found in our society. In Gore's book we find the same melange of New-Age therapy, nature-love, and recycled myths expressing dissatisfaction with civilization and technology that we found in McKibben's and Devall and Sessions' works.[62]

The narcissistic therapeutic sensibility provides the explicit framework for Gore's book. Gore tells us that *Earth in the Balance* arose out of his own midlife crisis or "life change" (14) precipitated by his son's near death after being struck by a car: "The search for truths about this ungodly crisis and the search for truths about myself have been the same search all along" (13). He wrote the book "to fully search [sic] my heart and mind about this challenge to which I feel called—and in the process to summon the courage to make a full and unreserved commitment to see it through" (16). Here New-Age self-help borrows the old rhetoric of evangelical Christianity and its doctrine of the "calling." Needless to say, Gore's experience—his consciousness of his own and his loved one's mortality and unique value and his recognition of a meaning larger than just his own life—reflects human *cultural* values, not natural ones. The nature Gore's book will idealize is utterly indifferent to the suffering and death of any individual life-form. Only civilization creates and celebrates the values animating Gore's journey to "restore a balance within ourselves between who we are and what we are doing" (12). Philosophy is unnatural.

But philosophy is too elevated a term to describe what Gore is up to. The twelve-step movement and its rhetoric of addiction and dysfunction provide the framework for Gore's ideas. In his view, Western civilization is "dysfunctional" (226), traumatized by the separation from nature effected by its intellectual "fathers" Bacon and Descartes. Hence our civilization is addicted to wasteful consumption of natural resources as a way of avoiding the psychic pain of that alienation, just as the victim of familial abuse turns to drugs or food or sex to avoid the painful memories of his parents' crimes (220-26). It is testimony to the intellectual incoherence of Gore's ideas that he uses a scientifically discredited theory about human nature as a received truth to develop an equally suspect, equally irrational theory about humanity's relationship to the natural world. Once more we see that constructing an emotionally gratifying myth is the environmentalists' real purpose here, not offering rational solutions to our social ills.

Gore, in fact, has not met a New Age shibboleth he doesn't like. The Noble Savage Ecologist Chief Seattle, of course, is trotted out.[63] A "modern prayer of the Onondaga tribe" is also quoted without any awareness that the prayer has probably been influenced by several centuries of Western Romantic culture (259). Gore treats us as well to a milder variety of eco-feminism, another therapeutic ideology that combines old stereotypes about women as more "nurturing" and "emotional" with peevish attacks on Western science and capitalism. As Carolyn Merchant, an influential eco-feminist, puts it, environmentalism and feminism both "are sharply critical of the costs of competition, aggression, and domination arising from the market economy's *modus operandi* in nature and society," and both ideologies attack the "view of both women and nature as psychological and recreational resources for the harried entrepreneur-husband."[64] Merchant's take on Western history reflects a profound historical ignorance, since it is *nature*, not the "entrepreneur-husband," that subjected women to painful childbirth, frequent pregnancy and lactation, physical inferiority to men, breast cancer, menstruation, and menopause, evils which only industrialized liberal democracies and technology have palliated for women. Gore, though, peddles this same eco-feminist snake-oil, presenting as established fact the dubious "right-brain/left-brain" dichotomy (214) and asserting that "for the last few thousand years, Western civilization has emphasized a distinctly male way of relating to the world and has organized itself around philosophical structures that devalue the distinctive female approach to life" (212). Therefore, to solve our problems we need "a healthier respect for female ways of experiencing the world" (213)— those "ways" comprising the stereotypes about nurturing emotional women that used to be a sign of sexist deviance.

Gore goes on to combine his mild eco-feminism with his dysfunctional family metaphor to indict Western civilization, in the process creating a fuzzy hodgepodge of bad history and therapeutic psychobabble: "But with God receding from the natural world to an abstract place, the patriarchal figure in the family (almost always the father) effectively became God's viceroy, entitled to exercise godlike authority when enforcing the family's rules." These testosterone-drenched hyper-rational "rules," of course, demand our "suppressing the emotions that might allow us to feel the absence of our connection to the earth" (227). In fact, it is in Noble Savage Third World and primitive societies that "patriarchal" authority brutally wielded against women and children is more apt to be found. The West doesn't practice purdah or sutte, or perform clitoridectomies, or require footbinding. In the West the scientific revolution and its political concomitant, liberal democracies, are what have been responsible for the liberation of women and children and their greater power and autonomy. It is women's liberation *from* nature by means of unnatural Western science and civilization that has improved their lives and decreased their suffering.

The truth or coherence of Gore's ideas, however, is not Gore's concern. What Gore is doing is indulging a whole series of cultural myths created to alleviate the disaffected modern's psychic pain. Nature-love, the West's perennial solace for civilization's discontents, recurs throughout the book in the assertions of a lost harmony between humans and the natural world. Gore frets that we have "lost our feeling of connectedness to the rest of nature" (1) and thus "the sense of awe and reverence that used to be present in our relationship to nature" (203).

What the urban-dwelling, technology-protected Gore fails to note, however, is that that "awe and reverence" of earlier people resulted from their *fear* of nature's destructive power and its indifference to human suffering or survival. Awe of the sheer *power* of nature, a power destructive as well as creative. Only when agricultural technology ensured a steady food supply could nature ever become an object of aesthetic pleasure and spiritual significance.[65] A modern like Gore, protected by a cocoon of sustaining technology, can afford to wax sentimental about the "vividness, vibrancy, and aliveness of the rest of the natural world"(220), the "deeper rhythms of life" (222), the "natural harmony that entails the music of life" (223), or the "awe, wonder, a sense of mystery—a spiritual response—when one reflects on [nature's] deeper meaning" (264).

The serpent in Gore's Eden that caused us to lose that once happy paradise of harmony with a kind Mother Nature was Western rationalism and science. Throughout, Gore decries our "technological hubris" (206) and "technological alchemy" (207) for their "increasingly aggressive encroachment into the natural world" (75) and the resulting "froth and frenzy of industrial civilization" (220). Our culture is further blamed for creating "an elaborate set of cultural rules designed to encourage the fullest expression of thought while simultaneously stifling the expression of feelings and emotions" (218). Anyone familiar with our vapid popular culture of talk-show confessions, or with our mindless political life knows our problem is definitely *not* a "stifling of feelings and emotions" or a full expression of "thought." Thoughtlessly expressing our feelings and emotions seems to be all we do.

Gore's attack on rationalism rounds up the favorite suspects of the Romantics: Descartes and Bacon, who are blamed for creating the division of mind and body, reason and feeling, and man and nature, and for an instrumental view of the natural world that has led to its degradation: "Descartes and Bacon ensured the gradual abandonment of the philosophy that humankind was one vibrant strand in an elaborate web of life, matter, and meaning"[66] (253). Gore's history repeats the old mischaracterization of Bacon as "the false prophet who led humanity, not to the promised land, but to the wilderness of rank materialism and crass utilitarianism,"[67] as Nieves Mathews puts it. But seventeenth-century philosophers like Bacon wanted to control nature to improve human lives, to alleviate the physical suffering that Gore—a creation of vaccination, sanitary food and water, and electricity—never faces precisely because of the success of the scientific revolution Bacon, Descartes, and others initiated. Bacon explicitly stated that the motive for investigating nature should be "charity for man and anxiety to relieve his sorrows and necessities."[68] And he rejected "both power and knowledge not dedicated to goodness and love."[69] Likewise with Descartes, who stated that one should search for knowledge in order to be useful to other humans, for we are under "the law which enjoins upon us the duty of procuring, as well as we can, the general good of mankind."[70] Gore's statement that Bacon is responsible for the idea that "new power derived from scientific knowledge could be used to dominate nature with moral impunity" (252) is simply false. It was the moral imperative to help their fellow human beings that motivated Bacon, Browne, and others, who wanted to liberate humanity from the superstition and falsehood that had for centuries caused human suffering and misery.

No more true is Gore's blaming of Bacon for the split between science and religion, which Gore thinks unleashed a Faustian science to manipulate a dead nature without any moral limits or larger meaning[71] (252). Clarence Glacken notes, "Bacon's philosophy of man's attaining control over nature by cultivating the arts and sciences and encouraging invention is not divorced from religion; it is a vital part of religion, being closely related to the history of creation and to the fall of man."[72] As well as charity to his fellow man, Bacon was driven by a "reverence for or disposition to magnify [God's] works," an attitude that required him "to approach with humility and veneration to unroll the volume of the Creation."[73] Likewise with Sir Thomas Browne, who said that "those highly magnifie him whose judicious enquiry into his acts, and deliberate research into his creatures, returne the duty of a devout and learned admiration."[74] To Bacon, the new scientific methodology would lead to a greater appreciation of God's glorious creation and providential order at the same time that it led to knowledge beneficent to human life by reducing the destructive chaos created in nature by the Fall. That there were unforeseen destructive consequences to that process is unarguable. What human ideal, no matter how noble, has not been accompanied by unintended destructiveness? But we modern Westerners, who live lives of material abundance and comfort because of the scientific revolution initiated by Bacon and others, should manifest some recognition that our psychic dissatisfactions and nostalgia for a beautiful maternal nature are luxuries made possible by our liberation from nature's destructiveness.

But these are rational objections to a gratifying myth. As with Devall and Sessions, McKibben, Thomas Berry, and numerous others, Gore ultimately is providing a quasi-religious therapeutic solace for people whose hectic lives are not soothed by the material comfort these people take for granted, and who fail to realize that the price we pay for that comfort is the psychological dissatisfaction Gore and the rest speak of. And however severe we may think that psychic pain to be, we have not yet witnessed vast hordes of urban dwellers giving up on those material comforts and voluntarily returning to a harder and more uncertain, but psychically more fulfilling, existence without antibiotics, electricity, and a dependable food supply. Indeed, other than cranks like the Unabomber, we are seeing quite the opposite—the rest of the world that *doesn't* have those material comforts desperately trying to catch up with the industrialized West. Apparently if we humans are given the choice between a deprived material existence rich in spiritual significance, and material comfort with psychic dislocation, we will choose the latter. It is hypocritical for those who enjoy that material comfort to decry the civilization that makes it possible.

THE ANTIHUMANIST IMPLICATIONS

Environmentalism's imperative "to decentre the human being, to question mechanistic science and its technological consequences, to refuse to believe the world was made for human beings"[75] and to replace humanism with "ecocentrism" necessarily leads to an antihumanism frightening in its implications, as the Unabomber's murders have shown. Bill Devall claims that "ecocentrism means rejecting the position that some life forms (such as humans) have greater inherent worth than other life forms."[76] If Devall is right, then we must confront the implications of this position. If humans are reduced to just another species with no more claim to life than any other, if human suffering is no more significant than the suffering of a whale or an owl, and if humans are threatening to destroy the integrity of the planet's wonderful biodiversity, then the destruction of humans is the logical answer to this problem.

These antihumanist implications can be uncovered by looking at the analogy made by some environmentalists between the Nazi death camps and the behavior of those who environmentalists think are destroying the planet. Overdramatizing humanity's threat to nature has led to what Charles Rubin correctly terms "a remarkably repulsive...moral equivalence between ecological problems and the Holocaust."[77]

The deep ecologist Bill Devall says, for example, that "students in natural resources sciences and management...are much like the guards in Nazi death camps," and he compares the cost efficiency of the timber industry to the ruthless "cost-effective" means the Nazis used to murder large numbers of people.[78] The "moderate" Al Gore indulges the same false analogy when he speaks of an "ecological *Kristallnacht*."[79] The net result of this odious analogy is merely to trivialize the murder of six million human beings by comparing it to the felling of trees.

There is, however, a real connection between the Nazis and the environmentalists—namely, that the Nazis were superb ones. Schama notes, "It is...painful to acknowledge how ecologically conscientious the most barbaric regime in modern history actually was—exterminating million of lives was not at all incompatible with passionate protection of millions of trees."[80] It is a continuing embarrassment to the environmental movement that the Nazi regime was the first state to make a high priority of environmental concerns. Hitler's regime passed a law in 1933 providing for the protection of animals, one in 1934 limiting hunting, and one in 1935 for the protection of nature. The Nazi ecologist Walther Schoenichen praised the diversity of nature and primitive cultures as much as contemporary environmentalists do, indeed basing an opposition to "miscegenation" on the grounds that it diluted diversity among humans.[81] "These laws," Ferry notes, "were the first in the world to reconcile a broad ecological plan with the concern for real political intervention."[82] Ferry goes on to point out the similarities between Nazism and deep ecology: "In both cases, we are dealing with a same *romantic and/or sentimental* representation of the relationship between nature and culture, combined with a shared revalorization of the *primitive* state against that of (alleged) civilization."[83] In other words, the Golden Age myth combined with Romantic idealization of raw nature.

Environmentalists will no doubt call these remarks a *reductio ad absurdum*, but there is no escaping the logical conclusions that follow from considering humans as just one life form among others, to be evaluated only in nature's terms. In nature's terms civilization is a monstrous aberration, rather than the humanizing force the Greeks considered it to be. "The hatred of the *artifice* connected with our civilization of rootlessness is also a *hatred of humans as such*," Ferry writes. "For man is the antinatural being par excellence. This is even what distinguished him from other beings, including those who seem the closest to him: animals. This is how he escapes natural cycles, how he attains the realm of culture, and the sphere of morality, which presupposed living in accordance with laws and not just with nature."[84] The Unabomber's terrorism, then, makes perfect sense, as do the limitations of human freedom or the suspension of democratic rights or the embracing of totalitarianism in order to protect the environment and create the various "ecotopias" imagined

by radical environmentalists.[85] In fact, the whole cargo of the
Enlightenment and humanism, the notion of inalienable rights possessed by individuals who should be free simply because they *are*
human and create themselves through choice, is to be jettisoned as
so much artificial anthropocentrism legitimizing our selfish destruction of the planet. What this threat to freedom can mean for individual human beings—for example, violence against those who
resist attempts to correct the human relationship with nature—
never seems to bother those modern environmentalists who take for
granted all those rights and humanistic values, as well as their own
unique human individuality.

WE ARE NOT NATURAL[86]

The attitudes and assumptions that we have traced through these
books on environmentalism have become more and more popular,
and so they increasingly determine the decisions we collectively
have to make about how to spend our resources, how to manage our
interactions with the natural world, and how to negotiate the conflicting demands of people and the environment. These decisions
should depend as much as possible on rational analyses of need and
consequence and cost and benefit, and on philosophical discussions
of human ethics, values, and responsibilities to ourselves and
nature—not on gratifying myths and false knowledge.[87]

If we ask first how these false ideas could gain such currency, we
have only to turn to the culprits identified in Part I. Our vulnerability to the "quantitative idols" of science is an important reason
why the woolier versions of environmentalism are given such credence. It is one of the paradoxes of an anti-science, antirationalist
environmentalism that most of its ammunition comes from the
activity of scientists. As Andrew Dobson notes, "It is remarkable,
indeed, to see the extent to which the success of modern political

ecology has been mediated and sustained by scientific research."[88] Unfortunately, much of that science is misleading or garbled when popularized, as has been shown by the numerous critical analyses of some of the more apocalyptic claims of environmental disaster.[89] Yet our culturally induced deference to scientific authority—and its armor of quantification, jargon, and formulae—convinces us that dubious opinions or interpretations are *facts* to which we must respond or suffer the dire consequences.

The schools must share part of the blame. Anyone with children in school knows that sentimental environmentalism is firmly ensconced in the curriculum. A recent sympathetic commentator on environmental education has gushed that this "is indeed a new, historic phenomenon—a whole generation of young people committed to the well-being of the planet and all its living things."[90] Obviously, this novel "commitment"—though "fashion" is a more accurate description—is created and daily reinforced in the schools. The gospel of recycling is preached to children day in and day out, usually without any awareness of the limitations of recycling, such as the cost in energy to sort and clean refuse, or without any recognition that urban waste-disposal still requires and will continue to require incinerators and landfills.[91] Earth Day is a major curricular event.[92] Classes raise funds by "selling" their parents rain forest products so kiddies can buy a fragment of the rainforest, which is then presumably protected from depredation. Posters of species threatened with extinction—usually cuddly mammals like the stuffed ones the kids sleep with—adorn classrooms.

My point is not that children shouldn't be taught to respect the environment and natural resources. They obviously should. Rather, I object to the false knowledge about these matters that is often presented without critical analysis and with a baggage of anti-Western ideology disguised as scientific fact. A laudatory survey a few years ago of environmental "educators" was replete with the usual mixture of sentimental nature-love and anti-modern complaints, all laced with apocalyptic anxiety: "I believe education can help prevent catastrophe if we will only bother, and we must," the article ends portentously, simultaneously displaying Romantic irrationalism and an Enlightenment faith in ameliorative reason.[93] Moreover, environmentalism in the schools is more often than not a matter of therapeutic emotionalism. Shaping values and attitudes, not providing information, is the admitted goal of environmental educators: "Many studies [of environmental education] have concluded that a sustainable and equitable future will require changes in personal beliefs, attitudes, and behavior as well as substantial alterations of economic, social, and political practices."[94] The creepy questions begged, of course, are *whose* "beliefs" and "attitudes" are going to be taught, who will teach them, how will they be defined and determined, and on what evidence will their validity be based. We can be reasonably sure that amorphous emotions will tend to shape these subjective beliefs and attitudes, not hard facts about the human use of resources and our relationship to the natural world, facts necessary to make the hard choices that that relationship must impose on us.[95]

The media are even more responsible than the schools for much of the hysteria, misinformation, oversimplification, and selective reporting that shape the average citizen's ideas about the environment. The media are addicted to dramatic images and emotion-laden conflicts between heroes and villains and so have little interest in evaluating the claims made by various studies or in presenting their full complexity. Everybody remembers the dramatic images of devastation that followed the *Exxon Valdez*'s dumping of eleven million gallons of crude oil into Prince William Sound in 1989. The pictures of thousands of dead birds and oil-blackened otters were accompanied by grim assertions of catastrophic environmental destruction. Yet three years later, Greg Easterbrook visited the sound and found barely any signs that the environment had been destroyed, as proclaimed by the media. On the contrary, the beaches were clean and most of the animals were thriving. But no cameras have recorded that spectacular recovery, because no drama and villains and emotional charge were involved. As Easterbrook notes, "The significance of ecological events to the government institutions and news organizations that cross-pollinate each other's pantomime hysteria is determined by factors unrelated to the ecology, such as the availability of pictures."[96] In fact, the greatest loss of plant and animal life in the sound occurred where the most aggressive cleaning up took place in response to the emotional public uproar caused by dramatic images of oily beaches and bedraggled sea-birds.[97]

A recent survey of studies investigating environmental reporting confirms that the media's appetite for drama causes them to diverge significantly from scientists when reporting environmental destruction or the risk of man-made chemicals. In fact, reporters spend comparatively little time evaluating risk. To report that some additive or chemical has been linked to human disease is easier than evaluating the seriousness of the risk. Bombarded by sinister images of environmental degradation, insidious chemical assault, and rampant pollution, we then are more ready than ever to turn to the therapeutic myths we have discussed.

Much of what passes for environmentalism, in short, is really a species of therapy for the disaffected, anxious modern looking for personal happiness. Indeed, environmentalism as therapy is now the conscious goal of some social workers, other peddlers of false knowledge in our society. The Sojourn program in Salt Lake City involves clients and nature in what the program's director calls "a course of therapy, one of letting go of the distractions that keep us from ourselves by physically attaching to what is more natural and eternal."[98] The usual vaporous therapeutic desiderata are bestowed on "clients" by this "course of therapy"—"Clients overcome fear and gain personal insights during their movement through the landscape.... Dobbin has noted increased confidence in relationships, improved communication skills, increased self-esteem, and greater compassion among participants."[99] Here the age-old pastoral dream of a sustaining and recuperative nature has been trivialized into the pseudo-scientific banality of therapeutic narcissism.

The therapeutic thrust of environmentalism explains its widespread appeal to New Age adherents. That nature-love may substitute for religion has long been obvious. Historian Keith Thomas traces this development to the later eighteenth century, when the appreciation of wild nature "had been converted into a sort of religious act. Nature was not only beautiful; it was morally healing. The value of the wilderness was not just negative; it did not merely provide a place of privacy, an opportunity for self-examination and private reverie (which was an ancient idea); it had a more positive role, exercising a beneficent spiritual power over man." Thomas quotes historian Archibald Alison, who said in 1815, "All the noblest convictions and confidences of religion may be acquired in the simple school of nature."[100] As seen, this sentiment is identical to modern environmentalism's anthropocentric idealization of nature.

"In the irony of ironies," Martin Lewis points out, "the ultimate concern of many eco-radicals...turns out to be not so much with the health of nature, but rather with the salvation of a human spirit that has supposedly been corrupted by civilization."[101] This religion, moreover, is millenarian: it sees apocalypse just around the corner if we don't abandon our cities and technologies and return to nature.[102] Needless to say, this solution is wildly improbable, as well as being the worst thing that could happen to nature if it were actually carried out.[103] But a more immediate concern, however, is the fanaticism and irrationalism that often accompany true believers, who eagerly anticipate the apocalypse and, in consequence, believe they are freed from any constraints on their behavior. Clearly the Unabomber exemplifies the sort of mischief and mayhem we can expect from such people.

Much of popular environmentalism, then, is false knowledge. We need what Easterbrook calls "ecorealism," the conviction "that logic, not sentiment, is the best tool for safeguarding nature; that accurate understanding of the actual state of the environment will serve the

Earth better than expressions of panic; that in order to form a constructive alliance with nature, men and women must learn to think like nature."[104] That is, we must stop indulging the old *unnatural* myth of nature-love or of a lost paradise freed from civilization and its discontents, and we must stop promoting self-gratifying eco-utopian fantasies whose ultimate purpose is to provide therapeutic solace for the anxious and disgruntled who nevertheless depend on high-tech civilization as much as anyone. Instead we must start making clear-headed discriminations between human needs and nature's, and we must start figuring out how we can rationally manage technology and growth in such a way that both humanity and nature can flourish. But those solutions will be found not in the quasi-religious, debased Romantic idealizations of a nature to whom our fate as a species is a matter of utter indifference, but rather in Socrates's "city," the "unnatural" social and political world of interconnected humans—the world in which we define ourselves as human beings and carry on the cantankerous communal conversations that try to sort out and define our human goods and values.

That social world of human connection is ultimately what gives value to nature. And at least one Noble Savage agreed. Chief Seattle, to whom was falsely attributed one of our most popular expressions of Romantic Indian ecology, really said something closer to this: "The ground beneath your feet responds more lovingly to our steps than yours because it is the ashes of our grandfathers. Our bare feet know the kindred touch. The earth is rich with the lives of our kin."[105] Chief Seattle knew what our urban Romantic ecologists do not: the people who live and die on the Earth are ultimately what give nature meaning. Without us nature would be, as Diderot said, "a sad and mute scene."

CHAPTER 6 ■ THE WHITE MAN'S GOLDEN AGE RED MAN

The friendly and flowing savage, who is he?

— WALT WHITMAN[1]

Indians have for centuries nourished our imagination, weaving in us a complex skein of guilt, envy, and contempt; yet, imagining that we see "the Indian," we often see little more than the distorted reflection of our own fears, fancies, and wistful longings.

— FERGUSON BORDEWICH[2]

False knowledge about noble Indians and ignoble whites permeates our society. The debased Romanticism of the New Age therapeutic sensibility has found in Indians a rich soil to cultivate. Time-Life books peddles a series of volumes that promise to reveal the secrets of Native-American therapeutic spirit-magic, sending along an "authentic" hand-made "dream-catcher" with your paid subscription. Bookstores and hotel conference rooms are crammed with the works of what one critic has called "Plastic Medicine Men," the "gaggle of pay-up-front impresarios and conductors of

'American Indian' spiritual exercises."[3] From the inventive Carlos Castaneda and Jamake Highwater to *Hanta Yo* and *Black Elk Speaks*, the old European vision of Indians as possessors of a primal nature-wisdom that can regenerate an angst-ridden materialist society continues to turn a handsome profit.[4] Even bottom-line-conscious businessmen aren't immune to the allure of primitive wisdom. Institutions like Mattel and the United States Air Force have sent their executives to management consultants Rainbow Hawk and Wind Eagle and their "tepeed training facility" in the Santa Cruz mountains. There, paleface executives learn "an ancient tribal approach to problem solving called a 'council ceremony'" celebrated around a fire pit fragrant with sage and other herbs.[5]

Why has this, as Mark Twain put it, "lost tribe of Indians who never existed" remained so popular? Because the Indian is a vehicle for the powerful myth of the Golden Age, which, as we have seen, has been the West's most persistent expression of dissatisfaction with the complexities and burdens of civilization.

THE AMERICAN GOLDEN RACE

The Golden Age myth imagines a time when humans lived in peace, leisure, health, and simple harmony with nature, all their needs freely provided by a maternal earth, their lives unencumbered by law and private property and free from the attendant evils of trade and war. This Golden Age, as the myth goes, ultimately degenerated into the Iron Age, a time of disease, greed for gold, war, cities and technology, hard work, and suffering. To Europeans, American Indians at first glance seemed to be a people who had escaped the fall into the Iron Age, and hence were free of the evils afflicting a decrepit Old World.

Columbus, as seen, characterized the Indians he encountered with Golden Age motifs of gentleness and communal life: they were "very gentle, not knowing what is evil, nor the sins of murder and theft," and "a loving people, without covetousness." So too Amerigo Vespucci in the *Mundus Novus* (1504-5) reported of the Indians that "neither do they have goods of their own, but all things are held in common," and that "they live according to nature." The famous Spanish defender of the Indian, Bartolomé Las Casas, agreed: "They are the most submissive, patient, peaceful, and virtuous. Nor are they quarrelsome, rancorous, or vengeful.... They neither possess nor desire to possess worldly wealth." And Arthur Barlow, the late sixteenth-century agent of Walter Raleigh, explicitly invoked the Golden Age myth: "Wee found the people most gentle, loving, and faithful, void of all guile, and treason, and such as lived after the manner of the golden age. The earth bringeth forth all things in abundance as in the first creation, without toil or labor."[6]

The Golden Age motifs of harmony with nature, leisure, and absence of property and greed recur over and over in the writings of the sixteenth and seventeenth centuries, too. Lescarbot, in his *Nova Francia*, called the Indian life "the most perfect and most worthy life of man," one which had characterized the "ancient golden age." Peter Martyr in his "Decades of the Newe World" (1532) likewise asserted that "amonge them [Indians] the lande is as common as the sonne and water: And that Myne and Thyne (the seedes of all myscheefe) have no place with them." Indians live in a "goulden worlde, without toyle, lyuinge in open gardens, not intrenched with dykes with hedges, or defended with waules. They deale trewely one with another, without lawes, without bookes, and without Iudges."[7] The New World thus is loaded with redemptive expectations, as hinted at in George Chapman's poem to Queen Elizabeth, in which he beseeches that monarch to "let your breath/Goe foorth vpon the waters, and create/A golden worlde in this our yron age." Likewise with Stephen Parmenius, a Hungarian who died on a voyage to Newfoundland in 1583: "The Golden Age began.../In such communities [as in the New World], and thus men lived/In blessedness." Their example leads to the hope that "Well could it be that that great time has come,/That round the globe we see peace-loving men/Promote the Age of Gold." The result will be a liberation from Iron Age necessity, for "Then Mother Earth/Will yield to all, from little effort, rich/Provisions from her ample store of goods." So too Michael Drayton, who in his "To the Virginian Voyage" (1605) apostrophized Virginia as "Earth's onely Paradise" where "the golden age,/still natures lawes doth give."[8]

In the eighteenth-century Baron de Lahontan, in his *New Voyages to North-America* (1703), explicitly contrasted Indian Golden Age virtue with European Iron Age vice: "Nations which are not deabuch'd by the neigbourhood of the Europeans, are strangers to the measures of meum and tuum [mine and thine], and to all laws, judges, and priests." Hence Indians are "utter strangers to distinctions of property, for what belongs to one is equally anothers."[9] Likewise Robert Beverley's *History and Present State of Virginia* (1705) extolled in Golden Age terms the Indians whose hands were not "harden'd by Labour, nor their Minds corrupted by the Desire of hoarding up Treasure...Neither fearing present Want, nor solicitous for the Future, but daily finding sufficient afresh for their Subsistence."[10]

Throughout the eighteenth century Indians continued to be useful devices for exposing the corruptions of civilization, as when the British essayists Richard Steele and Joseph Addison used the 1710 London visit of four Mohawk sachems or "council chiefs" to criticize London society and politics.[11]

By 1839, when Thomas J. Farnham was on his way to Oregon, this use of the Indian as Golden Age commentator on a corrupt civilization had become commonplace. Notice how his (probably) fictitious Indian reprises the Golden Age myth's demonization of agriculture: "As soon as you thrust the plowshare under the earth, it teems with worms and useless weeds. It increases population to an unnatural extent...spreads over the human face a mask of deception and selfishness—and substitutes villainy, love of wealth and power, and the slaughter of millions for the gratification of some royal cut-throat, in place of the single-minded honesty, the hospitality, and the purity of the natural state."[12]

Clearly, for most European and American observers, accurate observation and understanding of Indians early gave way to civilized men's need to express disillusionment with their own society.

By the nineteenth century, the Indian had to bear a burden of complex meaning. To the Enlightenment rationalist, the Noble Savage Indian lived in harmony with nature's laws because he had escaped the corrupt, artificial institutions like the church or aristocracy that had kept Europeans in thrall to priest and noble. But the Romantic Noble Savage "depended upon passion and impulse alone for a direct apprehension of nature in all its picturesqueness, sublimity, and fecundity."[13] In other words, to the Enlightenment's Golden Age and its lack of civil society has been added a Romantic Golden Age, which is characterized by nature-love and the sensibility that finds in natural beauty grist for man's emotions. The stunning natural scenery of America gave the Indian a sublime backdrop to his pathetic role as the doomed, suffering critic of a dull, conformist civilization that killed the spirit with its money-grubbing routines.

These sentiments abounded among the mostly urban artists, vacationers, and slummers of leisure who didn't have to contend daily with the harsh threats to existence that the pioneer, miner, and farmer confronted. As we saw in the last chapter, at the end of the eighteenth century the American poet and journalist Philip Freneau "contrasted his simple, moral life in the woods of Pennsylvania with the distorted existences of city-dwellers."[14] The French man of letters, Chateaubriand, in his *Recollections of Italy, England and America* (1816), said of northern New York's scenic beauty that "in this deserted region the soul delights to bury and lose itself amidst boundless forests...to mix and confound...with the wild sublimities of nature."[15] Likewise with Benjamin Rush, Estwick Evans, Thoreau in *Walden*, Cooper's Natty Bumppo, and Twain's Huck Finn lighting out for the territory: all to some degree see the American wilderness as a realm of individual freedom and communion with nature's beauty, both of which are stifled in the commercial din and artificial social strictures of Iron Age cities and in the oafish drudgery of the farm. The Indian, as the denizen of this sublime landscape, becomes the most attractive example of the freedom and sensibility available to those who dare to throw off the shackles of civilization and farm.

The fact that the Indian was doomed to lose his once-happy paradise made him only that much more useful as fodder for the Romantic sensibility. In 1841 the painter George Catlin brought together in one statement all of these meanings the West had loaded onto the Indian: "Nature has nowhere presented more beautiful and lovely scenes, than those of the vast prairies of the West and of *man* and *beast* no nobler specimens than those who inhabit them—the *Indian* and the *buffalo*—joint and original tenants of the soil, and fugitives together from the approach of civilized man; they have fled to the great plains of the West, and there under an equal doom, they have taken up their last abode, where their race will expire and their bones will bleach together."[16] An understanding of the Indian in all his human complexity has never been able to compete with that useful image of the Indian as vanishing emblem of a freedom, passion, and harmony with nature.

Yet all this idealization of the Indian has coexisted from the start with a demonization of him as pure savagery. The Dominican Tomas Oritz, for example, in a report to the Council of the Indies in 1525 catalogues the degenerate habits of the Indians, including cannibalism, sodomy, and nakedness, and he concludes that "God has never created a race more full of vice and composed without the least mixture of kindness or culture."[17] Both caricatures co-existed for the simple reason that Europeans found both useful for expressing their ambivalence about civilization, their recognition that while society is repressive and artificial, the absence of social restraints can lead to horror.[18] Thus alongside the gentle Taino of Columbus were found cannibals, devil-worshipers, and sexual monsters who by negative example proved the superiority of Christian, European culture and the benefits of rational progress. Both images represent a reduction of the Indian's humanity and a failure to see him as he really was, with all the nobility and ignobility, all the ambivalence and ambiguity that have always and will always characterize every one of us flawed human beings. As we will see next, these days the Golden Age Indian and his faithful companion, the Iron Age Westerner, dominate our imagination, providing us with a convenient fiction to express our own discontents with the burden of civilization.

INDIAN GIVERS

Jack Weatherford's *Indian Givers*[19] is informed throughout by the typical Golden Age/Iron Age contrast—the Europeans are "spurred on by a greed for gold that overshadowed the quest for silver, spices, or souls," whereas the Indians prized gold "more in an aesthetic or religious sense than in a mercenary one" (6, 7). This "wicked lust for having," as Ovid called it, is furthermore responsible for the great modern Iron Age institution, capitalism, from which flow all other Iron Age evils: "The capitalists built the new structure on the twin supports of the slave trade from Africa to America and the piracy of American silver" (38). The "technologically simple Indians," on the other hand, "usually lived in more just, equitable, and egalitarian social conditions" (122) "without strong positions of leadership and coercive political institutions" (121), again because they avoided the "incessant use of 'thine' and 'mine'" (123).

No more plausible is Weatherford's endorsement of the widespread belief that the Iroquois "invented democracy" and were the prime political sources for the founders of the United States. This historical canard also has its roots in the Golden Age and Noble Savage myths, both of which attributed a greater equality and har-

138 PLAGUES OF THE MIND

mony to those peoples who lived without law and judges and private property.[20] These days the myth has become historical fact,[21] repeated in countless textbooks, asserted in a Concurrent Resolution of the United States Congress in 1988, and given the presidential imprimatur: In April of 1994 Clinton said to several hundred Indian tribal leaders that "because of your ancestors, democracy existed here long before the Constitution was drafted and ratified."[22] The myth of Iroquois democracy is a pernicious form of false knowledge about our political heritage, one that has even infected the chief political leader of our nation.

Even a cursory description of the genesis and functioning of the Iroquois League, as far as these can be ascertained from the scanty evidence (most of it late and entangled in orally transmitted legends and myths), reveals how slight are the resemblances to the nascent American government and the political philosophy underlying it. The Iroquois League arose in the early sixteenth century as an attempt to curtail the violence and warfare endemic among the Five Nations.[23] Hence as American historian Dean Snow points out, the league was "more a mutual non-aggression pact than a political union."[24] As such, the league's council comprised the "sachems" or chiefs chosen from each nation's dominant clan. The sachems' positions were hereditary in the sense that titles given to chiefs belonged to a clan in a tribe, so a new chief had to come from the same clan.[25] Chiefs were not elected by "citizens" holding the franchise who were persuaded by the candidates' political principles, but were selected by the senior woman in each clan, who often chose a male relative, and who could remove or "dehorn" the chiefs if they proved unworthy. Nor were the chiefs proportionally representative of a nation's population: the Senecas were the largest nation, yet had the fewest number of chiefs.[26] And within nations, some clans could not contribute chiefs at all.[27] Finally, only the Onondagas could present matters to the league for discussion, and decisions of the council required unanimous assent before being carried out. As Elizabeth

Tooker correctly points out, "there is little in this system of governance the founding fathers might have been expected to copy."[28]

Yet Weatherford asserts the following:

> When Americans try to trace their democratic heritage back through the writings of French and English political thinkers of the Enlightenment, they often forget that these people's thoughts were heavily shaped by the democratic traditions and the state of nature of the American Indians.
>
> The modern notions of democracy based on egalitarian principles and a federated government of overlapping powers arose from the unique blend of European and Indian political ideas and institutions along the Atlantic coast between 1607 and 1776. Modern democracy as we know it today is as much the legacy of the American Indians, particularly the Iroquois and the Algonquians, as it is of the British settlers, of French political theory, or of all the failed efforts of the Greeks and Romans [129-30].

Apart from displaying sheer historical ignorance, Weatherford's claims are vitiated by his incoherent and vague use of the terms "freedom" and "democracy" and "egalitarian." That the American Indians were "freer" than contemporary Europeans is an obvious truism—all technologically simple societies with low population densities relative to their environments of course enjoy more freedom, and perhaps even more equality. From this perspective the Scythians were "freer" and enjoyed more "equality" than the Greeks, and the Germans more than the Romans. But this is a *de facto* freedom and equality, the result, not of conscious planning and a recognition of freedom and equality as abstract goods to be pursued, but of environmental and demographic forces. The trick for human political organization is to achieve *de jure* freedom and equality that are not vulnerable to and can survive the contingencies of history and change, that can weather the greater stress and complexity arising when societies get larger and more technologically sophisticated. Once population begins to increase and societies become more complex, once the state becomes more coercive in order to provide the infrastructure that maintains food production, it becomes more difficult to achieve freedom and egalitarianism.[29] Just look at the Inca or the Mexica, both highly complex indigenous American societies that were hierarchically stratified and definitely *not* egalitarian or democratic.[30]

So, in the end, we can say that the wisdom shown by the Five Nations in organizing such a federation in order to promote peace and stability is admirable, but in no way can we tout it as a major influence on the American Constitution and its institutions.

The true influences, as every schoolboy used to know, on the founding of the American Republic were, *inter alia*, the ancient Greeks and Romans, whose history and literature formed the basis of eighteenth-century education, the Florentine Republics, Whig political philosophers, and Enlightenment thinkers like Locke and Montesquieu.[31] Weatherford, though, airily dismisses this obvious truth:

> Egalitarian democracy and liberty as we know them today owe little to Europe. They are not Greco-Roman derivatives somehow revived by the French in the eighteenth century. They entered modern western thought as American Indian notions translated into European language and culture [128].
>
> Despite the ideal government sketched by Plato in *The Republic*, and the different constitutions analyzed by Aristotle in his *Politics*, the Old World offered America few democratic models for government[32] [134-35].

Weatherford's ignorance here is astonishing. The words "democracy" and "liberty" are literally derivatives of ancient Greek and Latin rather than of Iroquois, for a simple reason: Ancient Athens invented the idea of democracy as egalitarian rule by all the citizens regardless of birth or wealth. Women were excluded, of course, but then women couldn't serve as Iroquois Council chiefs either, no matter how much they kibitzed from the sidelines. And it was the Roman Republic, Alexander Hamilton's "nurse of freedom,"[33] that provided the most important example of a republic defined by representation and the separation of powers—the ideal "middle constitution" of a mixed, stable government defined by checks and balances so highly praised by the historian Polybius. The Iroquois League obviously was not a republic, since chiefs were not elected by "citizens" as delegates to a political institution. It was the example of republics ancient and modern that animated the Founders. As John Adams said in a letter to Lafayette in 1782, "Two republican powers, Athens and Rome, have done more honor to our species than all the rest of it. A new country can be planted only by such a government. America would at this moment have been a howling wilderness inhabited only by bears and savages, without such forms of government; and it would again become a wilderness under any other."[34] Such quotations could be multiplied, for the Revolutionary Age saw "the greatest outpouring of lessons from antiquity in the public arena that America was ever again to witness."[35]

As for the "French in the eighteenth century," that is the *philosophes*, the influence of classical civilization on them is a historical truism bordering on the banal.[36] But most important, what Weatherford calls the "light" from the "torch of Indian liberty that still burned brightly" when the Europeans arrived (124) dims beside the blaze of freedom ignited by a handful of Greeks on the plains of Marathon, in the passes of Thermopylae, and in the straits of Salamis, as even a casual reading of Herodotus will attest. Centuries before Europeans encountered the New World, the ideal of freedom, so many times nearly extinguished, was kept alive by Europeans in numerous anecdotes from ancient history, such as the reply of some Spartan envoys to the invitation of the Persian Hydarnes to submit to that Great King of Persia: "You understand well enough what slavery is, but freedom you have never experienced, so you do not know if it tastes sweet or bitter. If you ever did come to experience it, you would advise us to fight for it not with spears only, but with axes too."[37] Likewise, Romans like Cicero and especially Cato Uticensis provided classical models of martyrs to republican freedom; Joseph Addison's play *Cato* was frequently performed and went through eight editions before 1800.[38] For Weatherford to dismiss this classical tradition as a "failed effort" (even if we, like Weatherford, should ignore the fact that Athenian democracy lasted for nearly two hundred years and the Roman Republic far longer) bespeaks a reprehensible historical obscurantism.

Weatherford also argues for the Iroquois League's influence on the Articles of Confederation (135-42). As usual for those making this claim, Weatherford produces off-hand remarks by John Adams and Benjamin Franklin as evidence that, if not for the Iroquois League, the early American politicians would never have known about the idea of confederation. But Franklin's remark is actually dismissive of the Iroquois, whom he calls "ignorant Savages," and it merely acknowledges that they managed to create a confederacy. Nowhere does Franklin say that they are a *model* or that the structure and functioning of the Iroquois League should be emulated, if only because it is unlikely he or Adams or any of the founders could have had any genuine knowledge about the league's workings. As Tooker concludes about Franklin's statement and a few others mentioning the Iroquois League, "These statements confirm what is already well known: at least some whites and some Indians in the eighteenth century realized the advantages of confederation. None, however, go beyond the observation that the Iroquois tribes had successfully confederated before the colonies did."[39]

But the Founders did not need the Iroquois League to provide them with the idea of confederation. As Gottfried Dietze remarks in his study of *The Federalist*, various ancient Greek and modern federations (but not, notice, the Iroquois League) are mentioned repeatedly in *The Federalist* in order to illustrate the different models to be emulated and avoided.[40] An obvious model was the New England Confederation, formed in 1643 before the colonists knew of the Iroquois, and whose written constitution was called the Articles of Confederation.[41] That those who created the Articles of Confederation and the Constitution were also aware of the ancient Greek models of confederation is apparent from even a cursory reading of *The Federalist* papers. In Number 18, James Madison notes that the Amphyctionic Council, the ancient Greek league of city-states that administered Delphi and the Pythian games, "bore a very instructive analogy to the present confederation of the American States."[42] He goes on to say of the Achaean League of Peloponnesian city-states that, "could its interior structure and regular operation be ascertained, it is probable that more light would be thrown by it on the science of federal government, than by any of the like experiments with which we are acquainted." Likewise John Jay, in Number 4, uses as examples the city-state leagues of ancient Greece when discussing the problems of confederations: Men who were educated in the ancient classics and were knowledgeable about ancient history should need to turn to what they considered "ignorant Savages" for political inspiration and instruction strains credulity.

Weatherford suspects that the Greeks are important sources for American political ideas, which is why he spends time denigrating the ancient models. "The Greeks who rhapsodized about democracy in their rhetoric," he huffs, "rarely created democratic institutions. A few cities such as Athens occasionally attempted a system vaguely akin to democracy for a few years. These cities functioned as slave societies and were certainly not egalitarian or democratic in the Indian sense" (145). This is flat wrong: Athens was a functioning democracy for nearly two centuries, which is more than a "few years," and it is one of the few examples in history of a democracy that was literally "rule by the people," since all citizens *directly* participated in running the state. As for those people excluded from political power, Iroquois women had no more power than did

Athenian women, and the reference to slavery is simply an attempt
to tar the Greeks with a sinister brush. Slavery was universal among
mankind before the modern period and no more vitiates Athenian
democracy than Iroquois torture and mutilation of captives vitiates
the Iroquois league. Finally, Weatherford's whole game is given
away in the last prepositional phrase, "in the Indian sense." There is
no "Indian sense" of "egalitarian" and "democratic," for these *concepts*
didn't exist for the Iroquois, however much they may have acted in
ways that to a European observer *appeared* "egalitarian" or "democratic." But there is only the Western "sense" of these ideas, one that
Weatherford has projected back onto the Indians. Weatherford is
not engaged in recovering a historical truth obscured by a racist history establishment; he is perpetuating a falsehood.

   If Weatherford's myth-history were an anomaly, we could ignore
it. But as Clinton's statement demonstrates, the Iroquois origin of
democracy has become accepted as a fact about American history.
And just as bad money drives out good, so does false history drive
out true. In a society that knows less and less about ancient history
and its influence on the Western political heritage, the disappear-
ance of the Greeks and Romans from our collective memory and
political traditions holds frightening implications for the survival of
those values and political goods we all take for granted.

THE CONQUEST OF PARADISE[43]

In 1992 the quincentennial of Christopher Columbus's "encounter"
with the New World occasioned an orgy of indulgence in the
Golden Age idealization of Indians and the Iron Age demonization
of the West. The following pronouncement from the Coordinating
Body for the Indigenous People's Organization of the Amazon Basin
typified the rhetoric fashionable then: "Wanted: Christopher
Columbus...for grand theft, genocide, racism, initiating the
destruction of a culture, rape, torture, and instigating the big lie."[44]

This view of history as therapeutic melodrama is not new. In 1925 William Carlos Williams wrote, "The main islands were thickly populated with a peaceful folk when Christopher Columbus found them. But of the orgy of blood which followed, no man has written. We are the slaughterers. It is the tortured soul of our world."[45] In 1992 the Noble Savage and Golden Age myths in which, paradoxically, Columbus and other Europeans themselves indulged, reappeared with renewed vigor. Perhaps the quincentennial's best example of myth masquerading as history was Kirkpatrick Sale's interpretation of Columbus, the bestselling *The Conquest of Paradise.*[46]

Sale's descriptions of the Caribbean and North American Indians derive directly from the Golden Age myth. The Taino, the people first encountered by Columbus, "lived in general harmony and peace, without greed or covetousness or theft"; they were "well-fed and well housed, without poverty or serious disease" (101), and "seem...to have been a society without war" (98). Of course they were ecologically correct: they lived in a "balanced and fruitful harmony with their natural surroundings" (98). The North American Indians likewise are painted in golden-age tints. The Beothuks of Newfoundland were "a gentle and pacific people, who in fact retired from the mainland to Newfoundland to live in peace and seclusion" (220), though Sale never informs us how he divined the Beothuks' motives. Sale notes as well "the general egalitarianism of the typical nonstatified [sic] Indian society" (298). Unlike Iron Age European individualists, the Indians were "governed by the understood obligation of community" (299). And like modern politically correct professors, Northeastern Indians "in general" accorded women "high status" and "usually" made them "equal participants in both political and economic realms" (299-300). In Iron Age Europe, by contrast, "women's economic and social power, already constricted by a patriarchal culture, was further undercut by the new capitalist economies stressing production by men and outside the home"[47] (300).

Sale's careful loophole adverbs are there for a reason—he has no evidence for these sweeping assertions other than the subjective and anachronistic significance he gives to matrilineality and the women's role in selecting council chiefs. Particularly egregious is Sale's claim that Indian women "were full participants in economic life" because they did all the farming while the men hunted. In fact, as anyone who has done both can attest, hunting is much more enjoyable and gratifying work than the backbreaking drudgery of farming—that's why aristocrats hunt and peasants farm, that's why hunting today is a sport and farming is still work. The fact that Indian women not only farmed but also performed the unpleasant task of cleaning and butchering the animals their men killed testifies not to their higher status but precisely to their subordinate role in society.[48] Sale's assumption, widely shared by feminist idealizers of the Indian and of contemporary hunter-gatherers, that participation in food production, matriliny, and/or matrifocality meant higher social status and egalitarian gender relations, ignores still another fact—that, according to feminist scholar Gerda Lerner, "in all hunting/gathering societies, no matter what women's economic and social status is, women are always subordinate to men in some respects. There is not a single society known where women-as-a-group have decision-making power *over* men or where they define the rules of sexual conduct or control marriage exchanges.... While matriliny and matrilocality confer certain rights and privileges on women, decision-making power within the kinship group nevertheless rests with elder males."[49] Lewis Henry Morgan, the first ethnographer of the Iroquois and the source of the modern myth of Iroquois matriarchy, had grounds for asserting, "The Indian regarded woman as the inferior, the dependent, and the servant of man, and from nature and habit, she actually considered herself so."[50] If given the choice, these women no doubt would have much preferred hunting to skinning and gutting dead animals and laboriously cultivating the earth with wooden tools, just as the Iroquois women would have traded the right to select the sachem for the right to *be* one or even to speak in the council.

Contrary to Sale, then, Indian women's inferior status was more the norm in the New World than the exception. Analyses of Omaha Indian skeletal remains, for example, show that the women worked so hard their vertebrae weakened and often cracked, and that they had a less nutritious diet than their men enjoyed: "The disparity in diet weakened females from the start, while the physical stresses of women's traditional work sapped their remaining strength until disease finally took them off."[51]

Sale, though, prefers to idealize than to describe accurately. Continuing his encomium to the Northeastern Indians, he praises their "warm behavior and general civility" and a "climate, except in dead of winter, most benign and comfortable" (304). Like the Taino, the Indians are for the "most part pacific" (318) and avoid the Iron Age evil of property ownership (314). Most important, he notes their "intimate and abiding relationship with nature" (307) and their "rich interplay with nature" (368). They were "ritualistically conscious of and concerned about the effect of their actions on their surroundings and careful to see that limits and constraints were everywhere observed" (311)—they had an "*intrinsic* regardfulness for nature" (317). In Sale's descriptions we have all the Golden Age motifs: peace, absence of war and poverty and disease, and most important, the harmony with nature and an earth that, as Virgil put it, "pours out an easy living."[52] As Sale claims, the New World "was, in fact, as close to Paradise as noncelestial existence has [sic]" (177).

If the American Indians were living in a Golden Age, then of course contemporary Europeans were sunk in the misery and evil of the Iron Age. In three chapters (28-47, 74-92, 241-67) Sale details the misery, poverty, suffering, bigotry, sadism, racism, speciesism, and sexism of Renaissance Europe, a "desolate wilderness" (74). Moreover, all of the once-celebrated advances of the Renaissance that might have compensated for this misery are discounted. Sale portrays humanism, not as liberating the mind from the shackles of medieval church and superstition, but as provinding a rationaliza-

tion of power and authority and worldliness (38-39). The diviniza-
tion of man followed, which in turn led to the justification of discovery and conquest. Sale also indicts rationalism for creating the
scientific view of the world that divorced European man from nature
(42). Materialism, capitalism, the nation-state—all helped to create
a typically Iron Age society: "A milieu of restlessness, curiosity,
impatience, and zeal, the need to explain and explore and overturn
and unveil" (42). But not to forget greed, which is identified as the
quintessential European flaw: European society was the "first in
which the possession of material goods began so markedly to replace
other values at the center of ethical and religious pantheons" (43).

As a leading environmental romantic, however, Sale is virtually
obsessed with the purported ecological sins of the Europeans who
fell from the Golden Age harmony with nature still enjoyed by the
Indians. We are treated to banal generalizations about the West's
hostility to nature overlaid with two-bit psychologizing; those
repressed Europeans, Sale tells us, feared "most of the elements of
the natural world" (75) and saw it as "an antagonistic, oppositional
world" (76). Mountains are "diabolic, almost alive, dark and always
barren" (77), and Sale naively wonders why to Europeans the wild
was "so unreasonably fearsome" (78)—the question of a well-fed
city-dweller for whom nature has been rendered safe by the very
technology he is so eager to demonize. Because of this European
neurotic fear of nature, "European culture created a frightening distance between the human and natural," a distance that justified the
"imperative of human domination and control of the natural world"
(78-79). Because of Europe's "technophilia" (89)—its Iron Age
romance with technology—Europeans indulged in a "frenzy of defi-
ance and destruction" of nature, with the result that Europe's ecological heritage is "a record of deforestation, erosion, siltation,
exhaustion, pollution, extermination, cruelty, destruction, and
despoilation" (81-82) : mortal sins the Indians *never* committed.

We will see below how simplistic and misleading is Sale's view of the Indians' ecological correctness. But Sale is not writing history. He is resurrecting myth. To him, the "encounter" is a clash between a peaceful Golden Age race living in an "Edenic garden"—"peoples not fallen but risen, not damned but blessed, not inherently sinful but inherently salubrious"—and an Iron Age race comprising "peoples having ascended from a dark Other World, a world of sorrow and evil" (177), a people whose sole driving force was the "lust for gold"(145), a phrase that recalls Ovid's description of the Iron Age "wicked lust for having." [53] What gets lost every time is any recognition of the Indians' complex humanity, their right to exist apart from the anxieties and discontents of their idealizers. Rather than understanding the Indian, we idealize him as, to quote Bordewich, "little more than a warped reflection of ourselves; when Indians have stepped from the roles to which we have assigned them, we have often seen nothing at all."[54] Like his North American "paradise," Sale's Indians are figments of the Western imagination, what French Critic Jean-Jacques Simard has called "the Whiteman's shadow."[55]

RED EARTH, WHITE LIES

For more than twenty-five years Vine Deloria has been one of the most prominent caretakers of American received wisdom about Indians, even though he presents himself as a writer freed from "the cherished image of the noble redman."[56] Yet Deloria's latest work, *Red Earth, White Lies,*[57] indulges almost every cherished image we have of them. The result is a work of astonishing incoherence and zany racism as gratifying to New Age sensibilities as it is irritating to the deformed, guilty consciences of middle-class whites. Small wonder it offers nothing of use in solving the real problems of flesh-and-blood Indians.

Deloria makes his program explicit from the start: "Much of Western science must go" (15). Why? Because science doesn't discover truth—it simply manufactures rigged "knowledge" that serves the scientific establishment's power and privilege: "In our society we have been trained to believe that scientists search for, examine, and articulate truths about the natural world and about ourselves. They don't. But they do search for, take captive, and protect the social and economic status of scientists. As many lies are told to protect scientific doctrine as were ever told to protect 'the church'" (17-18). As such, scientists are no more adept at discovering and communicating the truth than are "lawyers and car dealers" (41). Scientists offer instead a mere "collection of beliefs," only some of which, Deloria grudgingly admits, are based on "considerable evidence" (50). This attack on science is as ridiculous as it is stereotypical. What's new about Deloria's use of this academic fad, however, is that he employs it to help him legitimize American Indian legends about their origins, which he considers (by fiat, not by argument) to be repositories of *factually true* information; and at the same time, he attacks as *factually untrue* what modern anthropologists and archaeologists have said about Indian origins and prehistoric behavior.

Deloria's attempt to substitute myth for science mires him in an egregious contradiction—he can attack the scientists' theories only by means of a *rational* analysis that attempts to expose their inconsistencies and contradictions, an attack that, if turned onto the orally transmitted Indian myths and legends he admires, would leave them utterly discredited. In other words, Deloria wants to have his scientific cake and eat it, too: objective critical analysis of evidence, the philosophical backbone of the scientific method, is valid when turned against his enemies, but *in*valid when pitted against the myths and legends he happens to believe.

This confusion becomes evident when Deloria tells us that "Western science must go, all of Western religion should go," for they have both bequeathed us "outmoded beliefs derived from the Near Eastern/European past which do not correspond to what our science is discovering today or to the remembered experiences of non-Western peoples across the globe" (15-16). This remarkable statement invites a whole host of questions. If "Western science" must be discarded, what possibly can remain to function as "our science," and what knowledge exactly is this science "discovering today" that presumably is more true? Why is one "Western science" invalid and "our science" valid? And if myths and legend are to be admitted to the bar as evidence for factual truth, by what principle does Deloria discriminate between Western religious beliefs and non-Western, both of which contradict modern science, not to mention each other? And why are the truths of non-Western spiritual traditions more valued than Western truths? The only possible coherent principle in Deloria's procedure is that everything Western is bad, and everything non-Western is good.

Deloria's real agenda is, not the explosion of poorly constructed theories about Paleo-Indians, but reconstructing the American Indian as a Golden Age Noble Savage, who sprang, unlike the invading white man, from the land itself and so always lived, also unlike the alien European, in harmony with the environment. Hence Deloria attempts to discredit two current theories concerning American Indians: that their ancestors migrated from Asia across the Bering land-bridge, and that they were at least to some degree responsible for overhunting many species of New World megafauna, contributing to their extinction. Deloria must attack these two theories because they weaken the mythic status of the peaceful Indian living in balanced harmony with a maternal nature: Migrating hunters who wipe out mastodons look uncomfortably like migrating Europeans who wipe out buffalo.

Despite a lot of rhetorical heat, Deloria's attack on these two theories generates little light. Significant archæological evidence shows that some ten thousand years ago Paleo-Indians armed with stone-tipped weapons were extremely efficient killers of whole species of large mammals, like antelope, horses, camels, mammoth mastodon, giant bison, oxen, and giant ground sloths. Indians in fact contributed to the extinction of some of these species—the so-called "Pleistocene overkill."[58] Deloria does manage to raise a few cogent objections to this theory, not by retelling Indian myths and legends, but mainly by quoting other "Western scientists"—without telling us how Loren Eisely, say, with whom Deloria agrees, escapes the truth-warping influences of professional jealousy and so is more reliable than Paul S. Martin, with whom Deloria disagrees. More important, though, is the *reason* why Deloria gets involved in this controversy: "Some people are offended by the idea that many people believe that Indians were more concerned and thoughtful ecologists than modern industrial users. Advocating the extinction theory is a good way to support continued despoilation of the environment by suggesting that at *no* time were human beings careful of the lands upon which they lived" (112-13).

In actual fact, like everybody else before the modern period, Indians were not ecologists at all, since "ecology" did not exist before the modern age when the science was invented. Indians exploited their environments to maximize living standards, their behavior limited not by *conscious* awareness of nature's potential vulnerability and complexity but by their technology and population levels.[59]

Deloria's critical analysis of the Bering land-bridge migration is similarly flawed. As Thomas Traumann reported recently, "Geneticists can now say with 100 percent certainty that all of the people who arrived in the Americas before Christopher Columbus came from Asia."[60] There is disagreement about when and how this migration took place, but at some point in the past, most likely around 12,000 B.C.,[61] the ancestors of the Indians migrated into the Americas. So why does Deloria attack this theory? "By making us immigrants to North America they [believers in Indian migration from Asia] are able to deny the fact that we were the full, complete, and total owners of this continent" (69; *see also* 251). Deloria wants the Indians to be "autochthonus," sprung from the earth itself, for that pedigree alone establishes their Golden Age right to possession of America and their innocence from land-grabbing and conquest, the peculiar crimes of Europeans (Note that Deloria calls the Indians "owners" despite the belief repeatedly preached by upholders of the modern Noble Savage myth that Indians had no conception of property ownership). Why else would Deloria attack the theory of evolution, which holds that all humans evolved from ancestors in Africa ,and thus enmesh himself in all sorts of logical absurdities? If evolution "may exist more firmly in the minds of academics than in any location on Earth" (67) and so perforce is false, then Indians did not descend from African ancestors but necessarily were created by some divine agency in the Americas. But this belief ultimately must depend not on reason and evidence, but on faith. Thus there will be no way of rationally adjudicating among all the "traditions and memories of non-Western peoples" (69) that Deloria wants us to privilege over scientific inquiry. Given that all those myriad "traditions and memories" will tell a thousand different conflicting stories about human origins, on what principle will we determine that, as Deloria claims, the Judaeo-Christian creation story is false and the Sioux or Cheyenne ones are true? Once more Deloria is defending the myth of the ecologically correct Indian, who now *literally* sprang from Mother Earth, not recovering a lost truth.

Deloria's refurbishing of myth in the guise of critical analysis also serves his version of the currently fashionable academic pastime of bashing the West, a sport Deloria indulges with an explicit racist gusto usually encountered in the zanier versions of Afrocentrism. In the course of recounting some Pre-Columbian American-Indian oral legends in which white-skinned people figure, Deloria spins a fantastic tale replete with killer comets and Caucasian giants. If there were wholesale destruction of animals in the New World, he speculates, this was accomplished not by Paleo-Indian hunters but by stinking, white-skinned giants, "mega-killers" who were probably "Europeans—demonstrating that even 12,000 years ago the whites had little regard for the environment or other forms of life" (153).

These giants, having mucked up North America, eventually "migrated east and invaded western Europe, routed the Neanderthals, and are known as the Cro-Magnon peoples" (167). In other words, Caucasians (which is whom Deloria means, since "Europeans" didn't exist until a few centuries ago) are *genetically* inferior peoples, programmed to violence, land-grabbing, and being mean to Mother Earth. Nor is this racism a mere rhetorical flourish for the sake of argument: in an earlier interview, Deloria had said of white people's propensity to evil, "It's got to be genetic. Why the fall of empires in world history, the total breakdown in the Middle Ages: Maybe they're programmed to exploit nature, for senseless killing."[62] This nonsense is the first step down a road that ends in advocating, like the Unabomber, the annihilation of such cancerous beings.

The more traditional myths about Indians that Deloria recycles are not any more worthwhile than his racist fantasies. What is the point of implausibly claiming, on no basis other than legends he never subjects to the same critical scrutiny with which he analyses modern scientific theories, that pre-Ice Age North America was a paradise, "a golden age when there was very little hardship" (172)? Why indulge fancies such as the one claiming "that there was no essential spiritual/intellectual difference between people and animals" (233), a sentiment more suitable for a Disney cartoon? That such false knowledge can be taken seriously and its originator afforded respect as a serious spokesman for modern Indians—whose pressing needs do *not* include any more mythic false knowledge about their ancestors—testifies to the corruption of intellectual life in America and the perversion of its character.

DEGILDING THE WHITE MAN'S RED MAN

When we turn from the myth to what we know of the real lives of Indians, we first must point out that the "Indian" they all refer to never existed, for the simple reason that the great diversity of languages, geography, climate, cultures, and societies in existence in the Americas on the eve of European contact makes it impossible to create the universal American Indian. Second, we must observe this vast ethnic, tribal, and linguistic variety was expressed in equally various practices and values, some good, some bad, some noble, some ignoble. There is no historical warrant for believing the mythic picture of an Indian people living in a Golden Age paradise, free from war and suffering and enjoying a harmonious relationship with a Mother Nature they cherish and respect.

THE HARSHNESS OF LIFE

While Indian life in pre-Columbian America was not, in Hobbes's famous phrase, "solitary, poor, nasty, brutish, and short," nonetheless life was much harder and more uncertain than the Romantic idealizations of tribal existence lead us to believe. As already seen, we moderns tend to value those attributes of tribal societies we do not possess—simplicity, closeness to nature, small scale, and so on—while taking for granted the positive benefits we derive from modern society and that tribal societies lack. Like the makers of *Dances with Wolves*, we assume Indians enjoyed our material benefits—health care, longevity, an adequate food supply, clean water, sanitation, protection from the elements—while escaping the evil side effects of the technology and urbanization that have created those benefits. Modern idealists fail to recognize, as did Mandeville in the *Fable of the Bees* (1714), the impossibility "of enjoying all the most elegant comforts of life that are to be met with in an industrious, wealthy, and powerful nation, and at the same time be bless'd with all the virtues and innocence that can be wish'd for in a golden age."[63]

All premodern life, including that of the American Indians, was subject to myriad evils, many of which have since been palliated, if not eliminated, by modern science and technology. There were life-shortening diseases, infections from wounds and broken bones, and bacterial contamination of food and water: "In all probability," W. H. Hutchinson has written, "the pre-Columbian Amerind did not live more than thirty years and infant mortality was high. Long before the European introduced virulent diseases to which the Amerind had no generationally acquired resistance, he suffered from respiratory and pulmonary ailments, tumors, gastro-intestinal ravages, dental problems, and infections."[64] An analysis of early Oneota Indian skeletons from west-central Illinois reveal "conditions that originate from nutritional deficiency or infectious disease," including tuberculosis and anemia from iron deficiency.[65] Nor were things any better in the more sophisticated Meso-American societies. Based on an analysis of pre-Columbian remains from Teotihuacan in central Mexico, Rebecca Storey concludes, "Before contact, the evidence of epidemic death all seems to be related to famine, and the diseases that accompany it are those to be expected among physically weakened individuals.... The types of diseases present were those from parasites, intestinal disorders, respiratory infections, and a few fevers."[66] Life expectancy at birth was about seventeen years, with more than half dying during childhood. The later Aztecs suffered from the same deprivation, at least for the lower class, whose living standard, according to one historian, "was even lower than it is for the rural population of central Mexico today."[67] Likewise the Maya were afflicted with diseases like malaria, yellow fever, and syphilis; they too suffered from chronic malnutrition, a low average lifespan, and high infant mortality.[68]

Social conditions among many American Indian societies were no more democratic and egalitarian than material life was paradisal. We noted earlier the subordinate position of women in some tribes, who often had to do heavier work on fewer calories. Jefferson and others frequently commented on the "unjust drudgery" to which Indian women were subjected.[69] Often the diets of pregnant women were restricted, and of course they were subject to attempted abortion, rape, beatings, and the complications and diseases attendant on childbirth that existed everywhere in the world before the advent of modern medicine.[70] Slavery, class stratification, and misogyny, institutions supposedly peculiar to Europeans, were practiced throughout the Americas (leaving aside for the moment the Aztec). The Chumash of California kept slaves, and their society was hierarchically stratified, with an upper class whose power derived from the accumulation of clam-shell money.[71] The Calusa and Natchez of the Southeast were controlled by upper classes that monopolized political power and probably economic as well. The "Mississipian" societies in the Mississippi Valley were characterized by a "wide social gulf that separated commoners from elites.... Skeletal evidence indicates that elites ate more meat, were taller, performed less strenuous physical activity, and were less prone to illness and accident than commoners."[72] So too the Kwakiutl of the Northwest Coast were dominated by "Titleholders" who owned slaves and dominated their people politically, socially, and economically.[73] Apparently, the "wicked lust for having" was not restricted to Iron Age Europe.

In addition to the evils of periodic famine, chronic malnutrition, slavery, oppression of women, infanticide, and ritual mutilation, we can add subjection to the powerful, banditry, violent death from enemy raids, cruelty, anxiety caused by fear of witches, sorcerers, demons, and ghosts—and, as we will see next, torture and warfare.

TORTURE AND WAR IN PARADISE

In the Golden Age myth, war and its attendant cruelties characterize more than anything else the evil of the Iron Age. And war is the direct consequence of the typical Iron Age sin, greed for gold.

But throughout the Americas, the movement of peoples and the competition for resources meant that organized violence was common. One study of Northwestern American Indian tribes found that only 7 percent never participated in warfare or raiding, and those tribes lived "in areas with extremely low population densities, isolated by distance and hard country from other groups."[74] Archaeological analysis of human skeletal remains and the surviving ruins of old fortifications also reveal evidence of frequent warfare and violent death occasioned by territorial disputes. Mass graves of victims killed and mutilated have been discovered at Crow Creek in South Dakota, where over five hundred men, women, and children "had been slaughtered, scalped, and mutilated during an attack on their village a century and a half before Columbus's arrival."[75] Similar finds in Colorado, California, and British Columbia tell the same story—"frequent deadly raids and occasional horrific massacres" were "an indigenous and 'native' pattern long before contact with Europeans complicated the situation."[76]

One study of fourteenth-century Oneota remains from the Illinois River valley reveals a high level of interpersonal violence, perhaps resulting from clashes between groups competing for territory. Skeletal remains from a site in west-central Illinois show signs of violent death and mutilation, including arrowheads stuck in bones, and skull fractures and holes caused by weapons. Fourteen people had been scalped and eleven decapitated, with males and females killed in equal numbers. The authors of the study conclude, "Death from conflict in eastern North America was by no means unusual. Skeletons with unambiguous trauma from interpersonal violence, such as projectile points embedded in bones and cut marks from scalping, have been found in Archaic to Historic cemeteries that are distributed from the Plains to the Atlantic Coast."[77] From the Iroquois' war against the Hurons, to the Sioux's empire-building in the Great Plains, war was a constant in much of American Indian life long before the coming of the Iron Age Europeans.

The archaeological evidence and later accounts from Europeans demonstrate that not just violence, but also cannibalism and torture were also frequent evils afflicting the presumed denizens of paradise.

Perhaps the most ferocious and inventive torturers were the Iroquois, the supposed inventors of democracy. Francis Parkman's classic *The Jesuits in North America in the Seventeenth Century* (1867) relates the brutal treatment of war-captives by the whole Iroquois people, including women and children. The purpose of torturing prisoners was to get them to cry out and hence confess their inferiority; since the prisoners knew this and refused as long as possible to gratify their captives, torture had to prolong agony without killing. Parkman relates one incident in which some Algonquin captives were tortured:

> It [the torture] consisted in blows with sticks and cudgels, gashing their limbs with knives, cutting off their fingers with clam-shells, scorching them with firebrands, and other indescribable torments.... On the following morning, they were placed on a large scaffold, in sight of the whole population. It was a gala-day. Young and old were gathered from far and near. Some mounted the scaffold, and scorched them with torches and firebrands; while the children, standing beneath the bark platform, applied fire to the feet of the prisoners between the crevices.[78]

One particularly defiant prisoner held out, and after he died, the Iroquois "tore out his heart and devoured it; then hacked him in pieces, and made their feast of triumph on his mangled limbs."[79] Sometimes the prisoner would be forced to eat his own flesh. This episode is not a fabrication of Jesuit propaganda—even historians sympathetic to the Iroquois and careful to explain the cultural contexts of such practices nonetheless admit them.[80] Nor are such practices unusual in North America. We have already seen the evidence of mutilation and torture from Illinois. Likewise in the Southwest, where "twenty-five sites containing cannibalized human remains have been found."[81]

The issue of torture brings us to the most notorious and representative example of Indian savagery in the American imagination, scalping, the origins of which has become a very popular bit of false knowledge. According to current received wisdom, scalping was invented by whites, not Indians. "Scalping," Vine Deloria matter-of-factly wrote in 1969, was "introduced prior to the French and Indian War by the English."[82] This belief in the English origin of scalping was given the authority of television in 1972 during an episode of the television series *Hec Ramsey*, in which a character fingers the Puritans.[83] But as James Axtell and many other scholars sympathetic to Indians have shown, the archaeological and linguistic evidence equally attest to the Indian practice of scalping long before the arrival of Europeans. As Bordewich points out, "Although popular convention now blames whites for the invention of scalping, words for scalping and more imaginative forms of dismemberment existed in many Indian languages from the earliest times."[84] The pre-white man Illinois burial site contains fourteen skulls with cut-lines on cranial bones, which indicates scalping.[85] Only an irrational fidelity to the myth of the Noble Savage Indian can explain the refusal of some people to accept that the Indians, like all humans everywhere, were capable of violent behavior worthy of condemnation.

Two Old World societies in particular exemplify the capacity for war, brutality, land-grabbing, and cruelty that supposedly only Europeans possessed. It is no accident that idealizers like Sale hardly mention the Mexica or, as they are better known, the Aztecs, a culture whose brilliance was matched by its grotesque cruelty. The Aztecs were imperialists, late-comers to central Mexico from the north, despised by the Toltecs they displaced.[86] They established an empire whose conquered peoples provided both material tribute and the victims for the ritualistic slaughter the Aztec religion believed necessary for life to continue. The scale of these sacrifices is mind-boggling—20,000 victims were dispatched at the dedication of the pyramid to the god of war Huitzilopochtli. The prisoners were dragged by the hair up the pyramid steps, their hearts torn out by the priests, then their bodies rolled down the temple steps. Then "each broken, emptied cadaver was taken up to be carried to the captor's home temple for dismemberment and distribution: flesh scraped from skulls and thighbones; fragments of flesh cooked and eaten; human skins, dripping with grease and blood, stretched over living flesh; clots of blood scooped up to smear the temple walls."[87] As historian Inga Clendinnen points out, this cruelty was not motivated by religion alone: "The killings were also explicitly about the dominance of the Mexica and their tutelary deity: public displays to overawe the watcher, Mexica or stranger, in a state theatre of power, at which the rulers of other and lesser cities, allies and enemies alike, were routinely present."[88] It is no wonder that the idealizers of the Golden Age Indian pass over the Aztecs in silence, for the culture too uncomfortably resembles these same idealizers' (false) portrait of Iron Age Europe.

The North American Indian peoples whose ferocity and relentless appropriation of other tribes' territories recall the Aztecs were the Sioux. They have been transformed, however, by the idealists into the diametric opposite of what they really were. Rather than *Dances with Wolves*'s peace-loving New Age flower children, the Sioux were cruel and magnificent warriors, whose relentless pursuit of honor in war, embodied in their maxim, "It is better to die on the battlefield than to live to be old,"[89] recalls the heroes of Homer. And the Sioux pursuit of war was directed towards the acquisition of territory. As Royal Hassrick puts it, the Sioux's "sole objective was a straightforward aggrandizement through impassioned action."[90]

Despite current mythology that the Sioux—whose name is a French corruption of the Chippewa word Naudiwisioux, meaning "lesser snakes"[91]—were indigenous to the Black Hills of South Dakota, their original home was near Mille Lacs Lake in central Minnesota. Starting in the late seventeenth century, having acquired the European advantages of the gun and the horse,[92] the Sioux started expanding westward. For the next two centuries they conquered and dispossessed tribes like the Omahas, Iowas, Arikara,

Kiowa, Crows, and Pawnee already inhabiting those lands.[93] It was, as Cash put it, "A march of conquest unequaled in the histories of the Indians in what is now the United States."[94] Along the way, Sioux warriors helped American troops destroy an Arikara village in 1823; the Crows were driven from the Plains, and the Pawnee from Nebraska; over one hundred Pawnee were massacred in 1873 by the Sioux, whom the Pawnee called *Tsu-ra-rat*, "throat-cutters."[95] The loss of territory and life by the Pawnee and Crows explains why they frequently aided the American army in its battles with the Sioux. But the mythologizing of the Sioux in films like *Dances with Wolves* has transformed the victims of Sioux territorial expansion into the traitorous, ignoble savages. And the question of evil Western technology is ignored, though European guns and horses were employed against Indians by other Indians hoping to facilitate a centuries-old practice of ethnic cleansing.

Contrary to *Dances with Wolves* and most popular wisdom, then, the nineteenth-century clash between the Sioux and the American Army culminating at the Little Big Horn was not precipitated by the attempt of a beleaguered people to protect their ancestral homelands and culture against land- and gold-hungry racists. The Sioux had themselves taken the Plains by force from other Indians. At least nineteenth-century Sioux were honest about their appropriation of others' lands. At the Fort Laramie peace conference of 1851, the Oglala Sioux Black Hawk asserted the Sioux right to the lands south of the Platte River by saying, "These lands once belonged to the Kiowas and the Crows, but we whipped those nations out of them, and in this we did what the white men do when they want the lands of the Indians."[96] Sioux culture as we know it didn't even exist before contact with whites, for it was the gun and the horse (and trade with whites) that created a nomadic, martial culture centered on the hunting of the buffalo and the stealing of enemy horses.[97] What happened in the Plains in the latter nineteenth century was "the clash of two expanding powers," one of which was simply too big and powerful not to prevail.[98]

Rather than living in Golden Age peace and harmony, many Indian peoples of the Americas were doing what all human beings have done throughout history—competing violently for land and resources and indulging the unfortunate propensity of humans to inflict suffering and pain on their fellows. To condemn the evil of Europeans and ignore or rationalize the evil of Indians is to dehumanize both—and to indulge the worst sort of false knowledge.

INDIANS AND NATURE

The most important motif of the Golden Age myth is the assertion of a now lost time of sustaining harmony between humans and nature, when a "free earth, untouched by the hoe and unwounded by the plow, on her own used to give all things to men."[99] For three-hundred years, this Western myth has been used to describe American Indians and their relationship to their environment. These days a patina of scientistic environmentalism overlays the myth, but its appeal ultimately is emotional, not rational. The myth of ecologically correct American Indians vicariously gratifies the age-old longing to return to the garden of nature and set aside the burdens of a complex civilization.

The Indian as ecologist is an idea now firmly ensconced in our collective mind. This belief became widespread in the late sixties and seventies as a consequence of popular environmentalism.[100] Remember that effective 1972 anti-litter advertising campaign featuring Cherokee actor Iron Eyes Cody squeezing out one manly tear as paleface slobs rape the environment? As a phenomenon of sixties anti-Western pique, the Indian-as-conservationist idea was usually accompanied by the trite condemnation of Western culture as mechanistic and destructively instrumental in its relationship to nature, as in J. Baird Callicott's assertion "that the world view typical of American Indian peoples has included and supported an environ-

mental ethic, while that of Europeans has encouraged human alienation from the natural environment and an exploitative practical
relationship with it."[101]

This bit of false knowledge about conservationist Indians is now
ubiquitous—Kirkpatrick Sale claims that Indians had "an *intrinsic*
regardfulness for nature," and Deloria likewise praises the Indians
who "were so in tune with their environment."[102] A whole recent
issue of *Sierra* magazine was devoted to perpetuating this myth.
Winona LaDuke rhapsodizes, "The earth is our Mother; it is from
her we gain our Life. Native peoples have courageously resisted the
destruction of the natural world at the hands of colonial, and later,
industrial society, since this destruction attacks their very identity."[103] Dennis Martinez concurs: Indians' "conservation ethics...are
nearly universal in their understanding of a sustainable land/
culture relationship."[104] Like Deloria, who believes Indians can talk
to animals, Martinez's analysis degenerates into the Disneyesque
assertion that "if you don't take care of the plants and talk to them
and relate to them, they get lonely and go away."[105]

In the summer of 1995 the animated hit *Pocahontas* proved once
more that the Disney Corporation is the master manipulator of
America's most cherished false knowledge. Indulging the old
American bad habit of viewing Indians through the lens of Euro-
American myth, the screenwriters transformed the historically shadowy Pocahontas into a *Sports Illustrated* swimsuit-issue babe and a
"poster child for eco-friendly multiculturalism," as *U.S. News and
World Report* put it.[106] The result was a spectacular example of history
as therapeutic melodrama.

Every hoary motif of the Noble Savage and Golden Age myths
is exploited by the film. Disney's Indians live in leisurely harmony
with nature, especially our leading lady, who is accompanied by a
loquacious hummingbird and raccoon and advised by a talking
"Grandmother Willow." In the film's hit song Pocahontas croons to
a Teutonic John Smith that "you [Europeans] think you own what-

ever land you land on" and that "the earth is just a dead thing you can claim," but *she* knows "every rock and tree and creature has a spirit, has a name." As the two cavort together in a soft-focus, pastel natural paradise, she instructs Smith (apparently she studied ecology with Mufasa the Lion King) that "we are all connected to each other in a circle, in a hoop that never ends."

Even more so than the myth of the ecologically correct Noble Savage, the Golden Age contrast between simple harmony with nature and a corrupt Iron Age civilization is the film's most important assumption. We see it in Pocahontas's lyrics about the "dead earth" and the European lust to own land, the same clichés we met in Al Gore's traducing of Western history. Thus the Europeans, typified by the obese villainous governor (whose dog is also an evil glutton), are characterized by insatiable greed and hair-trigger violence. As soon as they get off the boat they start clear-cutting the forest with cannon while they celebrate in frenzied song and dance the European lust for gold and domination—a validation of the medicine man's earlier vision of Europeans "prow[ling] the earth like ravening wolves, consuming everything in their path." The Hollywood moral is clear: Western civilization is dysfunctional, its technology serving an irrational need to dominate and control and devour and rape a maternal nature that only wants, as the gentle Indians in their primal wisdom understand, to nurture her wayward children—precisely the main theme of the West's Golden Age myth.

Even for a cartoon, the film's ahistorical mythologizing is embarrassing. Despite the absurd assertion of Russell Means—professional Indian (and voice of Powhatan)—that *Pocahontas* "is the finest film ever done in Hollywood on the Native American experience,"[107] the film has little to do with Indians and everything to do with gratifying the expectations and soothing the anxieties of middle-class Americans. It may be too much to ask of a cartoon that it respect history, so we can overlook the way the film glosses over exactly how Chief Powhatan created his empire and dominated the area around Chesapeake Bay and the Potomac without resorting to the violence and land-grabbing presumably the exclusive sins of Europeans.[108] But the character of Pocahontas is an insult to every Indian past and present: She represents nothing other than middle-class Romantic individualism and therapeutic self-fulfillment dressed up in buckskins and red skin. No historical Indian would ever entertain or express her aesthetic appreciation of nature, a self-conscious sensibility that was created in the West;[109] and the Wertheresque advice of Grandmother Willow to "listen with your heart" would be as meaningless to an actual Indian as the sentimentalized sexuality dominating the film's presentation of Smith and Pocahontas's love. *Pocahontas* ultimately transforms the American Indian into a vehicle for the white man's (and nubile white girl's) desires and wish-fulfillments, precisely the dehumanizing role the Indian has been compelled to play since Columbus.

The reader may want to forgive *Pocahontas*'s absurdities—it is, after all, a cartoon aimed at children. But this use of the contrived Indian as a projection of the psychic conflicts of whites dominates as well an earlier popular film, one that, despite its mythic anachronisms, was touted as a realist correction of Hollywood's long racist tradition of depicting Indians as bloodthirsty redskins panting to rape doughty white pioneer women. Despite the gushing of some historically illiterate film critics,[110] 1990's Academy Award-winning mega-hit *Dances with Wolves* is no more historically accurate about Indians than is *Pocahontas*, and it uses Indians in precisely the same way: as screens on which to project the disgruntled modern city-boy's anxieties and discontents. The main character, John Dunbar, is a "pre-enlightened Aquarian Age man,"[111] as Wayne Michael Sarf puts it, dropped off by cinematic fiat in the nineteenth century, a proto-ecologist who, disgusted by the waste and violence of Iron Age Civil War America, escapes into the frontier where he is reborn as a Lakota Sioux. The latter, contrary to everything we know about one of the most savage and imperialistic tribe of warriors in

America, are depicted as peaceful and tolerant communitarians who love animals and nature, practice gender equality, and somewhere discovered shampoo and high-tech dentistry. Nearly all the whites, in contrast, are greedy, polluting, foul, unwashed, sadistic monsters with bad teeth. And they're mean to animals, unlike our hero who, like Pocahontas, communes with animals and feels their pain.

Rather than a "revisionist" view of frontier history—a correction of some triumphalist, racialist tradition celebrating the massacre of Indians as the march of Western civilization[112]—*Dances with Wolves* is a "virtual compendium of currently popular attitudes towards Indians,"[113] a farrago of myths whose origins lie in Western culture and modern Western anxieties. As such, rather than realism the film is pure romance, the Indians merely providing a backdrop for the white hero's journey of erotic self-discovery—precisely the way Indians have been used for over 150 years. For example, Dunbar's love interest, a white woman raised by the Sioux, reprises one of the favorite motifs of late nineteenth-century dime-novel romances like Edward Willet's *Silver Spur* or Joseph E. Badger's *The Forest Princess*.[114] The Indian as peaceful ecologist, of course, invokes the Golden Age/Noble Savage myth in order to gratify the superior sensibilities of the well-off urban audience of curbside recyclers who can afford to sneer at their Iron Age ancestors whose brutality and violence created the world our enlightened yuppies take for granted. The mythic flip side of the noble savage, the ignoble savage, is present in the persons of the wicked, demonically painted Pawnee, who in point of historical fact were violently driven from their traditional lands by the relentless Sioux. And overlying all is the West's peculiar creation of nature-love, projected back onto people, Indian and white alike, who could not afford for one minute the modern sentimentalism of the anachronistic Dunbar. Like *Pocahontas*, *Dances with Wolves* offers a pastel paradigm of the modern individualist quest for self-fulfillment in sex and nature, a psycho-dramatic journey once embodied in the adventures of Kit Carson and Natty Bumppo. Only now this individualistic quest is given a cheap moral legitimization through a judgment on the past purchased with the coin of sensitivity to the suffering of feathered and beaded victims of a dysfunctional Western culture. Unfortunately, the film also reinforces and popularizes false knowledge about Indians and history and human nature.

Despite their indulgence of historical false knowledge, both of these films were big hits because they pander to the stereotypes about Indians that today dominate our collective imagination. Even when an ostensibly more balanced view of the European and American relations with the Indians is attempted, the pull of these stereotypes is too strong to resist. In the 1996 PBS series *The West*, despite periodic attempts to respect the complexity and mixed motives of the westward expansion, the fundamental assumption behind the show is, as summarized by Victor Davis Hanson, "the innately murderous, exploiting, and ultimately destructive nature of American culture."[115] In other words, it is the spectacle of indigenous Golden Age peace and harmony destroyed by what the book accompanying the series called "greed and arrogance," the typical sins of the Iron Age.[116] Hence the Indians are nearly all noble pitiful victims, while the white settlers are racist locusts or at best ignorant dupes manipulated by the capitalists' camouflaging ideology of Manifest Destiny. Behind the series lies the desire not to present history in all its complexity and ambiguity, its conflicting choices and competing goods, not to show the tragic costs of civilization, but rather to indulge an emotionally gratifying myth embodying the disaffected modern man's "protest against things as they are" and his "denial that things *are* as they are." As historian Walter A. McDougall goes on to say, the filmmakers ultimately return to "the same Monument Valley of myths they presumed to have escaped."[117]

But this New-Age fluff has nothing to do with the reality of the American Indian relationship to nature. Bordewich correctly notes that, "Like Euro-Americans, not to mention the rest of humanity, Indians used the means at their command to bend nature to their use, and within the limits of their technology, they were no less inherently exploitative of it."[118] Timothy Silver, in his study of South Atlantic Indians and the environment, also emphasizes the practical relationship to nature that Indians, like all the other humans, were compelled to take in order to survive: "For several millenia before European contact, Indians took whatever the land offered. Sometimes they took it efficiently; on other occasions they reduced animal populations, depleted soil, and demolished plant life."[119] A few examples of the Indians' impact on their environment reveal that the true source of modern views of environmentally correct Indians is Romantic myth, not historical fact.[120]

The idea that the Indians "lived lightly on the land," harmonizing their existence so smoothly with nature's that their presence scarcely disturbed her, is misleading to say the least. That the Indians intruded less into the environment than a more technologically advanced and more populous American society is a banal truism. Low population densities, stone axes, wooden digging tools, and lances and arrows necessarily mean less environmental destruction. But as soon as Indians acquired technologies like the horse and the gun, the Indians' destructive impact on the bison or the beaver increased exponentially. Even before the arrival of the Europeans, the complex societies of the Midwest and Southwest collapsed because those societies grew larger than the capacity of the land to sustain them. The Cahokia society of the Upper Midwest began to fall apart in the twelfth and thirteenth centuries when "expanded settlement, accompanied by especially hot dry summers, exhausted the soil, depleted the supply of timber for building and fuel, and reduced the habitat of the game that supplemented their diet."[121] Likewise in Mesoamerica—when populous complex societies began to outgrow the carrying capacity of their environment, ecological, social, and cultural disaster followed. This certainly was the case with the Maya, the collapse of whose magnificent civilization was precipitated in part by environmental abuse.[122]

In fact, evidence of Indian alterations of the environment "has become so pervasive that it makes use of the word wilderness (in the sense of land unaffected by human use) meaningless for huge areas of North America at the time of contact."[123] For example, numerous Indian tribes used fire to alter their environment and make it more conducive to providing whatever resources were necessary for survival. The Great Plains perhaps were created by Indian forest-burning in order to increase grazing for game and to make hunting more efficient.[124] Indians who farmed burned down forests to clear space for planting corn and beans, moving on to new forests when the soil was depleted. Burning forests also cut down on fleas, destroyed cover for enemies, and facilitated travel for both people and game.[125] The same phenomenon was observed in New England, where hardwood forests were burned, allowing more sunlight needed by trees like the birch and white pine, which the Indians valued, thus creating a new "nature" more suited to the Indians' needs.[126]

Contrary to the sentimental fantasies of modern romantics, the Indians' relationship to animals was no more brotherly and benign than their relationship to plants and trees. How could it be, when they depended on animal protein for survival? We have already noted the Paleo-Indian hunters' contribution to the extinction of Pleistocene megafauna. Their descendants across America likewise killed animals for various purposes, Indian efficiency limited, not by some inherent mystical bond with the animals, but by technology and small numbers. Across America, Indians used fire-drives and running herds off of cliffs to kill many more animals than they could use. Speaking of the Shonone practice of driving rabbits and antelope, Johnson and Earle comment, "These large-scale hunts sought to obliterate the local animal population in the interest of maximizing the immediate food supply; no attempt was made to save a breeding stock. A whole population was destroyed, and antelope were not hunted again until they reached numbers sufficient to justify another drive."[127] Peoples for whom starvation and famine were very real contingencies could not afford to consider whether their behavior threatened the existence of animals or disrupted some presumed primal harmony. They were worried about eating one more day.

In short, there is little evidence supporting the popular myth that Indians killed only what they needed in order to maintain some religiously sanctioned ecological balance in their environment. Robert Brightman's study of Crees and other forest Algonquians shows that before contact with Europeans, the Indians "were *not* practicing conservation, but instead killing more animals than they could use either domestically or commercially."[128] Cree religion, moreover, did not prohibit waste or seek to limit behavior for the benefit of Mother Earth and her children: "Rather than inhibiting overkill, religious definitions of the human-animal relationship encouraged it insofar as they premised an environment of primordial abundance in which game could not be destroyed but only temporarily displaced."[129] Indeed, these "religious definitions" held that the more game killed, the more there would be, for new animals were reincarnations of dead ones. Conservation of game was an idea imposed from without by the Hudson Bay Company for the coldly mercenary purpose of making sure there were enough hides to keep the company in business.

Like the Crees', the Plains Indians' killing of the bison was limited only by technology. As popular mythology has it, Indians killed only the bison they needed and were so averse to waste and so ecologically efficient that they used every last bit of it. Then those pathologically wasteful whites came along, shooting bison from trains for sport until the animals were nearly extinct. Like most myth, this is a partial truth expanded into false knowledge. The bison didn't even become an integral part of Plains Indian culture until after the Indians acquired from whites the horse and the gun, both of which allowed Indians to kill many more bison than they could immediately use in order to sell the buffalo robes and tongues. In this context, there is obviously no way Indians used every bit of the carcass. In the early nineteenth century the artist George Catlin, a champion of the Indian, said of the Sioux that they were "constantly calling for every robe that can be stripped from these animals' backs." In winter the animals were particularly vulnerable; after they were killed, "the skins are then stripped off, to be sold to the Fur Traders, and the carcasses left to be devoured by the wolves."[130] Tongues as well as robes were lucrative products of bison kills. Catlin reports the slaughter of 1,400 buffalo by Sioux hunters, who took only the tongues, which they then traded for whiskey.[131] Other Plains Indians were just as profligate. Dan Flores, in his study of the bison in the first half of the nineteenth century, calculates that in 1855 alone, about three thousand Cheyenne killed forty thousand bison.[132] In the northern Plains, Indians took 30 percent more bison than required for subsistence in order to answer the commercial demands for robes.[133] And why shouldn't the Indians have killed as many bison as possible? Doing so benefited them. Moreover, their religious conceptions of the animal gave it a supernatural origin that made it inexhaustible, a belief reinforced by the vast herds they could see with their own eyes.[134]

But, the idealist of the Indian counters, isn't this destructive behavior a result of the corruption of Indian culture by European? Sale, who admits the Indian involvement in the near extirpation of the beaver and the slaughter of caribou as well as of bison herds, explains that, the "aberrations of those later societies can be laid to the effects of decimating diseases and the disruptive pressures of war, trade, technology, and alcohol."[135] This rationalization, however, ultimately insults the Indian's culture and his presumed ecological beliefs, both of which are so fragile that they are wantonly abandoned for the whiskey and gee-gaws of white civilization. W. H. Hutchinson put it this way in one of the early attacks on the myth of the Indian ecologist. "If the Amerind was a truly dedicated ecologist, why did he so easily succumb to the artifacts offered him by Europeans that he stripped his land of furs and pelts to get them?"[136]

But the Indian was not an ecologist—like all humans, he took from his environment whatever he decided he needed to survive and flourish, using whatever technologies efficiently achieved his aims. Nothing in his religion or world view would have allowed him to entertain the possibility of extinction or ecological imbalance— ideas developed later by Western science. Silver points out that, "'Conservation and 'waste' are modern concepts that Indians would not have understood."[137]

No belief better represents the myth of the Indian's mystic closeness to the land than the widespread assumption that Indians worshipped Mother Earth, such as Winona LaDuke's claim: "The earth is our [Indians'] Mother." Unfortunately, Sam Gill's meticulous study of this idea shows that there is no evidence that American Indians worshipped a maternal earth deity. The two anecdotes most often presented as evidence of earth-worship—and hence of the Indians' superior ecological sensibility—cannot be disentangled from corruption by translation and transmission or from their historical moment. The first statement is attributed to the Shawnee Tecumseh, who in 1810 supposedly responded to an offer of a chair by saying, "The earth is my mother—and on her bosom I will repose." Gill's study of the statement's origins and transmission, not to mention what is known of Shawnee religious belief, leads him to conclude, "The extant evidence so far examined leaves us really no basis for holding that the statement attributed to Tecumseh is historically founded. There is no evidence to support this position and much to suggest that he did not make such a statement."[138] Tecumseh's statement reflects the growing idealization of the Indian as a noble savage once he had ceased to become a real threat to American expansion east of the Mississippi, not any Indian's actual belief. This phenomenon likewise accounts for James Fenimore Cooper's noble savages and the popularity of the Pocahontas story, both of which are contemporaneous with the Tecumseh legend. In other words, the mother-earth motif reflects a white Romantic idealization of the pathetic Indian sacrificed to the march of advanced civilization.

The second anecdote is much later than the Tecumseh one and even more tainted by white interpretations, influences, and mis-translations.[139] The statement is attributed to Smohalla, a Wanapum, when he refused to take up farming and the settled life around 1884 or 1885: "You ask me to plow the ground. Shall I take a knife and tear my mother's bosom? You ask me to dig for stone. Shall I dig under skin for bones? You ask me to cut grass and make hay and sell it, and be rich like white men. But how dare I cut off my mother's hair?" As Gill shows, this statement's meaning must be found, not in Indian religious belief, but in the crisis occasioned by the increasing encroachment of whites on Indian lands and by the collision of two radically different ways of life; the "references to the earth are metaphorical, not theological."[140]

To make the Indian a model ecologist was, as American histo-rian Calvin Martin puts it, "a silly and cruel charade.... Silly because it was yet another expression of this nation's superficial understand-ing of the Indian; cruel because it was bound to fail."[141] And bound to fail because it is a lie. Like all peoples everywhere, Indians sought first to survive in their environments and maintain living standards in the face of resource depletion, increases in population, and com-petition from other peoples. Whatever adaptations seemed to advance those goals were adopted, whether environmentally harm-ful or beneficial. The Indians' attitude to nature was fundamentally practical. And any religious awe or reverence they felt was occa-sioned by *fear* of powerful natural forces, not filial devotion.

WE ARE ALL THE IRON RACE

That the European incursion into the New World was a disaster for the people living there is obvious, even if most of the killing was accomplished by bacteria and microbes. But *all* of human history is a tragic record of vast movements of people in search of land and resources and a sad chronicle of the violent displacement of those who unfortunately are already in possession of those resources. The Romans in Gaul, the Arabs in North Africa, the Huns and Mongols in eastern Europe, the Turks, the Bantu, the Khmer, the Tonkinese—all wrought devastation on the peoples from whose blood and treasure new empires were fashioned. The European movement was merely larger and more devastating in its impact. Europe's advanced technology and cultural dynamism made it so, but it was ultimately no different in kind from the Aztec movement into central Mexico or the Sioux movement into the Plains—no different from, to quote Mexican novelist Carlos Fuentes, "the great epic of exodus and war at the root of life and movement in the empty continent."[142] Human cruelty, violence, and greed are constants, the property of no one race or culture.

But the critical consciousness that is borne of the recognition of the freedom and dignity of the individual, and so can acknowledge and condemn its *own* evil and injustice—that reflexive capacity is *not* universal. Jacques Ellul, no cheerleader of the West, has written: "The West alone has defended the inalienable rights of the human person, the dignity of the individual, the man who is alone with everyone against him."[143] This critical self-awareness was the creation of the West, a fragile plant sown by the Greeks and fitfully nourished for twenty-five centuries. The idealizer of the Indian, who is usually also a fierce critic of Western civilization, paradoxically exemplifies this critical consciousness. Like the Golden Age myth through which he views the Indian, the idealizer's universalistic moral categories do not come down to him from the New World but from the Old.

Moreover, the modern critic's intellectual forbears are not Indians but Europeans, some of whom from the very start of the clash with the New World deplored the violence and cruelty their fellows inflicted on the Indians. In 1511, the Dominican priest Antonio de Montesinos preached to his fellow Spaniards, "You are in mortal sin and live and die in it because of the cruelty and tyranny that you use against these innocent peoples.... Are these Indians not Men? Do they not have rational souls? Are you not obliged to love them as you love yourselves?"[144] So too Pedro de Cieza de León, who wrote, "It is no small sorrow to reflect that we Christians have destroyed so many kingdoms. For wherever Christians have passed, conquering and discovering, it seems as though a fire has gone, consuming everything."[145] And, of course, the heroic defender of the Indian, Bartolomé de las Casas, who in his *Confesionario* instructed priests to deny absolution to anybody who abused and owned Indians.[146] There is no record of a Sioux taking this sort of attitude toward a Pawnee, or an Aztec sympathizing with a Tlascalan, or an Iroquois championing the rights of a Huron. That Europeans *did* sympathize with and champion the rights of Indians; that they *did* recognize a common humanity shared with the Indian is an important moral achievement that must be acknowledged along with the cruelty and depravity of the European conquerors.

The tragic view of history, however, with all its contradictions and failed good intentions and messy complexity, is anathema to the idealizer, who finds it easier (and more profitable) to pander to the gratifying preconceptions and cheap guilt and smug compassion of contemporary whites. He condemns the very civilization that creates his mind and values and that provides him a level of material comfort and freedom reserved for only the most blessed of humans. Meanwhile, as Bordewich's valuable book shows over and over, the problems afflicting real-life Indians continue to fester, their solutions continually short-circuited by the false knowledge that most whites and too many Indians find more pleasing and simple than the hard work of coming to terms with the stubborn mystery of human good and evil.

CHAPTER 7 ■ THE FALSE GODDESS AND HER LOST PARADISE

And so feminism today has taken a distressing step away off the path to equality onto a detour down a yellow brick road. Feminist leaders are now telling women to perform the modern equivalent of the Sioux Indian Ghost Dance, to spend our energies frantically calling upon a mythical golden age in an effort to create a dreamlike future—because such rituals are better suited to our superior nature than fighting directly with men for our rights.

— RENE DENFELD, *THE NEW VICTORIANS: A YOUNG WOMAN'S CHALLENGE TO THE OLD FEMINIST ORDER*[1]

One of today's fastest growing cults worships a goddess that some modern academics have conjured into existence out of the bits and pieces of ancient myths and prehistoric artifacts. The popularity of the "Goddess," as she's usually called, is unquestioned and ubiquitous. Goddess worship gets its own enthusiastic chapter in *Megatrends for Women* and has its own magazines like *Sage-Woman* and *Crone Chronicles*,[2] and the Goddess herself is popularized in Jean Auel's best-selling novels set in Ice Age Europe. Bookstores are

filled with the self-help works of those like Felicity Wombwell and
Starhawk who transform the ancient "Goddess wisdom" into therapeutic solace for the angst-ridden, deracinated middle class. The
professional feminist conference circuit is increasingly a venue for
drum-banging Goddess rituals and chants, not to mention the sale
of statuettes, crystals, tracts, and jewelry.[3] Witches' covens are proliferating, since witchcraft is considered to be the oft-persecuted
remnant of the old Goddess religion "that centers on love and
respect for the Earth and the power of women," according to self-
styled witch Z. Budapest.[4]

As Ms. Budapest's statement reveals, Goddess worship reinforces
and validates the romantic environmentalism seen in Chapter 5, and
this accounts too for the Goddess's popularity, as well as for that subspecies of feminism known as "ecofeminism." As *Megatrends for
Women* puts it approvingly, "The Goddess is associated with reverence
for the earth and its environment. Her image is reemerging as
humanity seeks to make warfare obsolete and heal planet Earth."[5]
Goddess rituals are popular at environmentalist celebrations—on
Earth Day in 1991, half a dozen folks stood on a hill in Wisconsin
and prayed to Mother Earth, chanting "Clean soil, clean soil."[6] Like
environmentalism, romantic Indianism also finds the Goddess a
useful ally. As seen, American Indians are reputed to be natural ecologists worshipping Mother Earth; hence Goddess worship creeps into
the world view of many professional Indians as well. Paula Gunn
Allen opines, "I think the white man's rage against the Indian is
against this female force.... I think it was all the powerful women we
[Indians] had; their connection with the gods and the spirits scared
the bejeezis out of the whites."[7] (Apparently whites weren't scared
enough, or Indian women powerful enough, for whites not to steal all
the Indians' land.) This mixture of antirationalist feminism, romantic environmentalism, noble-savage Indianism, and creative scholarship is a recipe for false knowledge.

It is tempting to dismiss Goddess worship as another transitory

New Age fad flourishing among the tabloid semiliterate. Unfortunately, Goddess worship is strongest in the presumed bastions of clear thinking and rational discourse, the universities. Philip G. Davis notes, "Far from lagging behind, universities have become major vehicles for the spread of the Goddess movement. Many of the most important representatives of the movement are academics who lend the prestige of their positions and the fruits of their work to the cause."[8] As you might guess, women's studies departments are the major academic clearinghouse for the distribution of Goddess lore to students. The annual National Women's Studies Association Conference devotes much of its time and energy to the Goddess business and her "healing rituals."[9] But more traditional academic disciplines, especially archaeology, lend the authority of what is supposed to be empirically based research to an enterprise that can only be religious at best, and weirdly antirationalist at worst. The work of the late archaeologist Marija Gimbutas provides most of the intellectual cover for the Goddess myth, and archaeology continues to be, along with theology and religious studies, a major academic venue for Goddess "scholarship."

The secure place of Goddess worship in the presumed secular university means that this false knowledge can spread into the wider culture, not just through the college students forced by general education requirements into women's studies courses, but also through the students who become teachers and shape the K-12 curriculum and textbooks—not to mention the journalists who, half-educated to begin with, depend on academic "experts" for the information they pass on to their audiences.[10] As a result, a fabricated religious myth becomes to many a "fact" about history, with presumed moral implications and imperatives for all of us.[11]

In its academic guise, then, Goddess worship represents a dangerous conflation of New Age religion and dubious scholarship.[12] If Goddess worship would cast itself as a religion legitimized only by the faith of its adherents, then its capacity for mischief would be much more limited, though feminists should be concerned about a fad "drunk on disembodied nostalgia, ritualistic pretense, and New Age ideology," as two feminist critics put it.[13]

No doubt the inroads into mainstream Christianity by proponents of the Goddess are a concern to believers. The 1993 Re-Imagining Ecumenical Conference of major Protestant denominations was the occasion for statements such as the following, from feminist theologian (or "thealogian") Delores Williams: "I don't think we need folks hanging on crosses and blood dripping and weird stuff."[14] The question obtrudes: why do such people bother to consider themselves Christians if they want to eliminate the crucifixion and resurrection of Christ? And if anything is "weird," it's the incantation chanted at the conference by the Goddess devotees, with its panting *Penthouse*-esque references to the "hot blood of our wombs" and the "nectar between our thighs."[15] But ultimately it is up to Christians to defend their faith. Here the concern is with the spread of false knowledge that results when a therapeutic version of the Golden Age myth, one supported by little more than emotions, is passed off as *fact* established by the protocols of rational inquiry—the same unholy alliance of phony science and the obsession with emotional states that has been traced throughout this book.

THE THERAPEUTIC IMPERATIVE

As with romantic environmentalism and noble-savage Indianism, the Goddess movement gratifies the anxious urban-dweller's longing for a lost age of harmony with nature, simplicity, and peace.[16] In addition, the Goddess myth provides its believers an emotional gratifying sense of moral superiority. *They* see injustice and the general corruption of the Iron Age world—a world, of course, whose technology and affluence allow these gnostics to flourish in comfort. Cynthia Eller's study of feminist spiritualism confirms that middle-

class self-actualization explains the movement's ubiquitous therapeutic thrust and its popularity. Eller's sociological profile of the
typical adherent of the Goddess religion reveals that she is white,
middle-class, educated beyond high school, in her thirties or forties,
and "disproportionately lesbian."[17] That is, a cohort of women very
likely to be disaffected, in need of therapeutic solace, and able to
afford it. Eller's summary of the reasons for Goddess-worship's popularity among this group likewise points to Western radical individualism and its obsession with self-development as the
movement's engine.

     This therapeutic thrust is found everywhere in writings about
the Goddess, including so-called academic discussions. Feminist
conclaves typically involve such sentimentalism as the following
narcissistic injunction from Phyllis, a self-proclaimed Mohawk, to
the attendees at the 1992 National Women's Studies Association
Conference: "Take a moment to give ourselves a big hug. Let me
remind us that the person we're hugging is the most important
person we have in our life."[18] Try to imagine one of Phyllis's Mohawk
ancestors saying something so utterly Eurocentric. *Megatrends for
Women* likewise touts "enhanced personal power," and "confidence,
belonging, and self-esteem" as the therapeutic dividends of Goddess
worship.[19] But supposedly more intellectually sophisticated academics and scholars are equally prone to promises of personal fulfillment.
One of the early influential Goddess tracts, Merlin Stone's *When God
Was a Woman*, admits that "this is not intended as an archaeological
or historical text. It is rather an invitation to all women to join in the
search to find out who we really are, by beginning to know our own
past heritages as more than a broken and buried fragment of a male
culture."[20] This statement neatly joins self-actualization and self-discovery to a legitimizing victim-status. The editors of a collection of
essays by professional archaeologists feel no embarrassment at admitting that "in some of the essays...there is the emergent phenomenon
that the researchers themselves have been substantially changed by

their analyses."[21] On a more practical note, Z. Budapest recommends Goddess worship to feminists because it "would only enhance their labors and, in fact, fuel them when they feel depleted by too much political work."[22] So with Charlene Spretnak, who justifies the work of archaeologist Marija Gimbutas because its aim was "that we might be enriched by contact with Europe's original matrix, the bountiful earth-body of the Great Mother."[23] This celebration of a consoling, salvational research should give pause. Shouldn't the search for truth, rather than self-actualization or self-esteem, be the goal of intellectual endeavors?

And finally, the self-obsessed—and self-promoting—whining of the professional victim is frequently heard, as in Tina Passman's complaint that writing her article about the Classics profession's failure to endorse the idea of an ancient matriarchy "has been an arduous task, one which has required me to grapple with each of my own fragmented identities in a struggle toward some resolution." She goes on to tear out our hearts with her *cri de coeur* that "as a Lesbian, as a feminist, as a classicist, I have worked in physical, emotional, spiritual, and psychic isolation, relying upon the voices of other women who share many parts of a world and a language welcoming and common to women."[24] What language could possibly be used to describe the true plight of a single mother working in a truck-stop greasy spoon, if well-heeled academics are going to be allowed such a rhetoric of pathos and suffering?

The therapeutic imperative reaches bathetic intensity in the work of Carol P. Christ, a leading light of academic feminist spirituality. The introduction to her book *Laughter of Aphrodite* weaves radical individualism, self-actualization, romantic antirationalism, and nature-love environmentalism into a tapestry of earnest self-promotion and self-obsession. Christ is unabashedly frank about the origins of her work in her need for self-fulfillment and self-actualization: "As *I* look at *my* writing, *I* see that *I* have always been struggling to tell *my* story, to show the relation of the way *I* think to the way *I* live"—seven first-person pronouns in one sentence (emphasis added).[25] In other words, her scholarly writing is subordinated to her own therapeutic need "to want more than women of my generation were taught to want" (x), a good example of this culture's favorite narrative: bourgeois frustrated desire, dissatisfaction, and disappointment that exalted expectations have not been met.

Given that the self and its feelings are the focus rather than truth, Christ's starting point is not an objective, rational interpretation of evidence by means of a professional methodology, but rather that old Victorian sexist stereotype, "intuition" (ix), which provides Christ with the "insights with which we create feminist theology"[26] (xvi). The portentous "insights," however, revealed by this intuitive power are mere clichés that were earlier seen as deriving from eighteenth- and nineteenth-century Western romanticism: "the connections of my spirit to the spirits of all living things"; "our categories separate 'man' from 'nature,' denying the truth that 'we are nature'"; "spirituality is experiencing connectedness to the life force within all living things" (ix). These chestnuts are as old as Goethe's Werther and resemble the vacuities that Flaubert's Emma and Léon exchange. Such statements are the luxuries of a self-confessed "white, middle-class, well-educated, California born, feminist"(xii)—that is, an affluent urbanite protected by a sustaining womb of money and technology that together create the space for "mystical experiences...with nature" (ix), experiences that are never put to the gritty test of, say, actually obtaining sustenance from the earth or doing without mammograms or electricity or antibiotics. The role of the Goddess, then, is to validate this romantic quest for self-meaning in a nature pacified by the technology Christ deplores and to aid in the "empowerment" of women by correcting the "devaluation of female power, denigration of the female body, distrust of the female will, and denial of the women's bonds and heritage that have been engendered by patriarchal religion."[27]

When projected out onto the larger society, this self-transformational agenda found in the work of Goddess adherents not only legitimizes self-obsession, but also leads to grandiose utopian claims that the lost Golden Age paradise of the Goddess can be regained if only we can return to her ancient wisdom—as mediated, of course, by the modern academics who serve as her prophetesses. Mary Lynn Keller offers a shopping list of paradisal benefits that would accrue from embracing the Goddess: "peace might prevail for thousands of years"; "material sufficiency and well-being would become normal"; "egalitarian bonds based on mutual respect and benefit, affection and pleasure, would become normative between the sexes"; "the enjoyment of nature would be the basis of everyday living"; the interruption of life's pleasures would be a "relatively rare tragedy"; drug and alcohol use would disappear, and we would all become ecologists.[28] That is, all the utopian fantasies that have characterized millennial dreams for centuries, and that ignore the tragic limitations defining human existence, could all be ours. In the same vein, Christ parades her "concern for peace and survival that motivates me and drives me to despair"(xiii); "the knowledge that this earth could be destroyed with the press of a button or gradually poisoned to death by pollution fills me alternately with a sense of futility and urgency about my work" (ix).

Mary Lynn Keller is so excited by the prospect of a world-transforming knowledge bestowed by visionary Goddess study that her muse soars on purple wings:

> If we could allow ourselves an intuition or visions of the primary source of all life, or reality in its fullness; if we could allow ourselves to be illumined by this, as though beholding the brilliant, life-and-death-giving sun; and then, having opened ourselves to this radiance, if we would once again ask which set of working assumptions [matriarchal or patriarchal] leads to greater understanding of human culture, its past, present, and future possibilities, what might we believe?

What, indeed? From Hitler to Stalin to Mao to Pol Pot, this century has seen what sorts of unpleasant things people believe when they start to have irrational intuitions of "reality in its fullness" and then try to create their visionary utopias. As Isaiah Berlin points out, "The search for perfection [is] a recipe for bloodshed."[29]

Like Keller, Tina Passman extravagantly defines what the utopian stakes are in the academic struggle over the legitimacy of the Goddess: "The dismantling of patriarchy for an egalitarian, non-hierarchical ethic of self-governance and interaction between persons, groups, and nations," a deconstruction that would lead to "complete social transformation" predicated on a "utopian vision to strive for, a blueprint of the unknown land that is the aftermath of transformation."[30] One fears that Passman's "unknown land" might turn out to be Hamlet's "undiscovered country, from whose bourn/No traveller returns." *Megatrends for Women*, following the academic lead, also links the Goddess to grandiose dreams such as humanity's attempt "to make warfare obsolete and heal planet earth."[31] How convenient to have one's search for self-fulfillment glorified into the quest to save the planet. Needless to say, all of these laudatory ideals, not to mention the debased Enlightenment idea of social transformation through knowledge, derive from Western rationalism and the liberal political tradition that Passman and her ilk disparage as a mere mechanism of patriarchal oppression, not from ancient Goddess wisdom. Ancient prehistory and religion are not the issue in Goddess literature. Validating individualist self-actualization by liberationist and utopian claims is.

ANTI RATIONALISM, AGAIN

Despite their fuzzy rhetoric of self-help and their obsession with their own feelings, Goddess adherents assert that their interpretation of history and reconstruction of the Goddess religion are based on *facts* acquired through the procedures of rational inquiry, not primarily on visions or intuition. As Merlin Stone put it, their history corrects the distortions of sexist scholars who ignored or misinterpreted relevant evidence to gratify their "sexual and religious biases."[32] Stone maintains that "archaeological, mythological and historical evidence" that supports her view of a Goddess religion has been suppressed for centuries by patriarchal religions, and she touts the "archaeological evidence which proved that Her religion had existed and flourished in the Near and Middle East for thousands of years."[33] In her response to a critical article by Sally R. Binford, Stone claims that the reconstructed Goddess religion and the prehistoric society that presumably worshipped it are based on scholarly evidence and hence are incontrovertible historical facts. In support, Stone touts her ten pages of bibliography in *When God Was a Woman* and the "430 pages of additional evidence" in her other books as proof that a rational and objective analysis of evidence has established the truth of the Goddess.[34]

This claim to authority based on sound empirical procedure explains the importance of Marija Gimbutas for Goddess adherents. Gimbutas had a long and distinguished career as an archaeologist at UCLA, producing some first-rate research before she answered the call of the Goddess. Her authority—based on her earlier empirical research conducted according to the same methods and protocols that all such research follows—provides the Goddess movement with a patina of intellectual and scholarly respectability. Mary Lynn Keller says that "Marija Gimbutas's lifework has amassed material evidence for a revolutionary new picture of the cultural roots of Western civilization." In turn, Gimbutas's theory of a Golden Age early Europe destroyed by Indo-European invaders results from "lifelong study" and is "substantiated by the preponderance of evidence."[35]

If this truth is so firmly established, however, why do so many reputable archaeologists refuse to endorse it? If other archaeologists or scholars don't agree with Gimbutas, Carol Christ argues, it is because their "ideological convictions" prevent "serious scholarly consideration" of Gimbutas's work, which is the fruit of "decades of study."[36] The implication is that due to the work of Gimbutas and others, the existence of the Goddess and the Golden Age characteristics of pre-Indo-European culture are now to be considered *facts* established by an objective analysis of evidence. Critics, these people say, are ideologically driven, and so they are not giving Gimbutas's ideas "serious scholarly consideration." Gimbutas's own books, filled with diagrams, maps, charts, photographs of artifacts, and forbidding technical apparatuses, reinforce this implication of scientific support, particularly for the non-specialist. Those academics who follow Gimbutas provide copious scholarly documentation and references to monographs, books, and articles that purportedly represent a body of information establishing the *truth* of what's being asserted.

We will come soon to Gimbutas's interpretation of the evidence and the soundness of her theories. Here I want to bring up a serious contradiction in the work of most academic Goddess adherents. Despite their appeal to traditional empirical procedures to give these theories the authority of institutionally sanctioned truth, enthusiasts of the Goddess repeatedly appeal to nonrational "ways of knowing" and to the postmodern attack on science seen earlier. In the Introduction to their collection *Engendering Archaeology*, Gero and Conkey at least acknowledge that this contradiction might cause problems: "There is, for some [feminist scholars], an underlying tension between describing (the data, the interpretation, the past) and transforming these through a feminist lens."[37] But this serious issue is never really explored, and in the work of other scholars it is simply ignored.

Christ endorses "intuition" as the source of her knowledge. In this regard she follows Gimbutas, who in an interview claimed a double warrant for the truth of her work, a scientific one "based on a *lot* of evidence," and an "intuition" by means of which "you must feel that you are right in what you are saying."[38] Gimbutas's implication that there are two separate but complementary modes of establishing truth is misleading at best. Obviously, intuition plays a role in scientific discoveries, as no doubt do dreams and visions, but always in the final analysis such nonrational sources of inspiration must be *subordinated* to, not set complementary with, the hard test of objectively analyzed evidence and of professionally endorsed rational procedures. Intuitions and feelings must be tested for their soundness by comparison with evidence and subjection to procedures. How else convince others who do not share the intuition or feeling, the acid test of any theory?

Isaiah Berlin makes a similar point in his discussion of the limitations of Vico and Herder's intuitive historiography, ancestors of postmodern antirationalism:

> It is plain to us now that insight, no matter how brilliant and intuitive, and attempts to reconstruct the main lines of entire cultures by sheer imaginative genius, based on scattered erudition, are not sufficient. In the end it is only scrupulous examination of the evidence of the past and the systematic, self-critical piecing together of whatever can be empirically established, that can confirm one hypothesis and weaken or rule out others as implausible or absurd. History needs whatever it can obtain from any source or method of empirical knowledge.... Without reliable empirical evidence, the most richly imaginative efforts to recover the past must remain guesswork and breed fictions and romances.[39]

And when the intuition carries with it moral imperatives, when it creates a justifying narrative that merely gratifies the emotions and soothes the anxieties of the person endorsing it, the impulse to ignore—even to alter—the evidence becomes very powerful indeed.

This unresolved confusion between rigorous empirical method and fuzzy "intuition" or "feeling" runs throughout the writings of Goddess devotees. Merlin Stone at least is honest enough to confess to "a certain romantic mysticism," though she never tells us how that "mysticism" relates to all her empirical evidence.[40] Mary Lynn Keller, in the very same article in which she asserts Gimbutas's empirical bona fides, also alludes to alternative means of apprehending truth, without clearly defining those means and without giving us any procedure for testing their reliability or telling us how they relate to an empirical method. Quite the opposite, she makes reference to their incompatibility: "I question whether it will be possible to develop new frameworks of interpretation for the artistic and spiritual dimensions of ancient cultures that can be entirely satisfying to strictly empiricist and anti-spiritual scientists." The answer is it's *not* possible, given the paucity of evidence and the danger that subjective and anachronistic interpretation will fill the void. That's why the "artistic and spiritual dimensions of ancient cultures" should be a concern of speculative philosophy or more literary styles of history rather than of empirical research. But Keller then goes on to laud Gimbutas because she has solved this perennial conundrum: Gimbutas "has built a bridge between archaeology and mythology, between science and spirituality."[41] Well, no doubt creation science makes the same claim, but that doesn't mean those of us who do not share the faith or mystical experience ultimately holding the bridge together should be forced to walk over it. And we certainly should not teach creation science in schools as a *fact* about the creation of the world on no other warrant than its adherents' claims that they "feel" it is true.

Having taken this first step down the road of untestable "frameworks of interpretation," Keller goes on to attack "dispassionate objectivity." Contrary to her claims, however, no self-respecting scientist asserts "absolute certainty" about his theories. Instead of *bad*, cold rationality, Keller endorses a "paradigm" of knowing that is "participatory," "interdependent," "probabilistic," and "intersubjective": that is, all those *good*, warm "non-linear" things that come naturally to women but clearly denied to evil, murdering-to-dissect patriarchal science.[42] But Keller never explains how her new "paradigm" can lead to more reliable information than does the scientific method, and she never details exactly how, absent that method, it is possible to set about *verifying* the accuracy of the information she discovers. So, when all's said and done, Keller establishes Gimbutas's authority, not by appeals to the reader's "intuition" or to an "intersubjective" epistemology, but by assertions of "amassed material evidence" and a "preponderance of evidence"—the same empirical basis of appeal everybody else must establish in order for theories to be taken seriously by a community of scholars. It seems suspiciously as if Keller intends to rationalize Gimbutas's more fanciful speculations about prehistoric societies by locating them in the untestable and unverifiable realm of "intuition," all the while demanding our respect for them on the basis of the factual "evidence" Gimbutas presumably has "amassed."

This desire both to have and eat one's empirical cake recurs repeatedly in the work of Goddess adherents. Carol Christ, in the same sentence in which she legitimized Gimbutas's work as the result of "decades of study," claims that "I am able to appreciate Gimbutas's lifework in part because my religious perspective allows me to enter into the 'different world' of Old Europe in a way that makes it possible for the images to speak to me" just as they "spoke" to Gimbutas, whose empirical research had given them voice.[43] Apart from its naive ahistoricism, this sort of self-validation through subjective intuition could justify creation science as well, not to mention UFOs, angel visitations, or more unsavory beliefs such as the inferiority of certain races. Alison Wylie likewise tries to salvage unsupported speculations about prehistory by appealing to "feminist epistemology."[44] Admitting that "relativism and undecidibility" are the dangers of abandoning objective empirical procedures, Wylie recommends the "ambivalence" advocated by Sandra Harding, one of the foremost feminist critics of science as socially constructed mechanism of patriarchal power: "[Harding] recommends that we give up the compulsive search for 'master theories' and embrace postmodernism as an indispensable source of inspiration concerning possibilities that lie beyond existing modes of inquiry and understanding."[45] This passage begs a whole host of questions. First, the characterization of "postmodernism" here is false. Postmodernism is not, like divine revelation, a "source of inspiration" for knowledge lying beyond the ken of rationalism. Rather it is epistemic *nihilism*: it denies the possibility of *any* ground for knowing *anything*—except, of course, itself. Worse, how can we possibly discriminate among these various "possibilities" or determine which is more likely to be true if not by the objective analysis of the evidence purportedly supporting them? Once more, no matter what the source of the inspiration—drugs, dreams, visions, or divine revelation—for the rest of us nonbelievers the worth of an insight claiming to be a *fact* will have to be the same old empirical procedure that to the postmodernist perspective is flawed by its investment in oppressive and exclusive modes of patriarchal thinking.

In short, to establish *public* truths outside the chapel of the cultist or the private beliefs of the individual, there is no other "mode of inquiry and understanding" than the scientific, no "epistemic standards which are non-standard in scientific contexts."[46] Every other "mode" or "standard" invites relativism, subjectivism, special-pleading, fabrication, wish-fulfillment, and vagueness, not to mention justifying pure nonsense or outright frightening beliefs such as the "Aryan physics" of the Nazi physicist Philip Lenard or the "socialist genetics" of Soviet geneticist Trofim Lysenko. Indeed, the neo-pagan occultism that lay at the roots of much Nazi thought explains as well the antirationalism of some Goddess adherents. Common to both is what Philip G. Davis has called "intuitive immanentism": the idea, in the case of the Nazis, that knowledge arises from Teutonic "intuition and feeling" rather than from Semitic "intellectual observation and analysis."[47] As we have seen, and as Davis notes, "'Intuitive immanentism' is a fitting description of the worldview of Goddess folk and radical feminists as well."[48]

Only now, "male" rather than "Jewish" ways of knowing are to be spurned in favor of female "intersubjective" intuitive knowledge. The result, however, is the same: false knowledge whose acceptance is a matter of gratified feeling or political ideology rather than of convinced reason.

This attempt to have it both ways epistemically—that is, to appeal to the authority of empiricism when it suits, then to fall back on a self-validating intuition or feeling or "alternative ways of knowing" when evidence is inadequate or incoherent—once more recalls the methods of those advocating "creation science." Both represent a dangerous mingling of what should be two distinct activities: ascertaining the truths of the material world as opposed to determining the truths of the spiritual realm. The latter may be more important than the former, more central to our lives as humans, more meaningful and fulfilling to us, but ultimately spiritual truths are not subject to definitive proof or demonstration, being part of Hamlet's more things in heaven and earth than are dreamt of in philosophy. In a secular democracy comprising diverse religious and spiritual beliefs, to mingle the procedures for establishing material truth with those used to validate spiritual truth is to open the door to all manner of intellectual mischief—not to mention the unpleasant propensity of true believers to coerce rather than to convince.

Furthermore, if Gimbutas's theories are so solidly based on factual evidence, why do her followers even bother to make these appeals to "alternative" modes of knowing? Perhaps because those theories have in actual fact very little evidence supporting them, and what evidence there is must be interpreted with subjective latitude and with a whole host of unexamined assumptions in order for the theories to work?[49]

This fatal weakness in the Goddess/prehistorical paradise theory no doubt explains as well the unpleasant *ad hominem* attacks that mar the writings of Goddess adherents. Notice the way Keller loads this statement: "To accept Gimbutas's theory...an individual would

need to be willing to question the value of warfare, economic hierarchies of dominance and subordination, male dominance, and/or an
exclusively male-centered concept of God or ultimate reality."[50] The
implication, of course, is that if you *don't* accept Gimbutas's theory,
it's because you *do* endorse all those horrible beliefs. Tina Passman
flings a whole handful of question-begging epithets on critics of
early "matriculture" so that she doesn't have to bother with making
an argument: "The patriarchal denial of the possibility of early
matriculture found in traditional classics is elitist, (hetero)sexist,
and insidiously racist and anti-Semitic."[51] So there. Charlene
Spretnak accuses Gimbutas's critics of baser careerist motives:
"Attentive women wishing to curry favor with the backlash against
feminism, then, have realized that attacking Gimbutas as a 'feminist
extremist' opens certain doors."[52] But of course, *praising* Gimbutas
opens other lucrative doors. Carol Christ likewise dismisses
Gimbutas's critics, one of whose motivations is "to defend patriarchal Western hegemony." She too loads the issue by saying, "I
believe that it is almost impossible for a person uncritical of such a
world view [warfare, male dominance, the usual suspects] to understand or accept the conclusions of Gimbutas's work."[53] Again, not
accepting Gimbutas means you are *not* critical of war and hierarchies, mortal sins in the therapeutic university. Finally, Christ lapses
into hypocrisy when she dismisses Gimbutas's critics as "associated
with an academic establishment within which men whose values are
those of the European patriarchy still hold most of the significant
power and wherein those same men are launching a counterattack
against the challenges of feminism."[54] Christ, like Gimbutas and
most other Goddess apologists, is herself a part of the "academic
establishment." It is testimony to the corruption of intellectual life
in America that such sophomoric slander against one's critics is
accepted—no, rewarded—in academic discourse.

Such tactics as *ad hominem* attacks and appeals to "non-standard"
epistemology usually mask a shakily supported argument, and this
case is no different, as we will see when we examine Gimbutas's work.

THE CIVILIZATION OF THE GODDESS

In the work of Goddess adherents the name of Marija Gimbutas recurs like an academic talisman whose function is to avert critical scrutiny and assert the scientific bona fides of the Goddess theory. A mere reference to Gimbutas's work is thought sufficient to sweep from the board the issue of whether or not the picture of Old European society promoted by Goddess scholars has any basis in fact. Indeed, Gimbutas is the Moses who brought back from the Sinai of empirical archaeology the long-suppressed truth of pre-history. We have already heard Mary Lynn Keller's assertion that Gimbutas "amassed material evidence for a revolutionary new picture of the cultural roots of Western civilization."[55] Likewise Carol Christ touted the "challenge Gimbutas's work presents to the dominant world view of Western culture."[56] Clearly, it is Gimbutas's scholarship that provides the lion's share of the evidence, and most of the authority, for the idea that for several thousand years in Old Europe a peaceful, "matricentered" egalitarian society worshipped the Goddess.

Gimbutas's magnum opus, *The Civilization of the Goddess*, presents the most extensive description of that lost world and its tutelary deity.[57] This is a big, lavish book, crammed with photographs, charts, graphs, and technical apparatuses that create the perception of a mountain of empirical evidence establishing the historical truth of the Goddess. Yet throughout the book, fanciful interpretations and leaps beyond the evidence are woven into factual scholarly descriptions of artifacts and sites. The result is a shaky edifice of question-begging, special pleading, unexamined assumptions, and circular reasoning. In fact, the picture Gimbutas paints ultimately derives, not from the available material evidence, but from the inherited Western myth of the Golden Age.[58]

Gimbutas's Old European society is centered on the Goddess who represents "the sovereign mystery and creative power of the female as the source of life that developed into the earliest religious experiences." This "Great Mother Goddess...gives birth to all creation out of the holy darkness of her womb." She is the "metaphor for Nature herself, the cosmic giver and taker of life, ever able to renew Herself within the eternal cycle of life, death, and rebirth." Marilyn French, in her writing on prehistory, likewise asserts that "the qualities [associated with women] are fertility, regeneration, and a sense of humans as integrally connected with nature.... The goddess or principle of fertility or regeneration or vegetation was part of nature and worked within it."[59] This motif of harmony with nature is central to modern reconstruction of Old European culture and testifies to the continuing power of the Golden Age myth.[60]

Because they lived in harmony with a maternal nature, the Old Europeans created a society in which women, as human versions of the life-creating Goddess, enjoyed high status and important political functions: "Old European society was organized around a theacratic, communal temple community, guided by a queen-priestess, her brother or uncle, and a council of women as the governing body" (xi). Descent was matrilineal, and people enjoyed "economic egalitarianism." As in the Golden Age, when the earth was held in common,[61] there were no economic hierarchies or fetishized private property (324). Peace characterized a society that was free from war, violence, and "territorial aggression" (326,331). Gimbutas summarizes this society as "peaceful, sedentary, matrifocal, matrilineal, and sex [sic] egalitarian"[62] (352).

But starting in the fifth millennium B.C., the Golden Age degenerated into the Iron Age present of war, greed, and suffering, and Old Europe fell prey to the repeated invasions of the Indo-European-speaking peoples Gimbutas calls the Kurgans, after their burial mounds. In contrast to the Old Europeans, the Kurgans were "warlike, patriarchal, and hierarchical" (352). They were restless horse-riding nomads, pastoralists who worshipped the ubiquitous wandering sun rather than the stable earth. They "glorified the mag-

ical swiftness of arrow and javelin and the sharpness of the blade";
and they "exulted in the making of weapons, not pottery or sculpture."[63] They subordinated and despised women: "Females possessed
inferior status, elevated only by association with their male relations" (395). Unlike the Old Europeans, who believed that death
returned the individual "to the body of the Mother for regeneration
within the womb of nature," Indo-Europeans believed that the individual lived on in the underworld; an obvious origin for the West's
destructive individualism (400). In sum, the Indo-European Kurgan
culture was "warlike, exogamic, patriarchal, patrilineal, and patrilo-
cal, with a strong clanic organization and social hierarchy which
gave prominence to the warrior class" (396). They violently imposed
war, domination, hierarchy, the glorification of material wealth,
social stratification, slavery, and numerous other Iron Age evils on
the paradisal Old Europeans.

     Numerous critics have challenged the representational value of
this melodramatic interpretation of prehistory. Archeologist Brian
Hayden has questioned Gimbutas's "avalanche of highly subjective
interpretation"; speaking of the artifacts Gimbutas offers as evidence
of her thesis, he notes that "any attentive reader that examines the
illustrations [Gimbutas] provides to support her claims must be
bothered at times by identifications and claims that seem to be ver-
ifiable only with the eye of faith."[64] Brian Fagan, another archeologist, agrees that Gimbutas's "form of analysis stretches scientific
credibility beyond reasonable bounds." Her interpretations are
"remarkable for their uncritical subjectivity," and he notes further
that "her image of Old Europe is uncannily similar to that of the
Noble Savage so popular with nineteenth-century romantic novel-
ists."[65] Archaeologist Ruth Tringham likewise criticizes Gimbutas's
"morass of unqualified interpretations and value-laden statements."[66] Classicist Mary Lefkowitz, on her part, astutely notes the
contemporary political motivation behind Gimbutas's and other
Goddess adherents' ahistoric interpretations of the prehistorical evi-

dence: they are a "kind of pseudo-mystical mixing and matching of symbols and ideas that have nothing in common with each other except the contemporary use to which they may be put."[67] So too Lynn Meskell, in a valuable critique of Goddess scholarship, argues that Gimbutas's vision of the past and "the interpretations it presents are simply hopeful and idealistic creations reflecting the contemporary search for a social utopia." She also points out that Gimbutas's "dating, methodology, testing, typological and statistical analyses have all come under fire, not to mention artistic license and over-interpretation."[68] All of these criticisms are moot once we understand that Gimbutas's work is, as Juliette Wood characterizes Goddess scholarship, "an exercise in creative history";[69] it is a new version of the Golden Age myth and serves the same function: to offer solace for those psychically burdened with the complexities of civilization.

Yet the Goddess scholars insist that Gimbutas's theory of Old European culture and its destruction at the hands of Indo-European invaders is not a religious myth but an empirically established fact. A detailed critical analysis of Gimbutas's work lies beyond the scope of this essay. (For a more nuanced, alternative picture of prehistory that is not quite so free with the evidence, the reader should see the essays collected in *The Oxford Illustrated Prehistory of Europe*.[70]) But two points should be kept in mind when reading Gimbutas. First, she generalizes about an incredible variety of cultures existing over a very long time-span in an equally various number of environments: from the Upper Paleolithic, about 30,000 years B.C., down to the Neolithic, about 5,000 years B.C, a period that saw epochal environmental and technological transformations like the introduction of farming. That these changes will have had a profound impact on all aspects of prehistoric societies and cultures is obvious. Second, her entire discussion concerns preliterate peoples, whose complex rituals, rites, and social practices, therefore, have left no written evidentiary trail. This absence allows for a modern myth-making not possible for ancient Egypt or Sumer or Greece. These reservations aside, here follow some specific instances of Gimbutas's faulty reasoning, which focus on two key components of her theory: her claim that Old Europe was a peaceful paradise and her interpretation of the female figurines that provide the major evidence for her description of the Goddess's attributes and meaning.

Take one of the key assumptions of Gimbutas's argument, that prehistoric peoples would likely worship a creative Goddess on the analogy of human reproduction. "It was the sovereign mystery and creative power of the female as the source of life that developed into the earliest religious experiences," Gimbutas asserts (222). She goes on, "From the artifacts it seems clear that woman's ability to give birth and nourish children from her body was deemed sacred, and revered as the ultimate metaphor for the divine Creator" (223). In other words, Old Europeans, ignorant of the mechanics of reproduction and the male's role in conception, were awed by the mystical, earth-like power of woman to bring life out of her body. Hence they worshipped the female procreative force and made it the basis of their religion and social organization.

The assumption here, of course, is that prehistoric peoples did not understand the role of the male in reproduction—an assumption that defies common sense. As Hayden points out, "It is naive to believe that groups intelligent enough to invent language, fire, sewn clothes, complex technologies, and great art were so stupid that they could not make the associations between sex and reproduction."[71] Surely over time these peoples would have noticed that women do not conceive when men do not ejaculate into women. Perhaps that is why so many phalluses survive in prehistoric art—they represent the male power to provide visible seed for conception. If someone wanted to adopt Gimbutas's method of argument, he could assert that high prestige and awe attached to the male because he actively bestowed the fertile seed on the passive woman, just as seeds must be buried in the earth for plants to grow. And following Gimbutas's technique of using literary evidence from much later periods to support her assertions about prehistoric Europe, he could mention that this analogy between human reproduction and farming did dominate later Greek thinking.[72] This would then "prove" that the Old Europeans placed high value on males and afforded them commensurate social prestige and power.

Once Gimbutas has created this Goddess and her attributes out of such shaky assumption, she can find in the artifacts, like Hamlet and Polonius looking at clouds, whatever evidence she needs to support her definition, including circular arguments that recall one of M.C. Escher's self-consuming architectural fantasies. Speaking of the female figurines, for example, Gimbutas asserts that "the various shapes, gestures, and attributes portrayed on these sculptures, in addition to their provenance, lend themselves to a classification of types representing various aspects and functions of the Goddess" (222). But since the "aspects and functions" have already been deduced from the "shapes, gestures, and attributes," the "shapes, gestures, and attributes" cannot then be used as evidence that they represent "aspects and functions." Again, she says that "the life- and birth-giving mother was anthropomorphic and zoomorphic. Her main epiphanies were the deer, elk, and bear" (223). Her reasoning apparently goes like this: The Goddess was zoomorphic. Why? Because sculptures of deer, elk, and bear exist. These sculptures are epiphanies of the Goddess. Why? Because the Goddess was zoomorphic. But of course, there are any number of explanations for sculptures of deer, elk, and bear, the obvious ones linking these artifacts to hunting, the male pursuit par excellence, and one of humanity's oldest activities. Taking this assumption of a zoomorphic Goddess for granted, however, Gimbutas proceeds to pile up empirical evidence from a vast variety of locales and times and cultures, all balanced precariously on a rickety begged question.

Once she has conjured her Goddess into being, however, Gimbutas then proceeds to find the Goddess represented in artifacts and motifs that invite other, less fanciful interpretations. Consider the following: "The sacred animal of the Bird Goddess [a version of the Goddess] was the ram, which gained symbolic importance during the Early Neolithic when sheep became an important source of food and rams were needed for reproduction" (235). But why wouldn't the ram more obviously represent *male* reproductive power? If, as Gimbutas asserts, Old Europeans didn't understand the male's role in reproduction, why make the horned ram an icon at all? Why not the maternal ewe? In fact, the ram and its phallic horns more obviously symbolize male sexual potency.

Gimbutas's penchant for seeing the Goddess in every prehistoric sculpture or motif ultimately leads her to a manifest absurdity. Speaking of the so-called bucrania or "bull's heads" discovered all over the Near East and Europe, Gimbutas endorses the following astonishing leap: "The female womb with its fallopian tubes resembles the shape of a bull's head with horns, which may well account for the prevailing use of this motif to represent regeneration" (244). As archaeologist William Barnett points out, fallopian tubes "are barely visible upon dissection and have little cognitive connection to birth outside the realm of modern medicine."[73] Yet we are asked to believe that the same peoples who could not connect ejaculation with conception could nonetheless figure out the role in reproduction of the tiny fallopian tubes. Finally, all this fanciful interpretation is unnecessary, for the more obvious explanation for bucrania is that, like the ram, they and their phallic horns represent *male* sexual power as the power of regeneration.

These examples of Gimbutas's flawed reasoning could be multiplied, but now we need to look at the most important evidence for the existence of the Goddess, the so-called "Venus" figurines.

GODDESS, WHORE, AND EVERYTHING IN BETWEEN

The small sculptures called "Venus figurines" have been discovered all across Europe from Russia to Spain. As prehistorian Paul Mellars describes them, they are "small statuettes of rather well-developed (in some cases obese) female figures, with heavily accentuated sexual features and, usually, very attenuated or schematic representations of the heads, arms, and feet."[74] These statues have been discovered in caves, homes, and the prehistoric equivalent of garbage dumps, and most date from around 20,000 years ago. It is this vast variety of sculptures discovered in an equally vast variety of locales and times that Gimbutas asserts "represent various aspects and functions" of the "life-generating Goddess" who "personifies the eternally renewing cycle of life in all its forms and manifestations" (222).

The most obvious and ubiquitous criticism of Gimbutas's interpretation of these figurines is that it is reductive and simplistic. It ignores the "striking" diversity, as archeologist Margaret Conkey puts it, of Paleolithic art, a diversity of "media, subject matter, techniques, visual conventions, and spatiotemporal distributions."[75] Moreover, Gimbutas's fixation on the Goddess causes her to ignore the numerous figurines that are either sexless or male: "There are probably just as many phalli," Brian Hayden points out, "in the Paleolithic as there are Venuses."[76] Consequently, Gimbutas is often forced to interpret figurines or motifs signifying males in terms of the Goddess, as noted above where she attempts to make symbols of male sexual potency, such as a ram or a bull's head, represent aspects of the Goddess. This selective use of evidence is also coupled to a disregard for the vast stretches of time encompassing the figurines. Gimbutas asserts the continuity of the Goddess from the late Paleolithic to the Neolithic— a period of over ten thousand years.[77] That a religious view could have remained unchanged during significant environmental changes (such as the retreat of the glacial sheet from northern Europe) and during the critical transition from hunting/gathering to farming defies common sense. Nor is it likely that iconography would remain static during those momentous changes. As Lynn Meskell puts it, "To assume *a priori* that there is a Goddess behind every figurine is tantamount to interpreting plastic figures of Virgin Mary and of 'Barbie' as having identical ideological significance."[78]

As well as being reductive, the meaning Gimbutas assigns to the figurines depends on selective and highly subjective interpretations. The relentless focus on fertility and sex, for example, bespeaks modern preoccupations that ancient peoples may have subordinated to equally pressing issues such as famine or disease.[79] Likewise with the assumption that the figurines have some sort of sacred significance. How does this idea square with the fact that "most figurines are found broken and discarded as redeposited refuse"?[80] Perhaps this testifies to the ubiquity of the Goddess, or perhaps "it demonstrates that these figures are not sacred at all; or they may have multiple meanings which change as a figure is made, used and discarded."[81] There are other objections. If the figurines represent maternal fertility Goddesses, for example, why are there no statuettes showing mothers giving birth or suckling?[82] Most of the figurines are passive and abstract, their exaggerated sexual characteristics inviting any number of interpretations.

"In short," archeologist Peter Ucko summarizes, "it can be seen that the generally accepted Mother Goddess interpretation of prehistoric anthropomorphic figurines leaves several features of the figurines themselves wholly unexplained and, in addition, poses several theoretical problems of interpretation which it fails to solve."[83] Other suggested interpretations of the statuettes include: they were prehistoric erotica; they represented spirits of the house or home, or "pseudo-historical characters who formed part of the mythology or explanatory framework of the society"; they were objects of sympathetic magic to ensure fertility or pregnancy, the image discarded after it had worked (or hadn't)[84]; perhaps they were "dolls, toys, tokens of identification, primitive contracts, communication," or "teaching devices, tools of sorcery, magic, healing, or initiation."[85] Or maybe they were "items of ritualistic exchange between communities who…were dependent on wide ranging social and 'alliance' networks across large areas of the European continent."[86] Timothy Taylor, arguing that the figurines appeared "at a time of growing economic inequality between men and women," reads them not as the emblems of high female status, but rather as "part of a complicated sexual culture that, through sexual objectification and censorship, created and maintained power imbalances between men and women."[87] Ian Hodder links them to the household as the site of domestication of the wild, and the woman's ambiguous role in that process: "The underlying theme linking activities and concepts within the domus, is the woman as transformer of wild into domestic—the woman as domesticator, or as domesticated."[88] Nearly all of these interpretations show a greater respect for the variety and diversity of the evidence than does Gimbutas's theory of a totalizing cult of the Goddess which, as Mary Lefkowitz points out, "reduces all womankind to a genital identity."[89] Even the feminist prehistorian Margaret Ehrenberg concludes, "The likelihood of a significant continent-wide cult of a Mother Goddess has been greatly exaggerated."[90]

Once we see how fragile are the foundations for Gimbutas's Goddess, the "matricentered" social and cultural structure of Old Europe predicated on the Goddess's existence begins to totter also. Even if the figurines do represent female and natural fertility, it does not follow that women had high status, any more than the numerous images of the Virgin Mary evidenced the political and social power of Renaissance European women. Prehistorian Andrew Sherratt notes of early farmers of the Later Neolithic and Copper Ages—the climax of Gimbutas's Golden Age—that "their ideals were expressed in images of female procreation and abundance—even if women themselves bore most of the burdens of everyday life, and died after short lives exhausted by the work of cultivation and child-bearing."[91] Once more it is the perennial complexity and ambiguity and contradictions of human existence and culture that are ignored in Gimbutas's recycling of the Golden Age myth.

THE PREHISTORIC IRON AGE

Gimbutas's assertion of a peaceful, egalitarian, Old European society is no more firmly substantiated by the evidence than is her interpretation of the Venus figurines. Indeed, evidence of violence and intergroup conflict abounds throughout the whole period preceding the alleged Kurgan invasions. As Keeley notes, "Whenever modern humans appear on the scene, definitive evidence of homicidal violence becomes more common, given a sufficient sample of burials. Several of the rare burials of earliest modern humans in central and western Europe, dating from 34,000-24,000 years ago, show evidence of violent death." He concludes, "Warfare is documented in the archaeological record of the past 10,000 years in every well-studied region."[92] Violence between culturally differentiated groups probably arose out of increased competition for hunting grounds and other resources: "Increased density of settlement and territorial life in fixed hunting grounds created substantial progress in cultural differentiation. Emergence of territorial cultural units created conditions for border disputes or disputes over food resources and over space."[93]

Evidence for war and violence indeed has been discovered dating from the Mesolithic, the period of transition between the Upper Paleolithic and the Neolithic (ca. 10,000-5,000 years ago), Gimbutas's heyday of the Goddess's Golden Age. In the Ofnet Cave in Germany, Keeley notes, "two caches of 'trophy' skulls were found...comprising the disembodied heads of thirty-four men, women, and children, most with multiple holes knocked through their skulls by stone axes."[94] S. Vencl notes too the "occurrence of individuals killed by arrows in the Mesolithic cemeteries and depictions of archery battles."[95] Steven J. Mithen likewise discusses the numerous projectile points embedded in human and animal skeletons: "Numerous skeletons from these Mesolithic cemeteries have injuries caused by projectile points." At one cemetery "traces of cut marks and fractures on human bones suggest the extraction of marrow and cannibalism."[96] Evidence also survives of human sacrifice, sometimes of children.[97] The remains of fortifications also belie the peaceful nature of Old Europe: "Defensive architecture such as palisades, ditches and earthen banks appear by the fifth millennium

B.C.... and precede any evidence for [Kurgan] steppe intrusion, no matter how generously interpreted."[98] In sum, the many weapons that have been discovered, from arrow-points to maces, as well as the remains of fortifications in many sites, all testify to the reality of inter-group violence during this period of presumed peace and tranquillity.

But what about social organization? Was Old Europe as egalitarian and free of dominating hierarchies? Once more, evidence exists that suggests otherwise. The persistence of hunting throughout this period implies not just a penchant for and technology of violence, since any weapon that can kill an animal can kill a man, but also suggests castes and a developed hierarchical organization. Speaking of the Upper Paleolithic hunter/gatherers, Paul Mellars argues "that almost any social system which involved the regular formation of relatively large and stable social units would have required some form of division of authority or ranking within the societies, if only to provide the necessary degree of integration and co-ordination of the activities of the groups as a whole (as, for example, in the organization of communal hunting activities.)"[99] Success at hunting could have been a source of higher status in the community, as suggested by grave goods discovered in Mesolithic cemeteries, three of which "contain evidence for vertical social differentiation, indicating that the first ranked societies of Europe appeared during the Mesolithic."[100] David Anthony says of later cemeteries in the east Balkans, center of Gimbutas's Old European Golden Age, that they "contain clear evidence of hierarchical status differences, and the richest sexable graves are of males."[101] The same environmental and demographic pressures that made warfare likely would also have ensured that those males adept at the physical violence and leadership which secured game and protected resources would have enjoyed higher prestige and power.[102] In this context of competition for resources and the struggle to maintain living standards, it is hard to credit Gimbutas's picture of peaceful and egalitarian societies able to secure sufficient nutrition and security without conflict, coercive power, and violence.

Finally, like the idealizers of the Indian or of pre-agricultural peoples, Gimbutas ignores the everyday hardships and suffering that all human beings endured before modern medical and agricultural technology. Apart from war and violence, people suffered from diseases like arthritis, caries, and rickets, infections from broken bones, and parasites and bacteria spawned in tainted food and water. Insects, unseasonable storms, blight, drought, and fluctuations in animal herd populations frequently created famines that killed many people and weakened others, leaving them even more vulnerable to disease. The fury of nature and its predators must have been a constant source of anxiety and danger, as were superstitious fears of occult and supernatural forces. Women were particularly vulnerable to complications in pregnancy and childbirth and probably bore a greater toll from the hard physical labor necessary to ensure survival. In short, all of the destructive contingencies of human existence, from which modern Westerners are protected by technology and wealth, would have shortened life for our ancestors and made what life they had hard and dangerous—a far cry from the rosy picture painted by Gimbutas and her followers who take for granted a level of nutrition, material comfort, and personal safety impossible in ancient times.

Gimbutas's theory about the Kurgan invasion of Indo-European-speaking warriors who destroyed this once-peaceful culture is equally suspect. Gimbutas's picture of the nomadic, pastoralist Indo-Europeans derives as much or more from the nineteenth century as it does from the evidence. Prehistorian Colin Renfrew has challenged many of the assumptions that have gone into the popular depiction of the movements of Indo-Europeans and has offered an alternative model in which the gradual diffusion of Indo-European-speaking farmers from Anatolia replaces the more melodramatic saga of bloodthirsty, horse-riding killers swarming, like cattle-baron gunslingers in a grade-B western, out of the steppes to ravage and conquer the peaceful Old European farmers.[103] J. P. Mallory also finds Gimbutas's theory dubious, noting that "almost all of the arguments for invasion and cultural transformations are far better explained without reference to Kurgan expansions, and most of the evidence so far presented is either totally contradicted by other evidence or is the result of gross misinterpretation of the cultural history of Eastern, Central, and Northern Europe."[104] Though genetic studies have not completely verified Renfrew's model, one recent study has concluded that "the long-distance migrations postulated by Gimbutas remain an unnecessary element in the evolution of Indo-European populations, as reconstructed from the comparison of theoretical models and gene-frequency data. Migrations in the late Neolithic…are not reflected in the current genetic structure of Indo-European populations."[105] In short, like the myth of a Golden Age Old Europe, the theory of invading hordes of Indo-Europeans is at best an oversimplification of some nugget of historical reality, at worst pure fantasy.

MARKETING THE GODDESS

But that has not stopped the Goddess from spreading her message, and more than any other book, Riane Eisler's 1987 *The Chalice and the Blade* popularized the myth of the Goddess and her Golden Age prehistorical paradise. The book has gone through numerous printings and sold hundreds of thousands of copies, carrying the good news of the Goddess and her healing wisdom to an audience larger than one any academic could command. Part of the book's appeal, as Cynthia Eller points out, lies in the way it makes the Goddess more attractive by toning down the anti-male, radical feminist tone that characterizes the work of some Goddess scholars. For example, Eisler substitutes the neologism "gylany," ("woman-man rule,") for "matriarchy," thus avoiding the uncomfortable fact that no matriarchal societies can be documented to have ever existed and cleverly heading off the implication that women can be as power-driven and "hegemonic" as men. She turns Jesus into a feminist hero of sorts, and so defuses the more pagan, anti-Christian implications of those Goddess enthusiasts who, as seen above, excoriate the notion of a Big Daddy God making a yucky blood-sacrifice out of his son. And most important, the therapeutic objective of Goddess worship is expanded beyond strange female-centered rituals into a "partnership way" more attractive to middle-class heterosexual couples anxious to nurture their relationships and fulfill themselves. As Eller says, "Eisler has allowed feminist spirituality's sacred history to be marketed to whole new constituencies that might not have been receptive to feminist spirituality itself."[106]

That the therapeutic function of *The Chalice and the Blade* is its main focus is obvious from the accompanying workbook, *The Partnership Way*, which Eisler wrote to provide techniques for applying the lessons of the Goddess to modern lives—lessons on how to live without hierarchies and conformity and all those other nasty things that are the heritage of the "dominator" way introduced into European civilization by the Iron Age Indo-Europeans. In this, Eisler follows the academics who continually validate their writings by implicit or explicit transformational claims for both the individual and society. Eisler has an inflated estimation of her work's import: "This book opens a door," Eisler begins. "The key to unlock it was fashioned by many people and many books, and it will take many more to fully explore [sic] the vast vistas that lie behind it." This revolutionary achievement, Eisler goes on to explain, results from her "passionate concern about the human situation," a situation of imminent apocalypse her book can remedy, because it has answered the perennial questions that have exercised philosophy and religion for centuries.[107]

This therapeutic utopianism, however, is predicated on and legitimized by the claim that Eisler has discovered a new *truth* about the past and human nature, one based on evidence gathered by previous scholars:

Weaving together evidence from art, archaeology, religion, social science, history, and many other fields of inquiry into new patterns that more accurately fit the best available data, *The Chalice and the Blade* tells a new story of our cultural origins. It shows that war and the "war of the sexes" are neither divinely nor biologically ordained. And it provides verification that a better future *is* possible—and is in fact firmly rooted in the haunting drama of what actually happened in our past [xv].

Apart from its sheer hubris, this passage exemplifies the subordination of empirical procedure to the demands of therapeutic utopianism vitiating most of the work of Goddess adherents. It shows as well that the authority for Eisler's fantastic projections derives precisely from this aura of scientific truth bestowed by appeals to empirical procedures she has rejected. Reviewers of Eisler's book acknowledged its scientific authority by using phrases like "evidence indicates" and "well-documented and clear analysis,"[108] and they spoke of "archaeological clues" that "provide evidence."[109] Eisler herself in an interview used phrases like "my research shows," and confidently asserted that "evidence we now have indicates that this [her "partnership way"] was the original direction of our cultural evolution for over twenty thousand years."[110] Her fawning interviewer likewise gushed about Eisler's "incredibly transdisciplinary work, drawing from many fields of science," and referred to the "archaeological discoveries" that are as momentous as Columbus's discovery of America.[111]

This claim of discovered truth makes it easier for nonspecialists and scholars alike to credit the transformational powers Eisler asserts for this new information. One reviewer, for example, entertains the hope "that we can find our way through toward such an equalitarian, non-exploitative and nonviolent society" as the one Eisler's research presumably has shown to have existed in European prehistory.[112] Eisler herself modestly believes her book "will help free our

minds and our hands so that we may do what we are so uniquely able
to do: be creative, be caring, and pursue the human quest for truth,
justice, and beauty."[113] However, without the authority of factual
truth acquired through presumably flawed Western patriarchal
empirical procedures, most of us would not take these extravagant
transformational claims any more seriously than we take those of
New Age tabloid spiritualists or psychic hotline advisors. And a
closer look at Eisler's interpretation of that evidence reveals that, by
Eisler's own admission, the evidence is very uncertain.

The following passage taken from Eisler's work illustrates her
simultaneous confidence in the accuracy of her description of Old
Europe and her hesitancy about the evidence supporting that
description:

> These cave sanctuaries, figurines, burials, and rites all *seem to have been*
> related to a belief that the same source from which human life
> springs is also the source of all vegetable and animal life—the great
> Mother Goddess or Giver of All we still find in later periods of
> Western civilization. They also *suggest* that our early ancestors recog-
> nized that we and our natural environment are integrally linked
> parts of the great mystery of life and death and that all nature must
> therefore be treated with respect (3, emphasis added).

Notice that the confident description of prehistoric Europe's beliefs
in both sentences is linked to the evidence by the rhetorical loopholes
"seem" and "suggest." Notice too that the concrete evidence itself—
"cave sanctuaries, figurines, burials"—is slyly grouped with definitely *un*concrete "rites" for which little or no hard evidence remains,
and which thus have to be imaginatively reconstructed by modern
scholars. Furthermore, this concrete evidence from a vast variety of
locales and time periods is here promiscuously lumped together and
generalized into supporting this "belief" in a Mother Goddess, when
in actual fact this highly heterogeneous evidence can bear any

number of interpretations. Finally, the "belief" Eisler describes ultimately has its origins in Western Romantic assumptions about
nature, assumptions that Eisler projects back onto the scanty, diverse,
and fragmentary archaeological evidence. We don't know what our
"ancestors" thought, but it's a good bet that they—dependent for
their survival on an indifferent and fickle environment and vulnerable to predators and natural forces they could not control—looked on
nature with *fear* rather than with the sentimental "respect" that a
technology-protected, well-fed modern can afford.

Throughout this section of her book, Eisler laces her confident
re-creations of prehistoric European society with rhetorical escape
hatches and anachronistic projections. A few pages after the passage
quoted above, for example, Eisler damningly admits that "because of
the scarceness of their remains and the long time span between us
and them, we probably never will be entirely certain of the specific
meaning their paintings, figurines, and symbols had for our
Paleolithic forebears." So why should we credit Eisler's assertive
description of that "meaning," let alone take seriously the portentous ameliorative benefits that meaning supposedly will bring?

Eisler's recreation of European prehistory is not so much based
on factual evidence as it is a reflection of our old friend, the Western
myth of a peaceful Golden Age disrupted by a wicked Iron Age, a
myth Eisler cites, along with that New Age staple, the myth of
Atlantis, as evidence for a real-life prehistoric paradise (61-62). The
key motif of the Golden Age myth, the harmony of humans with a
beneficent nature that provides freely all of humanity's needs, dominates Eisler's reconstruction of Old European society: "Indeed, this
theme of the unity of all things in nature, as personified by the
Goddess, seems to permeate Neolithic art. For here the supreme
power governing the universe is a divine Mother who gives her
people life, provides them with material and spiritual nurturance,
and who even in death can be counted on to take her children back
into her cosmic womb" (19; note again the sly shift from "seems" to

"is"). In such a society the "primary purpose of art, and of life, was not to conquer, pillage, and loot but to cultivate the earth and provide the material and spiritual wherewithal for a satisfying life" (20). And like the dwellers of the Golden Age, the Old Europeans enjoyed "common ownership of the principal means of production" and a "basically cooperative social organization" (42). Needless to say, neither Eisler nor anybody else has *any* evidence for these fantastic idealizations, all of which reflect modern preoccupations and assumptions, particularly a vague socialist economics. They are projections gratifying the psychic needs of anxious, civilized moderns.

What happened to this Golden Age paradise? It was destroyed by invasions of Indo-Europeans, who possessed "a social system in which male dominance, male violence, and a generally hierarchic and authoritarian social structure was the norm"(45). Moreover, unlike those communal, cooperative Old Europeans, the Indo-Europeans "acquired material wealth…not by developing technologies of production, but through ever more effective technologies of destruction" (45). That is, war, political oppression, and greed were the awful consequences of these invaders from the East—precisely the same evils that the Iron Age myth identifies with civilization. The "blade" of domination and destruction gradually replaced the "chalice" of cooperation and love. In Eisler's hands, history no longer is the record of humanity's encounter with its tragic limitations but a therapeutic melodrama.

THERAPEUTIC MELODRAMA—AGAIN

Like Romantic environmentalism and Noble Savage Indianism, Goddess history offers a gratifying myth in the guise of empirical fact—precisely the combination of scientism and debased Romanticism we have already repeatedly encountered. Indeed, the origins of Goddess religions can be found, not in the new discoveries of archaeological science, but in the nineteenth-century's anti-

Enlightenment pique. It was then that theories of matriarchy arose out of a welter of "neopagan occultism and the radical feminist political agenda."[114] The writer often claimed as an intellectual ancestor of modern Goddess scholarship, J. J. Bachofen, must be understood in the context of nineteenth-century middle-class estimations of women as superior vessels of intuitive insight and nurturing power.[115] David Anthony, for his part, has pointed out the nineteenth-century roots of the Indo-European invasion myth in German Romanticism.[116] Then, of course, the civilizing Aryan invaders were the good guys bearing the gifts of civilization to European subhumans sunk in barbarism. We all know the horrific racist outcome of *that* distortion of history. But as Anthony points out, modern Goddess religion has endorsed the same fundamental myth: "Both interpretations share the same theoretical and logical form; it is only a politically motivated reversal of the 'good' and the 'bad' that separates them."[117] Like the myth of Aryan superiority, the myth of wicked Indo-Europeans destroying a paradisal Old Europe is a piece of pernicious false knowledge.

This myth is dangerous for two reasons. First, since it is a religious myth disguised as scientific fact, it distorts our historical understanding by presenting fanciful conjectures as empirically verified facts, thus obtaining for the former the authority and prestige of the latter. Moreover, the rational process by which we ultimately establish the truths of history is compromised. The admission of irrational "intuition" or "feeling" as the guarantors of truth is unwarranted. By these criteria, anything can be touted as true. Finally, as the previous two chapters attest, a false picture of the human condition is presented, one in which the tragic limitations of all humans, their subjection to a world of contingency and chance as well as to their own destructive passions, are wished away. We are left with impossible solutions for our problems, and utopian fantasies that can only gratify our inauthentic desire that the world and ourselves be other than they are.

Second, as feminist critic Rene Denfeld points out in this chapter's epigraph, the Goddess religion and its myths deflect energy and attention from the real problems pressing women today. As social critic Elizabeth Kristol has written, "Social groups that are confronted with political, cultural, and economic challenges are embracing utopian visions in a vain effort to comfort themselves in the present moment."[118] Those challenges will be best confronted from within the Western tradition of Enlightenment liberalism and rationalism that, more than anything in history, have improved the lot of those women who have been fortunate enough to be born in the societies shaped by that tradition. To deny that truth and demonize, in the name of emotionally gratifying fantasy, the very tradition that has made it possible for women today to live long and productive lives, that has liberated women from the drudgery of physical labor and the tyranny of biology, that has given them political rights and privileges still denied to masses of women today—the ability to reject the Western traditions that have made the minds and bodies of these Goddess worshipers what they are—is to indulge a false knowledge rendered even more noxious by hypocrisy and ingratitude.

CONCLUSION ■ THE EXAMINED LIFE

The unexamined life is not worth living for a human.

—SOCRATES[1]

The three versions of history as therapeutic melodrama that have been examined in the previous chapters are united by more than their reworking of the Golden Age myth. All three are also stories in the ideology misleadingly called "Multiculturalism," the dominant narrative used by popular culture and many intellectuals alike to explain our historical moment and public moral goals.[2] Despite what we are led to believe by its apologists, Multiculturalism is not about respecting cultural differences or the diversity of ethnic groups in America.[3] Multiculturalism is instead a melodramatic tale of the wickedness of the West and its role in destroying the peaceful paradises in which other peoples (usually "of color") lived before Europeans and then Americans came along to inflict on them racism, sexism, slavery, colonialism, imperialism, homophobia, technology, and environmental degradation.[4] As Arthur Schlesinger puts it:

Self-styled "multiculturalists" are very often ethnocentric separatists who see little in the Western heritage beyond Western crimes. The Western tradition, in this view, is inherently racist, sexist, "classist," hegemonic; irredeemably repressive, irredeemably oppressive. The spread of Western culture is due not to any innate quality but simply to the spread of Western power.[5]

As such, Multiculturalism is perhaps the most dangerous false knowledge circulating among us.

This version of history is false because it assumes a Romantic view of human nature as benign if only it remains uncorrupted by a dysfunctional Western culture and ideology. This description of history, as we have seen above, is a version of the Noble Savage myth,[6] and as such is wrong on simple empirical grounds. World history is filled with the evidence of universal human depravity and evil, a wickedness that knows no distinctions of race, religion, culture, or gender. Conquest, plunder, war, torture, cruelty, slavery, oppression of women or minorities—all stain the record of human life no matter what period or what part of the globe. The West has been more *efficient* at these evils because of its intellectual dynamism: its ability rapidly to adjust to new circumstances, its voracious appropriation and improvement of whatever advantages it encounters in others, and its creation of a rational procedure for acquiring knowledge that has allowed it to harness the forces of nature and subject them to its will.

Yet this is not the whole story of the West. Its evil may have been a magnified, more efficient expression of universal human evil, but its good has been its invention alone—the idea of the individual, rational human being who should be free to choose, and who possesses certain inalienable rights that should demand our respect regardless of gender, race, religion, or culture.[7] This vision of human identity had its beginnings in ancient Athens and Jerusalem, and over the centuries its slow, painful development has been marked by its betrayal over and over again by those who perhaps should have known better. But despite that betrayal, it is the West that has identified those universal human evils like slavery or racism or sexism *as* evils to be rejected and combated; it is the West that has discovered natural rights, which inhere in *all* humans simply because they are human. And despite that betrayal, that ideal of freedom for the individual has survived, and today this vision of human rights, and the form of governance that enshrines it, democracy, represent the best hope that all humans, Western or not, have for creating societies in which freedom, justice, and respect for individuals take precedence over the appetites or whims or superstitions of various elites. In this sense the whole world is either Western or trying to become Western, for, as Jacques Ellul reminds us, they have "inherited the consciousness of and desire for freedom. Everything they do today and everything they seek is an expression of what the western world has taught them."[8] That is why Chinese dissidents erected a model of the Statue of Liberty in Tiananmen Square.

Moreover, for all its destructive side-effects, the science and technology often vilified as the mere instruments of Western oppression and hegemony have improved material life for billions of people, freeing them from starvation, disease, suffering, and back-breaking labor. This is so simply because science is the most successful mode for knowing the material world that humanity has ever had, which is why every culture concerned about its survival and material well-being is compelled to master the scientific style of knowledge.[9] That this style of knowledge and the attendant material prosperity have had grievous costs and unforeseen consequences cannot be denied. There are no unalloyed human goods, and those goods often are mutually exclusive. In choosing among them we must make trade-offs—and be mature enough to pay the price and to accept the possibility that the price ultimately may be too high. But as we have seen, the therapeutic sensibility protests against this tragic truth. These days we want to possess simultaneously all goods—freedom *and* equality, material well-being *and* spiritual richness, the freedom to choose *and* the freedom from accepting the responsibility for our choices—without footing the bill.

Since the goods we choose, then, always have costs we often don't anticipate, we cannot afford a perfectly triumphalist endorsement of the world the West has created. Too much history waits to be lived, too much unforeseen change and chance lurks in ambush around the next corner, too many unpredictable choices will be made by people yet to come. The question is still open of whether our interventions in nature will have catastrophic consequences, or whether the complexity and stress of high-tech urban life will ultimately be unbearable, or whether someday we will realize too late that we have gained the whole material world and lost our souls. As a fervent believer in the tragic vision of human life, I incline toward pessimism. But even as we criticize the "air-conditioned nightmare" and bemoan the banal vulgarity of consumer hedonism, even as we decry the soul-killing "cash nexus" and the wasteland of popular culture, we must be honest and admit how well off we are: how much freedom we enjoy because our individual rights are protected by shared codes and laws; how much physical comfort and good health and leisure are ours because science and technology have liberated us from humanity's epic struggle for survival with an indifferent nature; and how much wealth and leisure lie at our disposal because of consumer capitalism.[10] And we must confront this truth: that humanity has chosen, and is continuing to choose, freedom and physical comfort at the price of spiritual and cultural impoverishment. Some of us may think that this is a bad choice, but until we have the courage of our convictions to live *without* the wealth and freedom and leisure the West has created, we will remain mere hypocritical scolds.

This brings us to the second reason anti-Western Multiculturalism is dangerous false knowledge—its sheer hypocrisy. As should be clear by now, the anti-Western melodramas of

Romantic environmentalism or Noble Savage Indianism or the Old European Goddess are all themselves expressions of Western ideas and versions of a Western myth that developed in response to conditions arising in the West. We should note, too, that the idea of ethnic identity at the heart of Multiculturalism—the belief that membership in a group defines the individual in unique ways peculiar to that group—is likewise a Western one. Its birth was in the anti-Enlightenment thought of German Romantic nationalism, an ancestor as well of both fascism and Nazism.[11] "Like the racists before them," French critic Alain Finkielkraut writes, "contemporary fanatics of cultural identity confine individuals to their group of origin. Like them, they carry differences to the absolute extreme, and in the name of the multiplicity of specific causalities destroy any possibility of a natural or cultural community among peoples."[12]

For this reason we must be wary of the anti-humanist implications of some strains of Multiculturalism, its willingness to subordinate the autonomous, rational individual into a group defined in terms of its absolute, non-negotiable differences from other groups. Our democracy is founded on a radically different assumption: our *shared* humanity—comprising reason and free will, both of which are more essential to what we are than the accidents of race or ethnicity—bestows on us inalienable rights and allows us to form a political community whose main purpose is the protection of those rights for *individuals*. And this "public thing" embodies abstract laws and procedures that guarantee the freedom and rights of individuals regardless of their group origin. That this ideal has in the past been betrayed, and continues to be imperfectly realized today, testifies to our weakness as human beings, not to its inadequacy as an ideal.[13]

However, the greatest irony is that Multiculturalism's anti-Western thrust is likewise utterly Western. The very idea that individuals should be free to criticize their society is a Western one, and no tradition has been harder on the West than the West itself.[14]

Western history is filled with those lone voices that "spoke truth to power" and paid the price of imprisonment, death, or exile; remember, the two men most influential for Western ethics, Socrates and Jesus, were both executed as threats to society. Indeed, Western culture can be defined in terms of its adversarial stance to every public system of values and power. This tradition of critical consciousness, of the "opposing self," as Lionel Trilling called it, who defines himself in opposition to his society and culture, and so can speak against tyranny and cruelty and evil, is a Western creation and one of the most valuable contributions to humanity's well-being.

This point about the self-critical imperative unique to the West needs emphasizing. Earlier we mentioned critics of the Spanish conquest like de las Casas, who protested against the brutal treatment of the Indians. Or consider the slave-holder Thomas Jefferson's prophetic words about the "peculiar institution": "And can the liberties of a nation be thought secure when we have removed their only firm basis, a conviction in the minds of the people that these liberties are of the gift of God? That they are not to be violated but with his wrath?"[15] What other slave-holding society has voiced self-criticisms such as these? We hear much about the West's sins of colonialism, but conquest and exploitation are sad constants; more unusual are sentiments like those eloquently given voice by Edmund Burke in the following passage taken from his prosecution of his countryman William Hastings for the latter's brutality and cruelty in India: "The sun in his beneficent progress round the world does not behold a more glorious sight than that of men, separated from a remote people by the material bounds and barriers of nature, united by the bond of a social and moral community, all the Commons of England resenting as their own, the indignities and cruelties that are offered to all the people of India."[16] The burden of the Multiculturalist should be to account for the West's unique recognition that slavery and oppression *are* evils that violate universal principles.

Finally, not just the minds of most Multiculturalists, but also their bodies are the product of Western technology and science.[17] Not only do they criticize the West from the political safety and freedom provided by the West, but they also enjoy the health care, sanitation, nutrition, and leisure that Western science has created. None of the enthusiasts for non-Western cultures wants actually to live in countries where safe food and water, dependable electricity and gasoline, efficient and competent hospitals, legally restrained police and military forces, and functioning public utilities are all a rarity. We have not seen hordes of Americans fleeing an allegedly racist, sexist, soul-killing, high-tech, fast-paced society for the simpler, more fulfilling, more egalitarian, less repressed "organic" lives of non-Western "primal" peoples. I admit this point sounds like that first version of the *ad hominem* fallacy I mentioned at the start— pointing out that a person's life is incompatible with his beliefs— but as Aristotle said long ago, virtue is a question of action, not words. The incessant vehemence of the self-righteous attack on Western society and values on the part of those who enjoy the material and political benefits of the West compels notice that no matter what they may say, they have already voted for the West with their feet.

Multiculturalism, then, for all its pretensions to being historical truth, is not an accurate description of history or a coherent ethical system. It is instead a therapeutic myth, a version of history that gratifies the feelings of those who are disaffected with modern civilization. In short, in Multiculturalism we find concentrated the false knowledge about history and the human condition we have traced throughout this book.

So what is to be done? What solutions to this state of affairs will I now offer, what techniques or innovations or reformations that can scatter the fog of false knowledge and set us back on the sun-lit road to utopia? To give in to the temptation to answer these questions would be to indulge the misplaced faith in enlightenment through knowledge that I criticized in Chapter 1. After three hundred years

of shattered Crystal Palaces, we cannot afford to indulge the optimism that Sir Thomas Browne expressed when he wrote of the
future, "What Libraries of new Volumes aftertimes will behold, and
in what a new World of Knowledge the eyes of our Posterity may be
happy, a few Ages may joyfully declare; and is but a cold thought
unto those, who cannot hope to behold this Exantlation [drawing
up] of Truth, or that obscured Virgin half out of the Pit."[18] Though
Browne's optimism was warranted in the case of the natural sciences,
in terms of human nature and action and ethics, it was not. We
know that the Virgin of Truth is still in the pit, that the well of
ignorance is deeper than we thought. We know now that knowledge
about human life and values cannot be as firm and predictable as
knowledge about nature: "For," Isaiah Berlin points out, "as Tolstoy
taught us long ago, the particles are too minute, too heterogeneous,
succeed each other too rapidly, occur in combinations of too great a
complexity, are too much part and parcel of what we are and do, to
be capable of submitting to the required degree of abstraction, that
minimum of generalization and formalization—idealization—
which any science must exact."[19] There is no science of humanity, no
"technicians of the soul," no procedures for manipulating human
beings and their unpredictable choices in order to achieve some ideal
goal. Every attempt to do so has led in the end to bloody disaster.

But even if we cannot offer firm suggestions for improving our
lot, even if we cannot devise stratagems and techniques that will
usher in the brave new world, we are not thereby justified in retreat-
ing into obscurantism or mysticism or quietism. With Socrates as
our model of humane skepticism, we can expose error and cant both
in ourselves and others, without necessarily providing the wisdom
we find lacking in them. That is, we can lead what Socrates calls the
"examined life": questioning assumptions, demanding coherent
explanations and evidence, challenging received ideas, and exercising the critical consciousness that is our priceless heritage. Though
we may not be able to discover the final, absolute truth about our-

selves and solve what Alexander Pope called this "riddle of the world"—humanity—at least we will know what is false. And with that ability to detect and expose error and cant and "Prejudice and Prescription," we will possess the most important freedom of all—the freedom of our minds, our intellectual autonomy that allows us to confront the hard choices and make the hard decisions that are the responsibility of every citizen in a democracy.

NOTES

PREFACE

1. *Sir Thomas Browne's Pseudodoxia Epidemica*, ed. Robin Robbins, 2 vols. (Oxford, 1981), 1.8. Subsequent references will appear parenthetically by section and chapter number.

INTRODUCTION

1. Thomas Browne, *Christian Morals*, ed. L. C. Martin (Oxford, 1964), 221.

2. In *English Literature in the Earlier Seventeenth Century*, 2 ed. (Oxford, 1962), 1.

3. *The Garden of Cyrus*, in *Sir Thomas Browne. The Major Works*, ed. C. A. Patrides (London, 1977), 386.

4. For the origins of the *Pseudodoxia* see Jonathan F. S. Post, *Sir Thomas Browne* (Boston, 1987), 32.

5. For witches see *Religio Medici* 1.30.

6. In *Suspira De Profundis*.

7. For a recent brief critical history of the rise of modern science and technology and its impact on human experience see Albert Borgmann, *Crossing the Postmodern Divide* (Chicago and London, 1992), 20-47. A more extensive analysis can be found in Lewis Mumford's *The Myth of the Machine* (New York, 1967-70), especially Volume 2, *The Pentagon of Power*.

8. *Technopoly: The Surrender of Culture to Technology* (New York, 1992), 69-70. For a descriptive and analytic critique of the "information society" and its effects see Frank Webster, *Theories of the Information Society* (London and New York, 1995), especially 6-29.

9.   For an exposure of these various tabloid frauds see Carl Sagan, *The Demon Haunted World. Science as a Candle in the Dark* (New York, 1996); Michael Shermer, *Why People Believe Weird Things. Pseudoscience, Superstition, and Other Confusions of Our Time* (New York, 1997). For New Age spiritualist fads like guardian angels and *The Celestine Prophecy*, cf. Wendy Kaminer, "The Latest Fashion in Irrationality," *The Atlantic Monthly* 278.1 (July 1996), 103-6; more comprehensively M. D. Faber, *New Age Thinking: A Psychoanalytic Critique* (Ottawa, 1996).

10.   In *The Vision of the Anointed. Self-Congratulation as a Basis for Social Policy* (New York, 1995), 2. Relevant also to this book is Sowell's *Knowledge and Decisions* (1980; New York, 1996), which examines the institutional processes for authenticating knowledge that then becomes the basis of decision-making. Nearly twenty-five years ago Charles Fair examined what he called the "new nonsense" in terms similar to Sowell's: "That body of contemporary ideas which, although widely discussed and taken by many with the utmost seriousness, either lack support from existing evidence or are clearly contradicted by it." *The New Nonsense. The End of Rational Consensus* (New York, 1974), 33.

11.   Cf. Fair, *The New Nonsense*, 34: "The element common to all departments of the New Nonsense is simply an inclination to willful personal belief so strong that it amounts to a compulsion."

12.   See Lisa Bannon, "How a Rumor Spread about Subliminal Sex in Disney's 'Aladdin,'" *The Wall Street Journal* 133.80 (24 October 1995), A1.

13.   See the discussion by Jean-François Revel, *The Flight from Truth. The Reign of Deceit in the Age of Information*, trans. Curtis Cate (1988; New York, 1991), 163-229.

14.   Revel, *The Flight from Truth*, 163. The chapter "The Need for Ideology" is filled with modern examples of distortions of truth arising from adherence to ideology.

15.   See John Ellis's discussion of the Marxist Frederic Jameson, the most influential and oft-quoted literary critic in America; in *Literature Lost. Social Agendas and the Corruption of the Humanities* (New Haven and London, 1997), 119-39. Cf. 119: "The considerable vogue of Jameson's writings compels us to confront an exceedingly strange fact: just at the time when in the real world Marxism was collapsing so completely that its viability as a political theory seemed almost at an end, its influence in the universities of the English-speaking world was increasing just as dramatically."

16.   See the discussion by Stuart Sutherland, *Irrationality. Why We Don't Think Straight!* (New Brunswick, NJ, 1992), 16-34.

17.   A convenient list can be found in C. C. Hamblin, *Fallacies* (London, 1970), 9-49.

18.   Michael Oakeshott's distinction between processes and practices discussed by Neil Postman, "Social Science as Moral Theology," in *Conscientious Objections* (New York, 1988), 5-6.

19. See the discussion in Douglas N. Walton, *Informal Fallacies. Towards a Theory of Argument Criticisms* (Amsterdam and Philadelphia, 1987), 217-240.

20. Richard Bernstein, *The Dictatorship of Virtue. How the Battle over Multiculturalism is Reshaping our Schools, our Country, our Lives* (1994; New York, 1995), 132. This definition is Bernstein's summary of one generated by a 1992 Columbia University Conference on Race, Religion, and Ethnicity.

21. To justify "racist" as an epithet in the absence of overt racist behavior, as Dinesh D'Souza points out, scholars "have devised an extensive vocabulary which seeks to perform the difficult task of uncovering disguised and hidden forms of white racism." This vocabulary contains exotic species ranging from "crypto-racism" to "feel-good racism." In *The End of Racism. Principles for a Multiracial Society* (New York, 1995), 15.

22. Thomas Gilovich, *How We Know What Isn't So. The Fallibility of Human Reason in Everyday Life* (New York,1991), 3. See too Shermer, who lists twenty-five ways "thinking goes wrong," *Why People Believe Weird Things,* 44-61.

23. Gilovich, 21.

24. Gilovich, 29-72.

25. For a recent insightful discussion of the ambivalence of science see Roger Shattuck, *Forbidden Knowledge. From Prometheus to Pornography* (New York, 1996), 173-225.

26. See Raymond Tallis, *Newton's Sleep. The Two Cultures and the Two Kingdoms* (New York and London, 1995), 13. Tallis's book is an excellent antidote to the oversimplistic criticisms of science too often found in humanist commentary, including no doubt my own.

27. In *The Age of Enlightenment,* (1956; New York, 1984), 29.

28. In *The Flight From Truth,* 6.

CHAPTER 1

1. *Notes from Underground,* trans. by Jessie Coulson (Harmondsworth, England, 1972), 29.

2. Nor is this assumption restricted to the liberal end of the political spectrum. The Republican-sponsored welfare reform bill vetoed by President Clinton in January of 1996 had a provision that would have given $75 million dollars to the states for "abstinence education" in order "to teach youngsters 'the social, psychological, and health gains to be realized from abstaining from sexual activity' until they are married." Al Kamen, "The Emphasis is on Dependence Prevention," *The Washington Post National Weekly Edition,* 13.11 (January 15-21, 1996), 15.

3. See the recent article by Stephen Glass, "Don't You D.A.R.E.," *The New Republic,* no. 4,285 (3 March 1997), 18-28.

4. Mary Gibbs, "How Should We Teach our Kids about Sex?" *Time* (24 May

1993), 60. See Sowell, *The Vision of the Anointed*, 15-21, for the fallacies underlying sex education programs.

5. Laura Hubbs-Tait, Lance C. Garmon, "The Relationship of Moral Reasoning and AIDS Knowledge to Risky Sexual Behavior," *Adolescence*, 30.119 (Fall 1995), 549-564.

6. 5.17.39, trans. J. E. King, *Loeb Classical Library*.

7. In *The Enlightenment: An Interpretation. Vol. 2: The Science of Freedom* (1969; New York, 1977), 5-6.

8. Isaiah Berlin, "Montesquieu," in *Against the Current*, ed. Henry Hardy (New York, 1980), 135. Not all Enlightenment philosophers wholeheartedly believed in progress; a strain of pessimism about the persistence of human ignorance and folly runs throughout their thinking. See Gay, *The Science of Freedom*, 98-108.

9. In "The Pursuit of the Ideal," in *The Crooked Timber of Humanity*, ed. Henry Hardy (New York, 1991), 5.

10. In *Social Studies* (London, 1892). Quoted in Phillip Rieff, *The Triumph of the Therapeutic. Uses of Faith after Freud* (New York, 1966), 4. A recent critical history of the myth of progress can be found in Christopher Lasch, *The True and Only Heaven. Progress and its Critics* (New York, 1991), 40-81.

11. *Democracy in America*, 1.18. Trans. Philips Bradley (1945; New York, 1994).

12. See as a particularly enlightening example the essays of Frederick Crews collected in *Skeptical Engagements* (Oxford, 1986), 3-111; and his recent *The Memory Wars. Freud's Legacy in Dispute* (New York, 1996). Also Ernest Gellner, *The Psychoanalytic Movement. The Cunning of Unreason*, 2 ed. (1993; Evanston, Illinois, 1996). For sociology see Stanislav Andreski, *Social Sciences as Sorcery* (New York, 1972); more briefly, Page Smith, *Killing the Spirit. Higher Education in America* (New York, 1990), 223-52.

13. In *Pluto's Republic* (Oxford and New York, 1982), 72.

14. Wendy Kaminer, *I'm Dysfunctional, You're Dysfunctional. The Recovery Movement and Other Self-Help Fashions* (New York, 1992), 3.

15. For the Recovery Network see Ruth Shalit, "Dysfunction Junction," *The New Republic*, no. 4,291 (14 April 1997), 24-26.

16. Michael Shermer elaborates on the parallels between witch-hunts and the recovered-memory accusations in *Why People Believe Weird Things*, 108-113.

17. See Frederick Crews, *The Memory Wars*, 17-18; Richard Webster, *Why Freud Was Wrong* (New York, 1995), especially 245-45.

18. *The Standard Edition of the Complete Psychological Works of Sigmund Freud*, trans. J. Strachey et al. (London, 1953-74), 1914: 14:16.

19. David S. Holmes, "The Evidence for Repression: An Examination of Sixty Years of Research," in *Repression and Dissociation: Implications for Personality Theory, Psychotherapy, and Health*, ed. Jerome L. Singer (Chicago, 1990), 96.

20. For exposure of recovered-memory abuses see the following studies: Elizabeth Loftus and Katherine Ketcham, *The Myth of Repressed Memory: False Memories and Allegations of Sexual Abuse* (New York, 1994); Ellen Bass and Laura Davis, *Making Monsters: False Memories, Psychotherapy, and Sexual Hysteria* (New York, 1994); Mark Pendergrast, *Victims of Memory: Incest Accusations and Shattered Lives* (New York, 1994). More briefly, "Remind Me One More Time...," *The Economist*, vol. 342 (18 January 1997), 75-77.

21. In July 1996 Franklin's retrial was abandoned by prosecutors after DNA testing cleared him of a second murder his daughter had accused him of, and after Eileen Lipsky's sister claimed that she and Lipsky had been hypnotized before the first trial; see Shermer, 112.

22. For a critique of the study see Christine Hoff Sommers, *Who Stole Feminism? How Women Have Betrayed Women* (New York, 1994), 137-56. More briefly cf. Richard Bernstein, *The Dictatorship of Virtue*, 194-99.

23. For the abuse of statistics in "studies" see Thomas Sowell, *The Vision of the Anointed*, 31-63.

24. In *A Mathematician Reads the Newspaper* (New York, 1994), 120.

25. Quoted by Marc Fisher, "Worth a Thousand Pictures. Joseph Mitchell's Words Defined a World," *The Washington Post* (25 May 1996), C1.

26. In "Fire in the Hole: Hard Times for These Times, Too," *The North American Review*, 280.4 (July/August 1995), 39-42.

27. *The Illusion of Technique. A Search for Meaning in a Technological Civilization* (New York), 1978. See too John Ralston Saul, *Voltaire's Bastards. The Dictatorship of Reason in the West* (New York, 1992).

28. "Montesquieu," in *Against the Current*, ed. Henry Hardy (New York, 1980), 160.

29. *Notes from Underground*, 33-34.

30. Ernst Gombrich's phrase *idola quantitatis* quoted by Medawar, *Pluto's Republic*, 167.

CHAPTER 2

1. *Faust*, Part 1. Line 3455, trans. David Luke, Oxford, 1987.

2. Letter, 31 August 1813, in Byron's *Letters and Journals*, Leslie A Marchland, London, 1974.

3. *Medea* 1079-80.

4. Walter Jackson Bate, *From Classic to Romantic. Premises of Taste in Eighteenth-Century England* (1946; New York, 1961), 130.

5. Isaiah Berlin, "The Counter-Enlightenment," in *Against the Current*, ed. Henry Hardy (New York, 1980), 14.

6. See Simon Schama, *Landscape and Memory* (New York, 1995), 102-3.

7. Isaiah Berlin, "The Apotheosis of the Romantic Will. The Revolt against the

Myth of an Ideal World," in *The Crooked Timber of Humanity*, ed. Henry Hardy (New York, 1991), 219.

8. In "On the Discriminations of Romanticisms," 1924; rpt. in *Essays in the History of Ideas* (Baltimore, MD, 1948), 247.

9. Quoted by Berlin, "The Counter-Enlightenment," 22-23.

10. *The Sorrows of Young Werther,* trans. Catherine Hutter (New York, 1962), 26, 83. Subsequent references parenthetical.

11. See Joseph Epstein on the subsidized and institutionalized "rebellion" of modern artists, in "What to Do About the Arts," in *Dumbing Down: Essays on the Strip Mining of American Culture,* ed. Katherine Washburn and John P. Thornton (New York, 1996), 179-93.

12. For the rise of romantic love and "affective individualism" see Lawrence Stone, *The Family, Sex and Marriage in England 1500-1800* (New York, 1977), 221-69.

13. This connection between consumerism and Romanticism thoroughly developed by Colin Campbell, *The Romantic Ethic and the Spirit of Modern Consumerism* (London, 1987).

14. In *Eros and Civilization* (Boston, 1955). 197.

15. "The Last Taboo," in *Dumbing Down*, 166

CHAPTER 3

1. Sigmund Freud, *Civilization and its Discontents*, trans. James Strachey (New York, 1961), 33.

2. *Landscape and Memory*, 14. See too William Cronon, "The Trouble with Wilderness. Or, Getting Back to the Wrong Nature," in *Uncommon Ground. Toward Reinventing Nature*, ed. William Cronon (New York and London, 1995), 69-90.

3. In *The New Ecological Order*, trans. Carol Volk (1992; Chicago and London, 1995), xxviii; see too 3-18.

4. Victor Davis Hanson, *Warfare and Agriculture in Classical Greece*, rev. ed. (Berkeley and Los Angeles, 1998), 2.

5. *Homeric Hymn to Demeter* 1-5; *Odyssey* 5.63-73; *Bacchae* 677-768.

6. *Idyll* 1.17-18.

7. *Georgics* 1.145-46. Trans. L. P. Wilkinson (Harmondsworth, Eng., 1982).

8. The most recent influential example of this indictment of Christianity is Lynn White, Jr., "The Historical Roots of Our Ecological Crisis," in J. White, ed., *Machina ex Deo*, Cambridge, Mass., 1968. For a brief criticism of this view see Keith Thomas, *Man and the Natural World. A History of the Modern Sensibility* (New York, 1983), 22-24.

9. For the ambiguous role of nature in Christianity see Mark Stoll, *Protestantism, Capitalism, and Nature in America* (Albuquerque, NM, 1997), 11-28.

10. *Purgatorio* 30.22-27.

11. In *La Nouvelle Héloïse*, 1.26; trans. Judith H. McDowell (University Park and London, 1968).

12. See Thomas, *Man and the Natural World*, 262-63, who points out that in England the success in bringing more land under cultivation, and the fad of symmetrical landscape-gardening, increased the aesthetic value of uncultivated landscapes.

13. "Lines," 21, 24-30.

14. "Ode: Intimations of Immortality," 67.

15. *Madame Bovary*, trans. Paul de Man (New York, 1965), 58.

16. *Landscape and Memory*, 573.

17. For the influence of tobacco company money on some environmental organizations' public policies see Margaret Morgan-Hubbard, "Money and Environmental Groups. How Clean is 'Green'?" *Environmental Action*, 27.4 (1996), 20-23.

18. *The Dream of the Earth* (San Francisco, CA, 1988), 4.

19. In "On Human Connectedness with Nature," *New Literary History* 24.4 (1993), 797-809.

20. Greg Easterbrook, *A Moment on the Earth. The Coming Age of Environmental Optimism* (New York, 1995), 119.

21. See Gregg Easterbrook, "Forgotten Benefactor of Humanity," *The Atlantic Monthly*, 279.1 (January 1997), 74-82.

22. Jean-Jacques Rousseau, *Discourse on Inequality*, trans. Julia Conaway Bondarella (New York, 1988), 16 n.9.

23. See Arthur O. Lovejoy and George Boas, *Primitivism and Related Ideas in Antiquity* (1935; New York, 1965), 288-90.

24. *Tusculan Disputations* 5.32, trans. J. E. King, Loeb Classical Library.

25. See the discussion by Simon Schama, *Landscape and Memory*, 81-87.

26. Roderick Nash, *Wilderness and the American Mind*, rev. ed. (New Haven, 1973), 47-48. A brief description of the Wild Man tradition can be found in Olive Patricia Dickason, *The Myth of the Savage and the Beginnings of French Colonialism in the Americas* (Edmonton, 1984), 70-80.

27. For European conceptions of Amerindians see, in addition to the works to be cited in the next section, *First Images of America: The Impact of the New World on the Old*, ed. Fredi Chiappelli (Berkeley and Los Angeles, 1976), especially Aldo Scaglione, "A Note on Montaigne's *Des Cannibales* and the Humanist Tradition," vol. 1, 63-70; and Wilcomb E. Washburn, "The Clash of Morality in the American Forest," vol. 1, 335-50; Dickason, *The Myth of the Savage*, 5-84. Cf. P. J. Marshall and Glyndwr Williams: "The concept of an innocent primitive had been present in western culture almost from its literate beginnings, but the age of discoveries had brought him from a remote past to the present, distant in space but no longer in time, available for scrutiny, dissection, perhaps emulation," in *The Great Map of Mankind. Perceptions of New Worlds in the Age of Enlightenment* (Cambridge, MA, 1982), 187.

28. In *The Conquest of Granada*, Part I, Act I, Scene 1. See Peter Gay, *The Science of Freedom*, 90-98, for the noble savage in Enlightenment thought.

29. *Discourse on Inequality*, 4.

30. In Hoxie Neale Fairchild, *The Noble Savage. A Study in Romantic Naturalism* (1928; New York, 1951), 8-11. Fairchild provides numerous other examples of Indians as noble savages. See too Robert F. Berkhofer, Jr., *The White Man's Indian. Images of the American Indian from Columbus to the Present* (New York, 1978), 6-31 and 72-80; Jean-Jacques Simard, "White Ghosts, Red Shadows: The Reduction of North American Natives," in *The Invented Indian.Cultural Fictions and Government Policies*, ed. James A. Clifton (New Brunswick and London, 1990), 333-69.

31. "Of Cannibals," in *The Complete Essays of Montaigne*, trans. Donald M. Frame (Stanford, CA, 1958), 152. Subsequent references parenthetical.

32. See Revel, *The Flight from Truth*, 175-77; D'Souza, *The End of Racism*, 149-51. More comprehensively see Derek Freeman, *Margaret Mead and Samoa. The Making and Unmaking of an Anthropological Myth* (Cambridge, Mass., 1983). For Diderot see Gay, *The Science of Freedom*, 146-59; for other idealizing accounts by South Sea travellers see Fairchild, 97-120.

33. For modern examples of the noble savage myth see Gaile McGregor, *The Noble Savage in the New World Garden. Notes toward a Syntactics of Place* (Toronto and Bowling Green, 1988), 177-308.

34. See D'Souza, *The End of Racism* 58-62, for the circumstances that inhibited the idealization of black Africans.

35. 1957; in *Advertisements for Myself* (New York, 1959), 337-58. References henceforth parenthetical.

36. In "The Decline of Utopian Ideals in the West," 30.

37. My translation. Aetna is a didactic poem once thought to be by Vergil but now dated around the first century A.D.

38. For the Golden Age/Iron Age myths related to the theme of Western decline see Arthur Herman, *The Idea of Decline in Western History* (New York, 1997), 13-45.

39. For primary texts readers should see the invaluable study by Lovejoy and Boas, *Primitivism and Related Ideas in Antiquity*.

40. *Prometheus Bound,* 506.

41. *Work and Days,* 109-120, trans. Hugh G. Evelyn-White, Loeb Classical Library. Subsequent line references parenthetical.

42. *Metamorphoses* 1.131.

43. For the Golden Age myth in modern goddess feminism, Afrocentrism, and "deep" ecology see Elizabeth Kristol, "History in the Past Perfect," *First Things* (April 1991), 43-49.

44. In "The Apotheosis of the Romantic Will," 236-37.

45. *Discourse on Inequality*, 13, 16.

46. In *From Classic to Romantic*, 160.

47. *Notes from Underground*, 35.

48. *The Higher Superstition. The Academic Left and its Quarrel with Science* (Baltimore and London, 1994), 3. See too the description of the New York Academy of Sciences spring 1995 conference "The Flight from Science and Reason" by Rita Zürcher, "Farewell to Reason: A Tale of Two Conferences," *Academic Questions* 9.2 (Spring 1996), 52-54.

49. Numerous critiques of these poststructuralist positions are available; see e.g. J. G. Merquior, *From Prague to Paris: A Critique of Structuralist and Poststructuralist Thought* (New York and London, 1986); Luc Ferry and Alain Renaut, *French Philosophy of the Sixties: An Essay on Antihumanism*, trans. Mary H. S. Cattani (Amherst, MA, 1990); John Ellis, *Against Deconstruction* (Princeton, NJ, 1991); Frederick Crews, *Skeptical Engagements* (Oxford, 1986).

50. Vincent B. Leitch, *Deconstructive Criticism. An Advanced Introduction* (New York, 1983), 58.

51. "We've Done it to Ourselves. The Critique of Truth and the Attack on Theory," in *PC Wars. Politics and Theory in the Academy*, ed. Jeffrey Williams (New York and London, 1995), 174. See too Christopher Norris, *New Idols of the Cave. On the Limits of Anti-realism* (Manchester and New York, 1997).

52. In *The Deconstruction of Literature. Criticism after Auschwitz* (Hanover, NH and London, 1991), 267.

53. Hirsch, 255.

54. *Higher Superstition*, 46. The case for science also clearly made by Raymond Tallis, *Newton's Sleep. The Two Cultures and the Two Kingdoms* (New York and London, 1995), and *In Defense of Realism* (London, 1988). Cf. 25: "Facts are selected and constructed, but they are not invented; they are made but they are not made up."

55. For an analysis of the work of Kuhn, Karl Popper, P. K. Feyerabend, and I. Lakatos—all of whom have provided the intellectual underpinnings of the attack on scientific knowledge—see David Stove, *Popper and After. Four Modern Irrationalists* (Oxford and New York, 1982).

56. See K. L. Billingsley, "Lost in Space," *Heterodoxy* 3.10/4.1 (Dec. 1995/Jan. 1996), 12. For other examples of scientific illiteracy see Robert L. Park, "Voodoo Science," in *Dumbing Down*, 149-56.

57. See Gerald Holton, "Science Education and the Sense of Self," *Partisan Review* 63.2 (1996), 205-214. Just how far this daffiness permeates the humanities/social sciences professoriate was revealed recently by the physicist Alan Sokal. He wrote an article parodying the vacuous ideas and pretentious jargon of the postmodern anti-science sensibility, making sure to lard his argument with the obligatory pseudo-liberationist cliches that legitimize the empty prose. Several editors of the "cutting edge" journal *Social Text* approved

the article for publication and it appeared in the May 1996 issue. See Janny Scott, "Postmodern Gravity Deconstructed, Slyly," *The New York Times* (18 May 1996), 1; Steven Weinberg, "Sokal's Hoax," *The New York Review of Books*, 63.13 (8 August 1996), 11-15.

58. In *Science and its Fabrication* (Minneapolis, MN, 1990), 115.

59. See *Higher Superstition*, 16-41.

60. *Postmodernism, Reason and Religion* (London and New York, 1992), 60-61.

61. Sagan is more confident that "[a]dvances in medicine and agriculture have saved vastly more lives than have been lost in all the wars of history," *The Demon Haunted World*, 11.

62. *Forbidden Knowledge*, 224. Cf. Tallis, *Newton's Sleep*, xix: "Science has suffered under the burden of spiritual claims and then been condemned because it cannot fill the absence of God, because it addresses the question How? and fails to address the deeper question Why?"

63. In *I'm Dysfunctional, You're Dysfunctional*, 117. See 101-17 for examples of New Age thought predicated on antirationalism.

64. For a critique of a feminist antirationalist classic, *Women's Ways of Knowing*, see Daphne Patai and Noretta Koertge, *Professing Feminism. Cautionary Tales from the Strange World of Women's Studies* (New York, 1994), 161-67.

65. *Notes from Underground*, trans. Jessie Coulson (Harmmondswordth, England, 1972), 36.

CHAPTER 4

1. *Hippolytus,* 207.

2. *How to Get Whatever You Want Out of Life* (New York, 1978), 7.

3. *The Culture of Narcissism. American Life in an Age of Diminishing Expectations* (1978; New York, 1980), 7. See too Robert N. Bellah et al., *Habits of the Heart. Individualism and Commitment in American Life* (1985; New York, 1986), 113-41; James L. Nolan, Jr., *The Therapeutic State. Justifying Government at Century's End* (New York and London, 1998), especially 1-21.

4. Charles J. Sykes, *A Nation of Victims. The Decay of the American Character* (New York, 1992), 49.

5. Cf. Nolan, 20: "[T]he therapeutic ethic appears to complement the utilitarian ethic. If offers to soften the harshness of life in the machine without removing the machine."

6. Bernie Zilbergeld, *The Shrinking of America. Myths of Psychological Change* (New York, 1983), 3.

7. *A Nation of Victims*, 21.

8. *Iliad* 21.462-66.

9. *Oedipus Turannos* 1076.

10. Peter Gay notes too that "what was new about eighteenth-century humanity was that it formed part of the general recovery of nerve: its optimistic decency was grounded in the rational foundations of scientific improvement as much as in religious prescriptions. Generosity was a luxury a progressive society could afford." *The Enlightenment: An Interpretation*, 30.

11. Colin Campbell, *The Romantic Ethic and the Spirit of Modern Consumerism*, 115;117-18. See 99-137 for a more detailed history of "Christian sentimentalism." For an examination of the cult of sensibility in the context of a growing consumerism and burgeoning feminism see G. J. Barker-Benfield, *The Cult of Sensibility. Sex and Society in Eighteenth-Century Britain* (Chicago and London, 1992).

12. R. S. Crane, "Suggestions Toward a Genealogy of the 'Man of Feeling.'" 1934; rpt. *The Idea of the Humanities. And Other Essays Critical and Historical* (Chicago and London, 1967), Vol. I, 194.

13. In Crane, 205.

14. Campbell, 151.

15. Crane, 213.

16. Crane, 188.

17. Brian Vickers, ed., Henry Mackenzie, *The Man of Feeling* (1771; London, 1967), ix.

18. J. M. S. Tompkins, *The Popular Novel in England 1770-1880* (Lincoln, NE, 1961), 103.

19. *La Nouvelle Héloïse*, trans. Judith H. McDowell, 1.26.

20. Fanny Greville, in Gardner D. Stout, Jr., Introduction to *A Sentimental Journey through France and Italy by Mr. Yorick* (Berkeley and Los Angeles , 1967), 22.

21. See Park Honan, *Jane Austen. Her Life* (New York, 1987), 276.

22. See Campbell, 138-60, for a more detailed history of the cult of sensiblity.

23. Lawrence Stone, *The Family, Sex and Marriage in England 1500-1800*, 237.

24. *On the Nature of Things*, 2.4.

25. See Bellah et al., *Habits of the Heart*, 117-21.

26. See Zilbergeld, *The Shrinking of America*, 42-45, quote on 43.

27. For American values and the beginnings of psychotherapy see Zilbergeld, *The Shrinking of America*, 33-49; also Christopher Lasch, *The Minimal Self. Psychic Survival in Troubled Times* (New York, 1984), 197-223.

28. *The Culture of Narcissism,* 13.

29. M. D. Faber's analysis of New Age tabloid therapy confirms the essential childishness of the New Ager: he is characterized by "infantile omnipotence," the urge to "fuse regressively" with the world and so overcome the individual's tragic separation from the world, and "narcissistic inflation," the belief in one's magical uniqueness compared to others, *New Age Thinking*, 7-8, emphases omitted.

30. For an early discussion of Sensitive Man see David Riesman's definition of the "other-directed" man in *The Lonely Crowd*, abridged ed. (New Haven and London, 1961), 19-24.

31. *A Nation of Victims*, 168. Emphasis in original.

32. See Florence King, "Sensitive Man," *The National Review*, 45.16 (23 August 1993), 72-73. Recently Michael Mandelbaum has argued that Clinton has brought the same therapeutic sensibility to his foreign policy, which helps to account for its less than distinguished record. "Foreign Policy as Social Work," *Foreign Affairs* 75.1 (Jan./Feb. 1996), 16-32.

33. Margaret Morganroth Gulette, quoted by Paul Hollander, "Reassessing the Adversary Culture," *Academic Questions* 9.2 (Spring 1996), 42.

34. See James Bovard, "Olfactory Correctness," *Heterodoxy* 3.6 (November 1995), 1, 10-13.

35. Bernstein, *The Dictatorship of Virtue*, 21-22.

36. For sensitivity training in universities, where it is part of the larger Diversity-Multiculturalism Industrial Complex, see Bernstein, *The Dictatorship of Virtue*, 60-96; Sykes, *A Nation of Victims*, 163-75; and two articles by W. R. Coulson, "Perils of Sensitivity Training," *Measure*, No.127 (February/March, 1995), and "Rejoinder," *Measure* No.130 (August/September 1995).

37. See D'Souza, *Illiberal Education*, 126-27; Thomas Sowell, *Inside American Education*, 155-69.

38. See Rene Sanchez, "A Required Course in Beating the Freshman Blues," *The Washington Post Weekly Edition*, 12.51 (October 23-29, 1995), 31.

39. Russell Jacoby, *Dogmatic Wisdom. How the Culture Wars Divert Education and Distract America* (New York, 1994), 73.

40. See Barbara Rhoades Ellis' discussion of the *Guidelines for Bias-Free Writing*, the product of the American Association of University Presses' Task Force on Bias-Free Language. In *Heterodoxy* 3.10/4.1 (Dec. 1995/Jan.1996), 4-5.

41. "Beyond Individualism: The New Puritanism, Feminism and Women," *Salmagundi,* Nos. 101-02 (Spring/Summer 1994), 83.

42. For the New Puritanism see the the essays collected under the titles "The New Puritanism?" *Salmagundi* Nos. 101-02 (Spring/Summer 1994), 35-150; and "The New Puritanism Revisited," *Salmagundi* Nos. 106-07 (Spring/Summer 1995), 194-256.

43. For the date-rape phenomenon on campus see Katie Roiphe, *The Morning After. Sex, Fear, and Feminism on Campus* (New York, 1993); a briefer survey of the topic can be found in Sykes, *A Nation of Victims*, 177-96. For the dangers to individual freedom posed by the New Puritanism see Camille Paglia, "No Law in the Arena," *Vamps and Tramps. New Essays* (New York, 1994), 19-94.

44. In "Puritans and Prigs," *Salmagundi* Nos. 101-02 (Spring/Summer 1994), 47.

45. See Thomas G. Moeller, "What Research Says about Academic Performance," *Education Digest*, 59.5 (January 1994), 34-38.

46. *In Defense of Elitism* (New York, 1994), 156.

47. In an international study of thirteen-year-olds, Korean students ranked first in mathematical skill, yet only 23 percent thought they were good at mathematics. Sixty-eight percent of the American students considered themselves good at math—and they ranked *last* in math skills. Thomas Sowell, *Inside American Education*, 3.

48. *A Nation of Victims*, 164.

49. Bloom quoted by Marvin Olasky, *The Tragedy of American Compassion* (Washington, DC, 1992), 194. Olasky's history of compassion in America shows its roots in the alliance of Romantic feeling with Enlightenment faith in technique.

50. Richard Stengel, "Compassion is Back," *Time* 147.6 (6 February 1996), 31.

51. Jean Bethke Elshtain, "Sense and Sensibility," *The New Republic*, no. 4,263 (30 September 1996), 29. For political compassion's roots in Rousseau see Clifford Orwin, "Moist Eyes—from Rousseau to Clinton," *The Public Interest*, no. 128 (Summer 1997), 3-20.

52. Compassion-at-a-distance provides the emotional fuel for Third Worldism, that self-loathing Western idealization of the Third World as the innocent victims of Western capitalist cruelty. See Pascal Bruckner, *The Tears of the White Man. Compassion as Contempt*, trans. William R. Beer (1983; New York, 1986), 43-82.

53. *The Flight from Truth*, 84.

54. See the article by Clifford Orwin, "Distant Compassion," *The National Interest*, No. 43 (Spring, 1996), 42-49.

55. See the summary of causes identified by Christopher Jencks in *The Homeless* (Cambridge, MA and London, 1994), 103.

56. Olasky, 213.

57. Christopher Lasch, *The Revolt of the Elites*, 105.

58. "Sense and Sensibility," 29.

59. See for example Bruce Blaine, Jennifer Crocker, and Brenda Major, "The Unintended Negative Consequences of Sympathy for the Stigmatized," *Journal of Applied Social Psychology*, 25.10 (16 May 1995), 889-906.

60. *The Revolt of the Elites*, 105.

61. In *The Image. Or, What Happened to the American Dream* (New York, 1962), 4.

62. "The Anxiety Constituency," *The Washington Post National Weekly Edition*, 13.21 (25-31 March 1996), 30.

63. See the review of several recent analyses of middle-class economic angst by Amity Shlaes, "Doom, Gloom, and the Middle Class,"*Commentary*, 101.2 (February, 1996), 19-24. See too Zilbergeld, *The Shrinking of America*, 70-86, for a link of psychic unease to rising expectations created by affluence.

64. In early December of 1996 five top economists asserted that the Consumer

Price Index, which measures inflation, has been calculated at a percentage point too high for twenty-five years—which, if true, means that income hasn't been declining as much, and the economy is bigger and growing at a rate greater than we have been led to believe. See Steve Pearlstein, "Fine-Tuning the Consumer Price Index," *The Washington Post National Weekly Edition*, 14.8-9 (23 December 1996-5 January 1997), 18-19; "Statistical Guessing Games," *The Economist*, 341.7995 (7 December 1996), 25-26.

65. See Steven Pearlstein, "Are We Better Off or Not?" *The Washington Post National Weekly Edition* 13.28 (13-19 May 1996), 6-7.

66. In *The Good Life and its Discontents. The American Dream in the Age of Entitlement* (New York, 1995), xv. Samuelson traces this optimism to the unprecedented postwar distribution of wealth and government services that raised everyone's expectations of what the "good life" entailed. As Samuelson puts it, "We transformed the American Dream into the American Fantasy," xiii.

67. For the Social Security and Medicare crisis see Peter G. Peterson, "Will America Grow Up Before It Grows Old?" *The Atlantic Monthly* 277.5 (May 1996), 55-86.

68. Government statistics that define poverty skew our definition of it because they omit the value of noncash benefits such as food-stamps, housing, health care, vouchers for child-care and school meals, etc., or the cash contributions from the underground economy or from people not officially defined as part of the household, such as a single mother's live-in boyfriend.

69. Bruce Bartlett, "How Poor are the Poor?" *The American Enterprise*, 7.1 (1996), 58-59.

70. *The Tragedy of American Compassion*, 136.

71. In Olasky, 53.

72. In Andrew Delbanco, *The Death of Satan. How Americans Have Lost the Sense of Evil* (New York, 1995), 186.

73. *I'm Dysfunctional, You're Dysfunctional*, 18.

74. Bellah et al., *Habits of the Heart*, 141.

75. Cf. Lasch: [T]he therapeutic morality associated with twentieth-century liberalism destroys the idea of moral responsibility, in which it originates, and...it culminates, moreover, in the monopolization of knowledge and power by experts," in *The Minimal Self. Psychic Survival in Troubled Times* (New York, 1984), 215.

76. G. E. Zuriff, "Medicalizing Character," *The Public Interest*, No. 123 (Spring 1996), 94-99.

77. L. J. Davis, "The Encyclopedia of Insanity," *Harper's*, 294.1761 (February 1997), 63.

78. *The Death of Satan*, 9. See particularly 185-217 for a discussion of how the modern intellectual's corrosive irony has contributed to the loss of the idea of evil.

79. *The Death of Satan*, 228.

80. *The Death of Satan*, 227.

81. "Pandora and the Problem of Evil," *Lancet* 347.8993 (6 January 1996), 1.

82. "The Time has Come to Study the Face of Evil," *The Humanist*, 55.6 (November/ December 1995), 38.

83. In *Dark Nature. A Natural History of Evil* (New York, 1995), x, xi, xvi.

84. I find it significant that Watson, for example, eschews a discussion of free will in his book, and when he does mention it in passing, puts it in those ironic quotation marks that signal the reader he is not to believe in the reality of the phrase in quotes. Cf. *Dark Nature*, 254, 255.

85. Rezak Hukanovic, "The Evil at Omarska," *The New Republic*, No. 4,230 (12 February 1996), 29

86. Trans. Aubrey de Selincourt.

87. Letter, 18 December 1831, in *The Collected Letters of Samuel Taylor Coleridge,* Vol. 6, ed. Earl Leslie Griggs, Oxford, 1971.

88. In *Narrative and Freedom. The Shadows of Time* (New Haven and London, 1994), 278-79.

89. In *The Works of Jane Austen*, vol. VI, *Minor Works*, ed. R. W. Chapman (Oxford, 1963), 140.

90. For the corruption of academic historiography by postmodern fashion see Keith Windschuttle, *The Killing of History. How Literary Critics and Social Theorists Are Murdering Our Past* (New York, 1997).

CHAPTER 5

1. *Phaedrus* 230d, trans. Harold North Fowler, Loeb Classical Library.

2. Commentators usually distinguish between two types of environmentalism, a moderate "light green" and a more radical "dark green." Andrew Dobson calls these two varieties "environmentalism" and "ecologism": "Environmentalism argues for a managerial approach to environmental problems, secure in the belief that they can be solved without fundamental changes in present values or patterns of production and consumption, while ecologism holds that a sustainable and fulfilling existence presupposes radical changes in our relationship with the non-human natural world, and in our mode of social and political life," *Green Political Thought*, 2 ed. (London and New York, 1995), 11. Since I am focusing on the underlying similarities between the two, I will use "environmentalism" to denote all ideologies that combine an idealization of nature with a dissatisfaction with modern society.

3. "FC," *The Unabomber Manifesto. Industrial Society and the Future* (Berkeley, 1995), 3. Subsequent references parenthetical.

4. "Is There Method to His Madness?" *The Nation*, 261.9 (25 September 1995),

305-9. Sale's article was based on a preview copy of the manifesto hand-delivered to him by the FBI: an example of just how integrated into the "establishment" are its so-called "dissidents."

5.   Cf. Robert L. Park: "Nevertheless, growing numbers of people, in one way or another, share some of the Unabomber's romantic longing for a simpler world. Unable or unwilling to comprehend the technology on which they depend, they are deeply distrustful of the science behind it, and reject the Western scientific tradition that created it. It is a romantic rebellion, led not by the semi-literate yahoos of fundamentalist religion, who are the traditional foes of science, but by serious academics who regard themselves as intellectuals," in "Voodoo Science," *Dumbing Down*, 149.

6.   Two of the "four essential postulates" of radical environmentalism identified by Martin Lewis are modern versions of the Golden Age and Noble Savage myths: "'primal (or 'primitive') peoples exemplify how we can live in harmony with nature (and with each other)"—Noble Savage; "technological advance, if not scientific progress itself, is inherently harmful and dehumanizing"—which means we must "abandon urban, industrial, capitalist civilization and return to the earth": Golden Age. In *Green Delusions. An Environmentalist Critique of Radical Environmentalism* (Durham and London, 1992), 3. But these "postulates" can be found in moderate environmentalist thought as well; cf. Al Gore's *Earth in the Balance*, discussed below.

7.   For Romanticism and modern environmentalism see David Pepper, *The Roots of Modern Environmentalism* (London, 1984), 76-90. See too Nash, *Wilderness and the American Mind*, 237-62. For environmentalism as a modern expression of the Western Romantic and anti-Enlightenment idea of apocalyptic decline caused by science and technology alienating humans from nature see Arthur Herman, *The Idea of Decline in Western History* , 400-440.

8.   In Nash, *Wilderness and the American Mind*, 55-56. Such enthusiasm was usually tempered by a recognition of nature's inhuman desolation and vast disorder: "In spite of such sentiments," Nash notes, "Romantic enthusiasm for wilderness never seriously challenged the aversion in the pioneer mind. Appreciation, rather, resulted from a momentary relaxation of the dominant antipathy," 65. For nature in the American imagination see too Stoll, *Protestantism, Capitalism, and Nature in America*.

9.   From *A Thousand-Mile Walk to the Gulf* (1916); in Roderick Nash, *Wilderness and the American Mind*, 124-25. For Muir see 122-40. For more examples of the American romantic idealization of wild nature as the spiritual alternative to corrupt civilization cf. 44-66. See too Cronon, "The Trouble with Wilderness," 70-80, where the American idealization of wilderness is traced back to the Romantic ideal of the sublime and the American experience of the frontier.

10. Psychologists and sociologists have long proclaimed the literal therapeutic value of wild nature; cf. Karl Menninger in 1959: "a proximity to larger non-urban areas of farm or wilderness" is "essential to the mental health of both child and adult," quoted in Nash, 249.

11. For the role of science good and bad in popularizing environmental issues see Charles T. Rubin, *The Green Crusade. Rethinking the Roots of Environmentalism* (New York, 1994), 12-17.

12. For a balanced evaluation of just how seriously the environment is in trouble see Gregg Easterbrook, *A Moment on the Earth*, 161-646; also the essays in Ronald Bailey, ed., *The True State of the Planet* (New York, 1995); Aaron Wildavsky, *But Is It True? A Citizen's Guide to Environmental Health and Safety Issues* (Cambridge, MA, 1995); Michael Fumento, *Science under Siege: Balancing Technology and the Environment* (New York, 1993); Gross and Levitt, *Higher Superstition*, 149-78.

13. Levitt and Gross, *Higher Superstition*, 154.

14. As Julian L. Simon points out, the world's population is eating better, natural resources are more available, the death-rate is falling, and our air and water are getting cleaner. See "Why Do We Hear Prophecies of Doom from Every Side?" *The Futurist*, 29.1 (1995), 19-23.

15. *Antigone,* 332-75; for Prometheus see Aeschylus's *Prometheus Bound,* 436-506.

16. For the "technophobia" of environmentalism see Lewis, *Green Delusions*, 117-49.

17. Cf. Ferry, *The New Ecological Order*, 89: "In all cases, the deep ecologist is guided by a hatred of modernity, by hostility towards the present," emphasis omitted.

18. *Metamorphoses* 1.109-111. Even critics of radical environmentalist myths indulge some of their same flawed assumptions. Cf. Lewis, who says we must "begin atoning for our very real environmental sins— for our fall from grace that began at the end of the Pleistocene epoch," *Green Delusions*, 251.

19. *Rogue Primate. An Exploration of Human Domestication* (Toronto, 1994), 19.

20. *So Shall You Reap. Farming and Crops in Human Affairs* (Washington, DC, 1994), 14.

21. Paul Shepard, *The Tender Carnivore and the Sacred Game* (New York, 1973), 7. For a discussion of Shepard's thesis see Rubin, 198-203.

22. Lawrence H. Keeley, *War Before Civilization. The Myth of the Peaceful Savage* (New York and Oxford, 1996), 170.

23. Simplifying misconceptions about contemporary hunting/gathering societies vitiate their use as analogies with pre-farming peoples. See Carol R. Ember, "Myths about Hunter-Gatherers," *Ethnology*, 17.4 (1978), 439-48.

24. See Allen W. Johnson and Timothy Earle, *The Evolution of Human Societies. From Foraging Group to Agrarian State* (Stanford, 1987), 28, 30. For analysis of modern idealizations of contemporary hunting-and-gathering societies, which provide most of the evidence for speculations about prehistoric hunters and gatherers, see Robert B. Edgerton, *Sick Societies. Challenging the Myth of Primitive Harmony* (New York, 1992).

25. Keeley, 25-26.

26. *Metamorphoses,* 1.101-102.

27. *The Tender Carnivore,* 144-45.

28. *Metamorphoses,* 1.89-100.

29. Edgerton points out that the Bushmen or San are not as peaceful and simple as the film portrayed them— they sometimes fight bitterly and violently over trespassing on hunting areas and the kidnapping of women. *Sick Societies,* 57.

30. *The New Ecological Order,* 5.

31. *Landscape and Memory,* 7; cf. Lewis, *Green Delusions* 8: "Pristine nature is non-existent—and has been, except perhaps in a few remote islands, for thousands of years."

32. See Victor Davis Hanson, *Fields without Dreams. Defending the Argrarian Idea* (New York, 1996).

33. Cf. Andrew Goudie on the impact of domestication: "The consequences [of domestication] are so substantial that the differences between breeds of animals of the same species often exceed those between different species under natural conditions," in *The Human Impact on the Natural Environment,* 3rd ed. (Cambridge, MA, 1990), 76.

34. *The New Ecological Order,* 131. Emphasis omitted.

35. *A Moment on the Earth,* 49.

36. Richard Leakey and Roger Lewin, *The Sixth Extinction. Patterns of Life and the Future of Humankind* (New York, 1995), 39.

37. *The Sixth Extinction,* 44.

38. Easterbrook, 98.

39. *The End of Nature,* 78.

40. *A Moment on the Earth,* 25.

41. Easterbrook, 27.

42. Easterbrook, 34. See too Leakey and Lewin, 52-53.

43. Leakey and Lewin, 251

44. As Stephen Jay Gould points out in *Full House: The Spread of Excellence from Plato to Darwin* (New York, 1996).

45. See Leakey and Lewin, 14-15.

46. For the dominance of bacteria see Gould, 176-86.

47. *The Sixth Extinction,* 144.

48. In Peter Gay, *The Science of Freedom,* 162.

49. J. E. Lovelock, *Gaia. A New Look at Life on Earth* (Oxford, 1979), 11.

50. As Dobson points out, the Gaia hypothesis undercuts much of the environmentalist hysteria about our destruction of the planet. See *Green Political Thought,* 43-48.

51. As Lewis points out, "Civil rights are much more difficult to defend in a discourse that purports to explain human nature in biological terms,"*Green Delusions*, 39.

52. Cf. Rubin, *The Green Crusade*: "To suggest that a concern for nature is best grounded in some explicit understanding of the human good is not merely to fall into mindless anthropocentrism. Indeed, it prevents some of the absurdities of anthropocentrism that are becoming all too evident in environmental debates," 249.

53. Quote in Ronald Bailey, *Eco-Scam. The False Prophets of Ecological Apocalypse* (New York, 1993), 10.

54. Rubin, *The Green Crusade*, 177. Cf. also 209: "Only a small number of people may subscribe to deep ecology in its entirety, but a whole constellation of ideas closely related to it are in the process of becoming the 'common sense' view of environmental issues." Likewise Lewis, 247: "Radical environmentalism enjoys substantial, and growing, intellectual clout." See Rubin (177-211) for an analytic history of deep ecology; for a philosophical discussion see Luc Ferry, *The New Ecological Order*, 59-90.

55. Bill Devall and George Sessions, *Deep Ecology. Living as if Nature Mattered* (Salt Lake City, 1985). Subsequent references parenthetical.

56. For a critical analysis of idealized primitivism in environmentalism see Lewis, *Green Delusions*, 43-81.

57. Cf. *Metamorphoses,* 1.90, 135-36.

58. Cf. Keith Thomas, *Man and the Natural World*, 301: "For adults, nature parks and conservation areas serve a function not unlike that which toy animals have for children; they are fantasies which enshrine the values by which society as a whole cannot afford to live."

59. Bill McKibben, *The End of Nature* (New York, 1989). Subsequent references parenthetical.

60. Senator Al Gore, *Earth in the Balance. Ecology and the Human Spirit* (New York, 1992). Subsequent references parenthetical.

61. Gore rejects the antihumanism of deep ecology (216-18)—after all, his book was a campaign document. Yet his ideas share many of the same assumptions that form the logical basis for radical environmentalism's antihumanism.

62. Theodore Kacyzinski, now proven to be the Unabomber, had a well-thumbed copy of Gore's book in his cabin. Herman, *The Idea of Decline*, 6.

63. *Green Delusions*, 242. See too Fergus M. Bordewich, *Killing the White Man's Indian. Reinventing Native Americans at the End of the Twentieth Century* (New York, 1996), 131-33. Cf. 133: "The speech as it is known to most Americans is, quite simply, an invention, a fact that seems to make little difference to well-meaning whites who are determined to portray Indians as icons of ecological correctness." And 159: "Although the legend of 'Chief Seattle' had indeed become a central part of modern Indian mythology, it no more repre-

sents universal native attitudes toward the earth than the Confucius of fortune cookies does the ambiguities of Chinese civilization." For the history of the speech and its reception see Albert Furtwangler, *Answering Chief Seattle* (Seattle and London, 1997).

64. Carolyn Merchant, *The Death of Nature. Women, Ecology, and the Scientific Revolution* (San Francisco, 1980), xvi. Cf. Ferry, 126: "To assert that women are more 'natural' than men is to deny their freedom, thus their full and whole place within humanity. That the ecofeminists hate Western civilization and modernity is their business. That they wish to find natural justifications for this hatred means playing the game of biological determinism, of which all women will suffer the consequences if it is to be taken seriously." See too Lewis, *Green Delusions*, 33-36.

65. Cf. for example the development of sentimental affection for pets and animals, which Keith Thomas points out "was first expressed either by well-to-do townsmen, remote from the agricultural process and inclined to think of animals as pets rather than as working livestock, or by educated country clergymen, whose sensibilities were different from those of the rustics among whom they found themselves," in *Man and the Natural World*, 182-83.

66. The attack on the scientific revolution is a cliche now in this species of environmentalism. Cf. Morris Berman: "Scientific consciousness is alienated consciousness: there is no ecstatic merger with nature, but rather total separation from it," in *The Reenchantment of the World* (Ithaca and London, 1981), 17.

67. Nieves Mathews, *Francis Bacon. The History of a Character Assassination* (New Haven and London, 1996), 409. For Gore's misreading specifically see James G. Lennox, "The Environmental Creed According to Gore: A Philosophical Analysis," in *Environmental Gore. A Constructive Response to* Earth in the Balance, ed. John A. Baden (San Francisco, 1994), 91-105.

68. In "The Natural and Experimental History for the Foundation of Philosophy," quoted by Clarence J. Glacken, *Traces on the Rhodian Shore* (1967; Berkeley and Los Angeles, 1976), 472.

69. *New Atlantis* 3.156; quoted in Mathews, 409.

70. In *Discourse on Method* 6; in Glacken, 477.

71. Again William Blake anticipates this by-now tired critique of the godless scientific revolution: Bacon is "a Contemplative Atheist" who "has no notion of any thing but Mammon," Blake wrote in the margins of his copy of Bacon's *Essays*. In *The Poetry and Prose of William Blake*, ed. David V. Erdman (New York, 1965), 615, 614.

72. Glacken, 472; see too Mathews, 412-14, for the importance of religion in Bacon's philosophy.

73. "Natural and Experimental History," in Glacken, 472.

74. *Religio Medici,* 1.13. For the neo-Platonic as well as Christian sources of this seventeenth-century attitude see Leonard Nathanson, *A Strategy of Truth. A Study of Sir Thomas Browne* (Chicago and London, 1967), 21.

75. Dobson, *Green Political Thought*, 11.

76. In *Simple in Means, Rich in Ends. Practicing Deep Ecology* (Salt Lake City, 1988) 15.

77. *The Green Crusade*, 190.

78. *Simple in Means*, 49, 88.

79. *Earth in the Balance*, 177. See Rubin, 189-91.

80. *Landscape and Memory*, 119.

81. Ferry, *The New Ecological Order*, 94.

82. Ferry, 91. For Nazi ecology see 91-107. The roots of Nazi nature-love go back, of course, to the German Romantics' "blood and soil" idealizations; cf. Schama, 82. Cf. too Herman, 418: "As Alfred Rosenberg and the Nazi Nordicists attacked the 'false spirituality' of Christianity and appealed to a return to the Aryan's original reverence for nature, back-to-nature types suddenly saw the National Socialists' Aryan man as heralding the new organic man, bonded to his race, his soil, and his environment."

83. Ferry, 93.

84. Ferry, xxviii.

85. As we saw above in Part One, the desire to create "new men" has invariably led to the worst crimes against those recalcitrant people who stubbornly refuse to be recreated. See Rubin, *The Green Crusade*, 198-211, for the totalitarian implications of environmentalist utopias. Cf. too Ferry, 78: "The idea that this control [of technology] must occur at the price of democracy itself is an additional step which deep ecologists, propelled as they are by a hatred of humanism and of Western civilization, but also by a nostalgic fascination with models of the past or potential models of the future (the Indians, communism), almost never hesitate to take."

86. A general descriptive analysis of the issues raised in this and the following section can be found in Tim Hayward, *Ecological Thought. An Introduction* (Cambridge, Mass., 1995), 53-86.

87. Cf. Gross and Levitt: Environmentalism's "unchanging casts of devils completely exclude the careful, unemotional weighing of costs and benefits, of relative risks and relative certainties that is a necessary part of making pragmatic judgments," in *The Higher Superstition*, 160.

88. Andrew Dobson, *Green Political Thought*, 11. Cf. too Ferry, *The New Ecological Order*: "But it is probably in the area of ecology that the feeling that the natural sciences will delivery [sic] *ready-made* teachings applicable to ethics and politics seems to be most confidently asserted," 84.

89. As in the works referenced in note 2 on page 174 above. For the scientific basis for Gore's claims see the essays in *Environmental Gore*.

90. Annie Brody, "Growing Up Green," *The Amicus Journal*, 15.3 (1993), 10-12.

91. See Roger Starr, "Recycling: Myths and Realities," *The Public Interest*, no. 119

(1995), 28-41; Chris Hendrickson, Lester Lave, and Francis McMichael, "Time to Dump Recycling?" *Issues in Science and Technology*, 11.3 (1995), 79-84.

92. See the lesson plan by James G. McGuire that organizes a unit on environmentalism around celebrating Earth Day, in *Journal of School Health* 66.5 (May 1996), 191-2.

93. Yvonne Baron Estes, "Environmental Education: Bringing Children and Nature Together," *Phi Delta Kappan*, 74.9 (May 1993), K1-12.

94. Walter H. Corson, "Priorities for a Sustainable Future: The Role of Education, the Media, and Tax Reform," *Journal of Social Issues*, 51.4 (1995), 38.

95. Ecological indoctrination has provoked a backlash in some schools, with the result that legitimate environmental issues have been banned from some classrooms. See Michael Satchell, "Dangerous Waters? Why Environmental Education Is Under Attack in the Nation's Schools," *U.S. News and World Report* 120.23 (10 June 1996), 63-4.

96. *A Moment on the Earth*, 57.

97. Easterbrook, 56.

98. Quote in Katherine McMain Park, "The Personal Is Ecological: Environmentalism of Social Work," *Social Work* 41.3 (May 1996), 321.

99. Park, 321. Park happily notes that "responding to the Earth and using the Earth interactively as a therapeutic method are on the increase," 322.

100. *Man and the Natural World*, 260.

101. "On Human Connectedness with Nature," 809.

102. As suggested by Ronald Bailey, *Eco-Scam*, 3-13. The Iron Age myth in Hesiod also has an apocalyptic finish: Zeus will destroy the Iron Race when humans have become so corrupted that babies are born with gray hair, *Works and Days* 180-81.

103. See Martin Lewis, *Green Delusions*, 8-9. Easterbrook too notes that "the worst thing that could happen to the Earth would be for humankind to continue to behave in an entirely natural manner, doing no more or less than other creatures would do if competitors did not stop them—that is, expanding to the maximum extent," *A Moment on the Earth*, 67.

104. *A Moment on the Earth*, xvii; see too 647-51. See too Lewis, *Green Delusions*, 242-51; cf. also his Appendix, in which he contrasts eco-radicalism and what he calls "Promethean Environmentalism."

105. William Arrowsmith's reconstruction of Seattle's words quoted in *Killing the White Man's Indian*, 161.

CHAPTER 6

1.   "Song of Myself," 39, lines 974-75, in *Leaves of Grass,* Loving, Oxford, 1990.

2.   *Killing the White Man's Indian,* New York, 1996, 17.

3. Alice B. Kehoe, "Primal Gaia: Primitivists and Plastic Medicine Men," in *The Invented Indian*, 199.

4. See Berkhofer, *The White Man's Indian*, 106-11. Cf. James A. Clifton: "The Indian's transcendental resources and heritage, many are discovering, possess a fabulous advantage over oil-bearing shales, timberlands, and condominium sites. Rather than being finite, they are infinitely replenishable—indeed, capable of perpetual expansion—limited in quantity, substance, and style only by the ingenuity of their inventors, delivered in annually exhibited new improved models as the consumer's wants dictate," *The Invented Indian*, 17.

5. "Managing, American Indian-style," *Fortune*, 134.7 (14 October 1996), 130.

6. In Berkhofer, 8, 11, 17, 73.

7. In Bernard W. Sheehan, *Savagism and Civility. Indians and Englishmen in Colonial Virginia* (Cambridge, 1980), 31, 22.

8. Sheehan, 14, 35. See Martin D. Snyder, "The Hero in the Garden: Classical Contributions to the Early Images of America," in *Classical Traditions in Early America*, ed. John W. Eadie (Ann Arbor, MI, 1976), 139-69.

9. In Marshall and Williams, *The Great Map of Mankind*, 200-1.

10. Robert Beverly, *The History and Present State of Virginia*, ed. Louis B. Wright (Chapel Hill, NC, 1947), 17, cf. also 156.

11. In the *Tatler* of May 1710, and the *Spectator* of April 1711. In Marshall and Williams, 196-7.

12. In Henry Nash Smith, *Virgin Land*, 71.

13. Berkhofer, *The White Man's Indian*, 79.

14. Nash, *Wilderness and the American Mind*, 55-6.

15. Nash, 49.

16. In Berkhofer, 89.

17. Quoted by Wilcomb E. Washburn and Bruce G. Trigger, "Native Peoples in Euro-American Historiography," in *The Cambridge History of the Native Peoples of the Americas* (Cambridge, 1996), Vol. 1, Part 1, 66-67.

18. See the essay by Stanley L. Robe, "Wild Men and Spain's Brave New World," in *The Wild Man Within. An Image in Western Thought from the Renaissance to Romanticism*, ed. Edward Dudley and Maximillian Novak (Pittsburgh, 1972), 39-53.

19. *Indian Givers. How the Indians of the Americas Transformed the World* (New York, 1988). Subsequent references parenthetical.

20. For the origins of this myth in the increasing idealization of the Indian in the nineteenth century see Elisabeth Tooker, "The United States Constitution and the Iroquois League," in *The Invented Indian*, 115-22. See too the longer version of this article in *Ethnohistory* 35.4 (1988), 305-36. This validation of racial identity and superiority by claiming to be the source of democracy likewise has its roots in the nineteenth century. Then, racialist propounders of

Teutonic superiority extolled an "Anglo-Saxon democracy" and freedom whose roots supposedly lay in their Germanic genes. See Herman, *The Idea of Decline*, 161-62.

21. The influence of the Iroquois league argued for by Bruce E. Johansen, *Forgotten Founders* (Ipswich, MA, 1982), and Donald A. Grinde Jr., *The Iroquois and the Founding of the American Nation* (San Francisco, 1977). Both Johansen and Grinde are criticized by Samuel B. Payne, Jr., "The Iroquois League, the Articles of Confederation, and the Constitution," *William and Mary Quarterly*, 3rd Series 53.3 (1996), 605-620; and in the same issue, Philip A. Levy, "Exemplars of Taking Liberties: The Iroquois Thesis and the Problem of Evidence," 588-604. Cf. Levy's assessment of Grinde and Johansen's work: "a crazy quilt of inaccurate assessments, free-floating speculations, incorrect or disembodied quotations, and thesis-driven conclusions," 603-4.

22. In Bruce E. Johansen, "Debating the Origin of Democracy: Overview of an Annotated Bibliography," *American Indian Culture and Research Journal*, 20.2 (1996), 155-72.

23. See the description of the League's origins and functioning in Dean R. Snow, *The Iroquois* (Oxford and Cambridge, MA, 1994), 52-67; Elisabeth Tooker, "The League of the Iroquois: Its History, Politics, and Ritual," in *Northeast*, ed. B. G. Trigger (Washington, DC), 1978, 418-41.

24. Snow, 62.

25. Tooker, 114.

26. Tooker, 114; Snow, 63-64.

27. Snow, 62.

28 Tooker, 114.

29. Cf. Mark Nathan Cohen: "The emergence of complex social institutions among hunter-gatherers represents a response—repeatedly evolved—to two sets of problems that egalitarian structures were poorly equipped to handle: (1) the problem of organizing subsistence and maintaining economic home-ostasis in the face of pressures that reduced mobility and required the exploitation of more and more temporally and spatially limited and incongruously distributed resources and (2) the problem of organizing individuals to minimize crowding stresses in human aggregates of increasing size and permanence." In "Prehistoric Hunter-Gatherers: The Meaning of Social Complexity," *Prehistoric Hunter-Gatherers. The Emergence of Cultural Complexity*, ed. T. Douglas Price and James A. Brown (Orlando, 1985), 99.

30. For egalitarianism and its lack in Indian societies see Leland Donald, "Liberty, Equality, Fraternity: Was the Indian Really Egalitarian?" in *The Invented Indian*, 145-67; Edgerton, *Sick Societies*, 75-79.

31. See Meyer Reinhold, ed., *Classical Tradition in Early America* (Ann Arbor, 1976); *Classica Americana: The Greek and Roman Heritage in the United States* (Detroit, 1984), especially 94-115.

32. Weatherford obviously doesn't know that Plato and Aristotle are *critics* of

democracy, which they believed inevitably degenerated into mob rule and tyranny. And he is equally ignorant of a rich, first-hand narrative of democratic practice found in Aeschylus, Sophocles, Euripides, Herodotus, and Thucydides.

33. Quoted in Reinhold, *Classica Americana*, 98. For the influence of Classical Republicanism see Philip Rahe, *Republics Ancient and Modern. Classical Republicanism and the American Revolution* (Chapel Hill and London, 1992).

34. Quoted in Jennifer Tolbert Roberts, *Athens on Trial. The Antidemocratic Tradition in Western Thought* (Princeton, 1994). See 179-93 for a discussion of the Classical influences on the founders; more comprehensively, Carl J. Richard, *The Founders and the Classics. Greece, Rome, and the American Enlightenment* (Cambridge, MA and London, 1994); for the influence of ancient republics, 74-80. Weatherford seemingly is unaware that the founders were wary of radical democracy on the Athenian model, which they saw was characterized by leveling "turbulence" and which threatened the property rights of landowners. See Roberts, 180-84. Hence they favored the "mixed government" whose ancient model was the Roman Republic; cf. Richard, 122-68.

35. Reinhold, *Classica Americana*, 95.

36. See Peter Gay, *The Rise of Modern Paganism*, 31-203.

37. Herodotus 7.135, trans. Aubrey de Sélincourt.

38. Reinhold, *Classica Americana*, 98; Richard, 57-61.

39. Tooker, 112.

40. *The Federalist. A Classic on Federalism and Free Government* (Baltimore, 1960), 290-91; Cf. Reinhold, 103: "Great attention was directed at the time of the Convention to the theoretical and practical aspects of federalism, and in this connection the debates and polemical literature analyzed the merits and failures of the Greek leagues." See too George Kennedy, "Classical Influences on *The Federalist*," in Reinhold, *Classical Traditions*, 119-38; Richard, 104-14.

41. See Payne, "Iroquois Influence," 611-12.

42. *The Federalist*, ed. Jacob E. Cooke (Middletown, CT, 1961). Cf. Richard, 105: "The Amphictyonic League was the focus of nearly as much discussion as the Constitution itself, especially among the Federalists, who seemed never to tire of recounting the league's history and attributing its downfall to decentralization."

43. This section first appeared in a different form as "Curse You, Christopher Columbus! Or, History as Manichaean Melodrama," *Measure*, 109 (October 1992), 1-8.

44. Quoted approvingly by Charlie Signet and Joanna O'Connel, "Discovering the Truth about Columbus," *The Utne Reader*, 38 (March/April 1990), 26.

45. *In the American Grain* (1925; New York, 1933), 41.

46. *The Conquest of Paradise: Columbus and the Columbian Legacy* (1990; New York, 1991). Subsequent references parenthetical. See the critical discussion of Sale's

book by Robert Royal, *1492 And All That. Political Manipulations of History* (Washington, DC, 1992).

47. The assertion of gender equality at least among the Iroquois is now an accepted fact. Cf. Gary B. Nash in the textbook *Red, White, and Black: The Peoples of Early North America* (Englewood Cliffs, NJ, 1992), 21-22: "The European idea of male dominance and female subordination in all things was conspicuously absent in Iroquois society."

48. See William Cronon, *Changes in the Land. Indians, Colonists, and the Ecology of New England* (New York, 1983), 44-47.

49. Gerda Lerner, *The Creation of Patriarchy* (New York, 1986), 30.

50. Quoted by Elisabeth Tooker, "Women in Iroquois Society," in *Extending the Rafters. Interdisciplinary Approaches to Iroquoian Studies*, ed. Michael K. Foster, Jack Campisi, Marianne Mithun (Albany, 1984), 109.

51. Bordewich, *Killing the White Man's Indian*, 175-78; cf. too Edgerton, *Sick Societies*, 81-86.

52. *Georgics* 2.460.

53. A point made too by Royal, *1492 and All That*, 21-25.

54. *Killing the White Man's Indian*, 343.

55. In "White Ghosts, Red Shadows: The Reduction of North American Native," *The Invented Indian*, 333.

56. In *God is Red* (New York, 1973), 50.

57. *Red Earth, White Lies. Native Americans and the Myth of Scientific Fact* (New York, 1995). Subsequent references parenthetical.

58. See *Pleistocene Extinctions. The Search for a Cause*, ed. Paul S. Martin (New Haven and London, 1967).

59. Cf. Martin Lewis, *Green Delusions*, 73.

60. "The First Americans," *World Press Review*, 43.4 (1996), 37-38; see too Ann Gibbons, "The Peopling of the Americas," *Science*, 274 (1996), 31-33.

61. See Dean R. Snow, "The First Americans and the Differentiation of Hunter-Gatherer Cultures," in *The Cambridge History of the Native Peoples of the Americas*, 1.1.130-38. Cf. 135: "Skeptics [of claims of Indian occupation before 12,000 B.C.] have not been without their own scientific failings in this controversy, but for the moment, at least, it appears that all of the really convincing evidence for early Indians is less than 14,000 years old (12,000 B.C.)".

62. In *The Progressive*, 54.4 (April 1990), 27.

63. In *The Great Map of Mankind*, 197.

64. "The Remaking of the Amerind," *Westways*, 64.10 (1972), 20.

65. George R. Milner, Eve Anderson, Virginia G. Smith, "Warfare in Late Prehistoric West-Central Illinois," *American Antiquity*, 56.4 (1991), 590.

66. "An Estimate of Mortality in a Pre-Columbian Urban Population," *American Anthropologist*, 87 (1985), 522.

67. Richard E. W. Adams, *Prehistoric Mesoamerica*, rev. ed. (Norman, Ok. and London, 1991), 367.

68. Adams, 265.

69. Jefferson in *Notes on Virginia*, Query 6; quoted in Marx, *Machine in the Garden*, 121.

70. See Edgerton, *Sick Societies*, 114-15; for subordination of women cf. 81-86.

71. Edgerton, 75-79.

72. Neal Salisbury, "The Indians' Old World: Native Americans and the Coming of the Europeans," *William and Mary Quarterly*, 3rd series 53.3 (1996), 439.

73. Leland Donald, "Liberty, Equality, Fraternity," 151-58

74. Keeley, 28.

75. Keeley, 68.

76. Keeley, 69.

77. Milner, Anderson, and Smith, "Warfare in Late Prehistoric West-Central Illinois," 583, 584, 592; quote on 594-95.

78. In *France and England in North America*, vol. 1 (New York, 1983), 574.

79. Parkman, 575.

80. E.g. Snow, *The Iroquois*, 32, 53-55, 127-28; also Mathew Dennis, *Cultivating a Landscape of Peace. Iroquois-European Encounters in Seventeenth-Century America* (Ithaca and London, 1993), 88-90; cf. 88: "Ritual cannibalism remained important in Iroquois life."

81. Keeley, 104.

82. In *Custer Died For Your Sins. An Indian Manifesto* (London, 1969), 6.

83. See James Axtell, "The Unkindest Cut, or Who Invented Scalping?" in *The European and the Indian. Essays in the Ethnohistory of Colonial North America* (New York and Oxford, 1981), 16-35.

84. *Killing the White Man's Indian*, 36-37.

85. "Warfare in Late Prehistoric West-Central Illinois," 584. See Figure 2 for a photograph of a skull with a scalping cut-line.

86. Carlos Fuentes, *The Buried Mirror. Reflections on Spain and the New World* (New York, 1992), 99.

87. Inga Clendinnen, *Aztecs. An Interpretation* (Cambridge, 1991), 261.

88. *Aztecs*, 92.

89. Royal B. Hassrick, *The Sioux. Life and Customs of a Warrior Society* (Norman, 1964), 32.

90. Hassrick, 69.

91. Joseph H. Cash, *The Sioux People* (Phoenix, 1971), 3. Because the Chippewa were pressed by the Sioux and the more powerful Iroquois, the "greater snakes."

92. For the impact of the gun and the horse on the Plains Indians see Loretta Fowler, "The Great Plains from the Arrival of the Horse to 1885," *The Cambridge History of the Native Peoples of the Americas*, 1.2.5-21.

93. See Richard White, "The Winning of the West: The Expansion of the Western Sioux in the Eighteenth and Nineteenth Centuries," *Journal of American History*, 65.2 (1978), 319-43.

94. Cash, 19.

95. Martha Royce Blaine, *Pawnee Passage: 1870-75* (Norman and London, 1990), 134-39.

96. White, 341,

97. Hassrick, 72.

98. White, 342. See the perceptive discussion of the Plains wars by John Keegan, *Fields of Battle. The Wars for North America* (New York, 1996), 249-314.

99. Ovid, *Metamorphoses,* 1.101-2.

100. Richard White, "Native Americans and the Environment," in *Scholars and the Indian Experience. Critical Review of Recent Writing in the Social Sciences*, ed. W. R. Swagerty (Bloomington, 1984), 180.

101. "Traditional American Indian and Western European Attitudes toward Nature: An Overview," *Environmental Ethics*, 4 (1982), 293. Callicot at least admits that his is a "romantic point of view."

102. Sale, *Conquest of Paradise*, 317; his emphasis; Deloria in *The Progressive*, 26.

103. "Like Tributaries to a River," *Sierra*, 81.6 (1996), 41.

104. "First People, Firsthand Knowledge," *Sierra*, 81.6 (1996), 50.

105. "First People," 50.

106. *U.S. News and World Report*, 118.24 (19 June 1995), 61.

107. In *Time*, 145.25 (19 June 1995), 61.

108. See James Axtell, "The Rise and Fall of the Powhatan Empire," in *After Columbus. Essays in the Ethnohistory of Colonial North America* (New York and Oxford, 1988), 182-221; cf. 184: "All of the tribes between the James and Piankatank rivers were under Powhatan's thumb, obedient to the relatives and trusted councillors he intruded as local chiefs. Even tribes on the Eastern Shore across Chesapeake Bay and on the Potomac paid him tribute to remain free from his imperial embrace." Also Christian F. Feest, "Pride and Prejudice: The Pocahontas Myth and the Pamunkey," in *The Invented Indian. Cultural Fictions and Government Policies* (New Brunswick and London, 1990), 49-61.

109. Cf. Åke Hultkrantz: "The American Indians were practical people, nature to them the means of subsistence, housing, dress, transportation, and so on," in *Belief and Worship in Native North America*, ed. Christopher Vecsey (Syracuse, 1981), 125.

110. E.g. Robert Stam, who claims that "the film constitutes a relatively progressive step...in its adoption of a pro-indigenous perspective, and...in respecting

the linguistic integrity of the Native Americans." Quoted by Michael Walker, "Dances with Wolves," *The Book of Westerns*, ed. Ian Cameron and Douglas Pye (New York, 1996), 284. The business about "linguistic integrity" is particularly egregious, since the film mistakenly has the Sioux men speaking the *feminine* form of Lakota, according to David Seals in "The New Custerism," *The Nation*, 252.18 (13 May 1991), 637.

111. Wayne Michael Sarf, "Oscar Eaten by Wolves," *Film Comment*, 27.6 (1991), 67. See too Richard Grenier, "Indian Love Call," *Commentary*, 91.3 (1991), 46-50, for more of the film's historical absurdities.

112. Walter A. McDougall points out that this tradition is largely the creation of post-Vietnam War critics looking for an American "ideology validating the virtual genocide of peoples of color," one "which allegedly conditioned American behavior from Plymouth Rock to Vietnam." As McDougall notes, popular culture this century has traded on both positive and negative stereotypes of Indians and whites alike. In "Bury My Heart at PBS," *Commentary*, 102.6 (December 1996), 44.

113. Bordewich, *Killing the White Man's Indian*, 17.

114. See Henry Nash Smith, *Virgin Land. The American West as Symbol and Myth* (1950; New York, 1970), 113-14.

115. Victor Davis Hanson, "Ken Burns's West," *The Weekly Standard*, 2.2 (1996), 39.

116. *The West: An Illustrated History*, Geoffry Ward (New York, 1996), 4.

117. McDougall, 46.

118. *Killing the White Man's Indian*, 211.

119. *A New Face in the Countryside. Indians, Colonists, and Slaves in South Atlantic Forests, 1500-1800* (Cambridge, 1990), 65, 66. Cf. too Cronon, *Changes in the Land*, 12: "It is tempting to believe that when the Europeans arrived in the New World they confronted Virgin Land, the Forest Primeval, a wilderness which had existed for eons. Nothing could be further from the truth.... Indians had lived on the continent for thousands of years, and to a significant extend modified its environment to their purposes."

120. We should heed too Hultkrantz's reminder that the geographical and ethnic diversity of American Indians means that "there does not exist, and has not existed, a common Indian attitude toward nature," in *Belief and Worship*, 119.

121. See Salisbury, "The Indians' Old World," 444-49; quote on 445.

122. See Adams, *Prehistoric Mesoamerica*, 263-71.

123. White, "Native Americans and the Environment," 181.

124. Easterbrook, *A Moment on the Earth*, 92-94.

125. Silver, 50-51, 59-64.

126. Cronon, *Changes in the Land*, 30, 49.

127. In *The Evolution of Human Societies*, 34.

128. "Conservation and Resource Depletion: The Case of the Boreal Forest Algonquians," in *The Question of the Commons. The Culture and Ecology of Communal Resources*, ed. Bonnie J. McCay and James M. Acheson (Tucson, 1987), 122; Brightman's emphasis.

129. Brightman, 132.

130. George Catlin, *Letter and Notes on the Manners, Customs, and Condition of the North American Indians*, vol. 1 (1841; Minneapolis, 1965), 249, 253.

131. Catlin, 256.

132. "Bison Ecology and Bison Diplomacy: The Southern Plains from 1800 to 1850," *The Journal of American History*, 78.2 (1991), 483.

133. William A. Dobak, "Killing the Canadian Buffalo, 1821-1881," *Western Historical Quarterly*, 27.1 (1996), 49.

134. Flores, 484; Dobak, 49-50.

135. *Conquest of Paradise*, 321.

136. "The Remaking of the Amerind," 94.

137. *A New Face in the Countryside*, 66.

138. Sam D. Gill, *Mother Earth. An American Story* (Chicago and London, 1987), 26.

139. Cf. Gill: "Neither Huggins nor MacMurray [the two source of the Smohalla quote] knew the native languages and had to depend upon translations through even more than one language. Neither was trained in observing and recording such encounters. Indeed, Huggins's account may well be based on recall of an incident that happened years earlier," 54.

140. Gill, 66.

141. "The American Indian as Miscast Ecologist," *The History Teacher*, 14.2 (1981), 244.

142. *The Buried Mirror*, 98.

143. In *The Betrayal of the West*, trans. Matthew J. O'Connell (1975; New York, 1978), 18.

144. In Royal, *1492 And All That*, 66.

145. Ronald Wright, *Stolen Continents. The Americas Through Indian Eyes Since 1492* (New York, 1992), 13.

146. Royal, 70.

CHAPTER 7

This chapter appeared in a different form in *Arion,* 7.1 (1999), 72-97.

1.   Rene Denfeld, The New Victorians: A Young Woman's Challenge to the Old Feminist Order, New York, 1995, 132-33. uder (New York, 1995).

2.   Patricia Aburdene and John Naisbitt, *Megatrends for Women* (New York, 1992), 267-88.

3. See Denfeld's description of the 1993 International Women's Day conference, *The New Victorians*, 127-30.

4. "A Witch's Manifesto," *Whole Earth Review*, 74 (Spring 1992), 35.

5. *Megatrends for Women*, 268.

6. Richard N. Ostling, "When God Was a Woman," *Time*, 137.18 (6 May 1991), 73.

7. In *Whole Earth Review*, 74 (Spring 1992), 45.

8. "The Goddess and the Academy," *Academic Questions*, 6.4 (Fall 1993), 49. Davis has recently published a book-length study, *Goddess Unmasked: The Rise of Neopagan Feminist Spirituality* (Dallas, 1998).

9. Christine Hoff Sommers, *Who Stole Feminism?*, 31.

10. For the Goddess religion in universities cf. Denfeld, 131-32.

11. Cf. Cynthia Eller, in her by no means unsympathetic study of feminist spiritualism: "It [Goddess history] pulses out into the greater culture where it gradually leaches into the popular mentality as something between folk wisdom and historical fact," *Living in the Lap of the Goddess. The Feminist Spirituality Movement in America* (New York, 1993), 150-51.

12. Cf. Lynn Meskell: "The literature of the Goddess lies at the interface where academic scholarship meets New Age gynocentric, mythologized interpretations of the past," in "Goddesses, Gimbutas and 'New Age' Archaeology," *Antiquity*, 69.262 (1995), 74. See too Lawrence Osborn, "Women Warriors," *Lingua Franca* (November 1997).

13. Donaleen Saul and Jean Napali, "Goddess Worship: Toxic Niceness?" *New Directions for Women*, 20.4 (1991), 4. See also the reservations summarized by Jennifer Sells and Helen Cordes, "New Goddess Worship Troubles Skeptics," *The Utne Reader*, 45 (May/June 1991), 19-20.

14. Susan Cyre, "Fallout Escalates Over 'Goddess' Sophia Worship," *Christianity Today*, 38.4 (4 April 1994), 74.

15. Cyre, 74.

16. As even sympathetic commentators admit; cf. Juliette Wood, "The Concept of the Goddess," in *The Concept of the Goddess*, eds. Sandra Billington and Miranda Green (London and New York, 1996), 18.

17. Eller, 18.

18. Quoted in Sommers, 31.

19. *Megatrends for Women*, 268.

20. Merlin Stone, *When God Was a Woman* (New York, 1976), xxv.

21. Margaret W. Conkey and Joan M. Gero, "Tensions, Pluralities, and Engendering Archaeology: An Introduction to Women and Prehistory," in *Engendering Archaeology. Women and Prehistory* (Oxford, 1991), 7.

22. "A Witch's Manifesto," 35.

23. "Beyond the Backlash. An Appreciation of the Work of Marija Gimbutas," *Journal of Feminist Studies in Religion,* 12.2 (Fall 1996), 97.

24. "Out of the Closet and into the Field: Matriculture, the Lesbian Perspective, and Feminist Classics," in *Feminist Theory and the Classics*, eds. Nancy Sorkin Rabinowitz and Amy Richlin (New York and London, 1993), 185, 201.

25. *Laughter of Aphrodite. Reflections on a Journey to the Goddess* (San Francisco, 1987), xiii. Emphases added. Subsequent references parenthetical.

26. On "intuition" in the Goddess movement see Denfeld, 143.

27. "Why Women Need the Goddess: Phenomenological, Psychological, and Political Reflections," 1978; rpt. in *Womanspirit Rising. A Feminist Reader in Religion*, ed. Carol P. Christ and Judith Plaskow (San Francisco, 1979), 286.

28. "Gimbutas's Theory," 89.

29. "The Pursuit of the Ideal," 1988; in *The Crooked Timber of Humanity*, ed. Henry Hardy (New York, 1991), 18.

30. "Out of the Closet," 181, 200.

31. *Megatrends for Women*, 268.

32. *When God Was a Woman*, xxiii.

33. *When God Was a Woman*, xiii, 9.

34. In *The Politics of Women's Spirituality. Essays on the Rise of Spiritual Power within the Feminist Movement*, ed. Charlene Spretnak (Garden City, 1982), 550.

35. In "Gimbutas's Theory," 73, 78.

36. In "A Different World": The Challenge of the Work of Marija Gimbutas to the Dominant World-View of Western Cultures," *Journal of Feminist Studies in Religion*, 12.2 (Fall 1996), 55, 64.

37. *Engendering Archaeology*, 7.

38. In "Rediscovering the Goddess," 125.

39. *Vico and Herder. Two Studies in the History of Ideas* (New York, 1976), xxv.

40. *When God Was a Woman*, 2.

41. "Gimbutas's Theory," 77-78. The use of mythology as evidence raises a whole other set of problems. Cf. Sally R. Binford: "We do not attempt to reconstruct biological evolution or the history of the universe by recourse to myth, and the data of cultural evolution are no more amenable to this kind of methodology than are these other attempts to understand evolutionary processes," in "Myths and Matriarchies" (*The Politics of Women's Spirituality*, 544).

42. "Gimbutas's Theory," 78.

43. "A Different World," 64.

44. "Gender Theory and the Archaeological Record: Why Is there No Archaeology of Gender?" in *Engendering Archaeology*, 31-54.

45. Wylie, 44.

46. Wylie, 48.

47. "The Goddess in the Academy," 61.

48. Davis, 62.

49. Cf. Sally R. Binford: "In the many discussions I have had with partisans of this myth over the past several years, I am persuaded that logic, reason, and arguments based on knowledge of the data cut no ice at all," "Myths and Matriarchies," 542.

50. "Gimbutas's Theory," 88.

51. "Out of the Closet," 181.

52. "Beyond the Backlash," 91.

53. "'A Different World,'" 56.

54. "'A Different World,'" 59.

55. "Gimbutas's Theory," 73.

56. "'A Different World,'" 55.

57. *The Civilization of the Goddess. The World of Old Europe*, ed. Joan Marler (San Francisco, 1991). Subsequent references parenthetical. A briefer exposition can be found in "Women and Culture in Goddess-Oriented Old Europe," 1980; rpt. in *Weaving the Visions. New Patterns in Feminist Spirituality*, eds. Judith Plaskow and Carol P. Christ (San Francisco, 1989), 63-71.

58. See Elizabeth Kristol's valuable discussion of the return of the Golden Age myth in Goddess literature: "History in the Past Perfect," *First Things* (April, 1991), 44-46.

59. *Beyond Power: On Women, Men, and Morals* (1985; New York, 1986), 47.

60. See Denfeld, 134-35, for other examples from Goddess adherents.

61. Cf. Ovid, *Metamorphoses* 1.135-36: *communemque prius...humum.*

62. The motif of "sedentary" also appears in Ovid's myth of the Golden Age, in which "mortals knew no shores except their own" (*Metamorphoses* 1.96). The Iron Age is the age of sailing and travel, which is motivated by greed and unholy curiosity (132-34).

63. "Women and Culture in Old Europe," 70-71.

64. "Old Europe: Sacred Matriarchy or Complementary Opposition?" in *Archaeology and Fertility Cult in the Ancient Mediterranean*, ed. Anthony Bonanno (Amsterdam, 1985), 21, 22.

65. "A Sexist View of Prehistory," *Archaeology*, 45.2 (March/April 1992), 15, 18.

66. Review of *Civilization of the Goddess* in *American Anthropologist*, 95.1 (March 1993), 197.

67. In "The Twilight of the Goddess," *The New Republic*, No. 4.046 (3 August 1992), 29.

68. "Goddesses, Gimbutas, and 'New Age' Archaeology," 74, 76. See too the discussion of Denfeld in *The New Victorians*, 133-42; Juliette Wood, "The Concept of the Goddess," 19-21.

69. "The Concept of the Goddess," 22.

70. *The Oxford Illustrated Prehistory of Europe*, ed. Barry Cunliffe (New York, 1994).

71. "Old Europe," 22-23.

72. See my *Eros. The Myth of Ancient Greek Sexuality* (Boulder, 1997), 145-46.

73. In "Language of the Goddess," *American Journal of Archeology*, 96.1 (1992), 170. Quoted in Denfeld, *The New Victorians*, 139.

74. "The Upper Palaeolithic Revolution," in *The Oxford Illustrated Prehistory of Europe*, 69.

75. "Ritual Communication, Social Elaboration, and the Variable Trajectories of Paleolithic Material Culture," in *Prehistoric Hunter-Gatherers. The Emergence of Cultural Complexity* (Orlando, 1985), 303; see too 312-16.

76. "Old Europe," 23.

77. In Nilsen and Woolport, "Rediscovering the Goddess," 122; cf. Denfeld, 137.

78. "Goddesses, Gimbutas, and 'New Age' Archaeology," 82.

79. Lefkowitz, "Twilight of the Goddess," 32.

80. Ian Hodder, *The Domestication of Europe. Structure and Contingency in Neolithic Societies* (London, 1990), 60.

81. Meskell, "Goddesses," 82.

82. A point raised by Timothy Taylor, *The Prehistory of Sex* (New York, 1996), 159.

83. *Anthropomorphic Figurines* (London, 1968), 419.

84. Margaret Ehrenberg, *Women in Prehistory* (Norman and London, 1989), 74-75.

85. Meskell, "Goddesses," 82.

86. Mellars, "Upper Palaeolithic Revolution," 69. See too Clive Gamble, "Culture and Society in the Upper Paleolithic of Europe," in *Hunter-Gatherer Economy in Prehistory*, ed. Geoff Bailey (Cambridge, 1983), 211.

87. *The Prehistory of Sex*, 122, 115.

88. *The Domestication of Europe*, 68; cf. too 287: "It thus seems possible that the culturing or ordering of the female form was part of a more general process of controlling the wild and the dangerous."

89. "Twilight of the Goddess," 33.

90. *Women in Prehistory*, 73.

91. "The Transformation of Early Agrarian Europe: The Later Neolithic and Copper Ages 4500-2500 B.C.," in *The Oxford Prehistory of Europe*, 201.

92. *War before Civilization*, 37, 39.

93. S. Vencl, "War and Warfare in Archaeology," trans. Petr Charvát, *Journal of Anthropological Archaeology*, 3 (1984), 121.

94. *War before Civilization*, 38.

95. "War and Warfare in Archaeology," 120.

96. "The Mesolithic Age," in *The Oxford Illustrated Prehistory of Europe*, 121, 123.

97. David Anthony quoted in Denfeld, *The New Victorians*, 140.

98. J. P. Mallory, *In Search of the Indo-Europeans* (London, 1989), 242.

99. "The Upper Palaeolithic Revolution," in *The Oxford Illustrated Prehistory of Europe*, 64-65.

100. Mithen, 125.

101. "Nazi and Eco-feminist Prehistories: Ideology and Empiricism in Indo-European Archaeology," in *Nationalism, Politics, and the Practice of Archaeology*, ed. Philip L. Kohl and Clare Fawcett (Cambridge, 1995), 94.

102. Mithen, 133.

103. Colin Renfrew, *Archaeology and Language. The Puzzle of Indo-European Origins* (New York, 1987).

104. *In Search of the Indo-Europeans*, 185.

105. Guido Barbujani, Robert R. Sokal, Neal L. Oden, "Indo-European Origins: A Computer-simulation Test of Five Hypotheses," *American Journal of Physical Anthropology*, 96.2 (1995), 127.

106. *Living in the Lap of the Goddess*, 156.

107. Riane Eisler, *The Chalice and the Blade. Our History, Our Future* (New York, 1987), xiii-xiv. Subsequent references parenthetical.

108. Shaun Madison Krahmer, in *Journal of Religion*, 70.2 (1990), 277, 278.

109. Gina Allen, in *The Humanist*, 48.1 (1988), 46.

110. Fran Hosken, "The Chalice and the Blade. An Interview with Riane Eisler," *The Humanist*, 47.4 (1987), 28, 27.

111. Hosken, 27, 29.

112. Krahmer, 278.

113. Hosken, 42; see *The Chalice and the Blade*, 185-203, for the extravagant utopian benefits that will accrue to all of us if we heed Eisler's call.

114. Phillip G. Davis, "The Goddess and the Academy," 61.

115. Cf. Mary Lefkowitz: "One suspects that his [Bachofen's] notion of ancient realities was based on a contemporary appreciation of the role of women in his own society, and that the fixed laws he saw in the confused and contradictory record of the past were the patterns he most wanted to find," in "Princess Ida and the Amazons," 1981; rpt. *Women in Greek Myth* (Baltimore, 1986), 24. For Bachofen in the context of nineteenth-century German irrationalism see Richard Noll, *The Jung Cult. Origins of a Charismatic Movement* (1994; New York, 1997), 161-76.

116. "Nazi and Eco-Feminist Prehistories," 88-90.

117. Anthony, 82.

118. "History in the Past Perfect," 49.

CONCLUSION

1. Plato, *Apology* 38a, my translation.

2. Cf. David O. Sacks and Peter A. Thiel: "No longer just concerned with learn- ing about new ideas, multiculturalism is, as the word suggests, a cultural phe- nomenon, with rules of etiquette, codes of conduct, and precisely assigned roles for each of the participants," *The Diversity Myth: Multiculturalism and the Politics of Intolerance at Stanford* (Oakland, 1995), xviii.

3. For a discussion of the various "false portraits" that have allowed multicultural- ism to be misunderstood and misrepresented see Alvin J. Schmidt, *The Menace of Multiculturalism. Trojan Horse in America* (Westport, CT, 1997), 9-24.

4. For the anti-Western bias in Multiculturalism see Arthur Herman's discussion in *The Idea of Decline in the West*, 364-71. This anti-Western bias characterizes as well a new history textbook which embodies the National Standards of United States History; see Walter A. McDougall, "The National Standards Take Hold," *Heterodoxy*, 5.6 & 7 (June 1997), 16-17.

5. *The Disuniting of America. Reflections on a Multicultural Society* (New York, 1992), 123. Perusal of the work of Multicultural theorists reveals its antipa- thy for Enlightenment humanism; see e.g. *Multiculturalism: A Critical Reader*, ed. David Theo Goldberg (Oxford and Cambridge, MA, 1994).

6. John Ellis correctly identifies the Noble Savage myth as an important Western origin of Multicultural political correctness, in *Literature Lost: Social Agendas and the Corruption of the Humanities* (New Haven, 1997), 12-32.

7. See Jacques Ellul, *The Betrayal of the West*, 1-34.

8. Ellul, 21.

9. See Ernest Gellner, *Postmodernism, Reason and Religion*, 78-79.

10. Cf. Raymond Tallis, *Enemies of Hope. A Critique of Contemporary Pessimism, Irrationalism, Anti-Humanism and the Counter-Enlightenment* (New York, 1997), 42: "I think that few critics of modernity would prefer untreatable cystitis to anomie, chronic malnutrition to alienation; and few would find being under the thrall of the priest, the local squire, an unaccountable govenment or an unchallengable workplace bully in an organic community better than living in an atomic society."

11. See the valuable essay by Alain Finkielkraut, *The Defeat of the Mind*, 1987; trans. Judith Friedlander (New York, 1995).

12. *The Defeat of the Mind*, 79.

13. For the threat of Multiculturalism to American political ideals see John J. Miller, *The Unmaking of Americans. How Multiculturalism Has Undermined the Assimilation Ethic* (New York, 1998).

14. Cf. John Ellis, *Literature Lost*: "Those in the grip of this impulse [anti-Western political correctness] are critical of the Western tradition and define them- selves by their opposition to it, yet the impulse itself is so much a part of the

Western tradition that the attitudes it generates can be said to be quintessentially Western," 12.

15. *Notes on the State of Virginia*, Query 18.

16. Quoted in Ian Crowe, "Introduction: Principles and Circumstances," *The Enduring Edmund Burke*, ed. Ian Crowe (Wilmington, DE, 1997), 18-19.

17. See Tallis, *Enemies of Hope*, 199-217.

18. *Christian Morals*, 2.5.

19. "On Political Judgment," *The New York Review of Books*, 63.15 (3 October 1996), 29.

INDEX